THE FRENCH TRADITION
IN EDUCATION

PETRUS RAMUS
(Pierre de la Ramée)
(1515–1572)

THE FRENCH TRADITION
IN EDUCATION

RAMUS to Mme NECKER DE SAUSSURE

BY

H. C. BARNARD, M.A., B.Litt.

Sometime Senior Hulme Scholar of Brasenose College, Oxford
Author of *The Little Schools of Port-Royal*, etc.

CAMBRIDGE
AT THE UNIVERSITY PRESS
1922
REPRINTED
1970

Published by the Syndics of the Cambridge University Press
Bentley House, 200 Euston Road, London, N.W. 1
American Branch: 32 East 57th Street, New York, N.Y. 10022

PUBLISHER'S NOTE

Cambridge University Press Library Editions are re-issues of out-of-print standard works from the Cambridge catalogue. The texts are unrevised and, apart from minor corrections, reproduce the latest published edition.

Standard Book Number: 521 07771 0

First published 1922
Reprinted 1970

First printed in Great Britain at the University Press, Cambridge
Reprinted in Great Britain by John Dickens & Co. Ltd, Northampton

TO

MY FATHER

FOREWORD

THIS book, which was published in 1922, has been reprinted photographically. For this reason it has not been possible to make any alterations in the text, but the following emendations should be noted:

p.9, note. for Logicien read Physicien and for Physicien read Logicien.

p.104, line 8 for '*moral*' read '*morale*'. ....

p.154, line 26 for 'Mans' read 'Le Mans'.

p.193, lines 4 & 14 and p.311 (index) for 'Dumoustier' read 'Dumonstier'.

p.232, line 25 for 'Abbé de Saint-Pierre' read 'Bernardin de Saint-Pierre'.

p.235, line 16, for 'joins' read 'join'.

There are also one or two comments which may nowadays appear to be 'dated'—*e.g.* the reference on p.48 to the 'overlap' and 'confusion' which have been to some extent, at any rate, obviated by the 1944 Education Act. Also there might now be a reference in chapter IV to my *Fénelon in Education* (1966); and in *Education and the French Revolution* (1969) I have endeavoured to supply the 'separate treatise' mentioned in the Preface. Both of these books are published by the Cambridge University Press.

H.C.B.

PREFACE

THE history of Education in France affords an extensive and profitable field for research. Much valuable work has already been accomplished; the teachings of such reformers as Rabelais, Montaigne, and Rousseau are familiar to every training-college student, while the school practice of the Jesuits and the Port-Royalists is described in every text-book of educational history. But there are many aspects of the subject which have not yet been presented to readers in this country or even, in any detail, in France itself, although the original sources which are available present a vast amount of material. It is with the object, therefore, of filling in some of the existing *lacunæ* that the present volume has been prepared.

It is doubtless true that education is coterminous with life itself, for, in a sense, all experience is educative. At the same time it is advisable to give terms their customary connotation and in the present case to limit education to those formative processes which aim at preparing the future citizen for a life of usefulness and service. In this book the outlook is still further restricted, for I have dealt primarily with the education of children and adolescents up to the end of what to-day would be called secondary school age; I have purposely set aside a consideration of higher education such as is the special province of the modern university. I have tried to picture certain aspects of education in France during the centuries which succeeded the Renaissance, and to sketch in somewhat greater detail, against this vaguer background, the career of certain educationists or educational institutions which have hitherto received far less attention than they would seem to deserve. The period of the Revolution I have left untouched because the educational activities which are associated with it seem to me of so great importance that they would merit a separate treatise consecrated solely to this subject.

I wish to acknowledge with sincere gratitude my indebtedness to Prof. J. W. Adamson whose criticism and encouragement have continually been of the greatest assistance; to the Rev. Mother Superior of St Ursula's Convent, Oxford, who very kindly allowed me access to unpublished manuscripts and other material dealing with the life and work of the Venerable Anne de Xainctonge; to Miss M. Claxton who rendered valuable help in the compilation of the bibliography; and to Miss J. Sorrell, B.A., who read through the proofs. For the picture of Anne de Xainctonge I am indebted to the Rev. Mother Superior of St Ursula's; for that of Madame Necker de Saussure to her grandson, M. Henry Necker of Geneva, and to Mr Henry F. Montagnier; while the remaining six portraits were procured for me by my friend Mr P. H. Dannatt, M.A. To all of those who have thus helped to add to the value and interest of this book I should like to express my sincere thanks.

H. C. B.

May 1922.

CONTENTS

MAPS

LIST OF PLATES

CHAPTER I

THE UNIVERSITY OF PARIS (1)—RAMUS

IT is impossible to assign any precise date to the foundation of the University of Paris. As early as the eleventh century the schools of that city were already sufficiently famous to attract students from a distance, but it was not until about the year 1210 that the nascent University received from the Pope its first written statutes. It had developed out of a guild or corporation of masters teaching under the licence of the Chancellor of the cathedral of Notre-Dame. But early in the twelfth century Abelard, whose teaching did much to make Paris an intellectual centre, had set up an independent school under licence from the Chancellor of Ste Geneviève, at that time a collegiate church. Thus in course of time there came to be two authorities—the Chancellors of Notre-Dame and of Ste Geneviève, ecclesiastical officials who represented the Pope—who granted the *ius ubique docendi* to those who were to be admitted to the master's degree[1]; in virtue of it the licentiate was given (in theory, at any rate) the right of teaching in any institution over which the authority of the Pope extended—*i.e.* in practically any school or university of western Christendom. But the granting of the *maîtrise*—the degree itself—belonged to the University, and although the Chancellors kept their licensing privilege down to 1789, their actual powers greatly diminished.

From mediaeval times the University had inherited its division into four faculties—those of theology, law, medicine

---

[1] The Chancellor of Notre-Dame alone conferred licences in theology, law, and medicine; but for the licence in arts application might be made either to him or to the Chancellor of Ste Geneviève. Cf. "Quant aux maistres-es-arts, à l'un ou l'autre Chancelier selon le choix qui en est fait par celuy qui veut prendre sa licence." Pasquier, *Recherches*, p. 840.

and arts, the first three being "superior" and the fourth introductory to them. It was customary for boys to enter the Faculty of Arts at the age of twelve or thirteen, or even considerably earlier than this[1]; and thus, although they were members of the University, they followed what to-day would be regarded as essentially a secondary school course. There even developed a tendency for the Faculty of Arts to overlap the Little Schools which gave a kind of preparatory course[2], and numerous disputes arose for this reason during the sixteenth and seventeenth centuries. Besides these Little Schools, which catered for children of both sexes, there were several "Latin schools" or *grandes écoles* which were open to boys only and in which the curriculum did not differ materially from that of the Faculty of Arts. The Latin school, like the Little School, was under the control of a cathedral official called the *écolâtre*[3], but no degree was given at the end of its course. In course of time the *grandes écoles* were superseded by the Faculty of Arts and thus it became customary for a boy to proceed straight from the Little School to the University. The existence of the Faculty of Arts also tended to prevent the rise of independent secondary schools in France; it assumed a practical monopoly of secondary education until the advent of the various teaching orders in the seventeenth century. It is easy to understand the bitterness with which the University regarded the establishment of Jesuit schools in France.

It is no part of our purpose to attempt even a sketch of the development of the University of Paris; we have here merely to describe the stage which it had reached in the sixteenth century, and as our concern is primarily with the education of children or adolescents we shall leave on one side the consideration of the higher faculties and deal more particularly with the Faculty of Arts. The students were grouped into "nations"—a custom which still obtains in

---

[1] *E.g.* Henri IV became a member of the college of Navarre at the age of nine; his friend Du Plessis-Mornay was eight years old when he entered the college of Lisieux.

[2] See *infra*, pp. 47–48.   [3] See *infra*, p. 41.

some of the universities of Scotland. At Paris there were four of these groups; the nation of France (*Honoranda Gallorum Natio*) included students from the neighbourhood of the capital as well as those from Spain, Italy, the Mediterranean islands and Africa. Picardy (*Fidelissima Picadorum Natio*) comprised natives of Northern France and the Low Countries. Students from Normandy had a nation of their own (*Veneranda Normanorum Natio*), while Germany (*Constantissima Germanorum Natio*) included not only Germans, but also Danes, British[1], Poles, Swiss and Hungarians. Each nation elected its own proctor who acted as chairman at meetings of the nation and represented it at University functions; the proctors in their turn elected a rector who was head of the Faculty of Arts. He held office for a term of three months and originally was not allowed to occupy the position more than once; but especially after 1600 this rule was not observed and there are many instances of rectors who remained in office for several years. The higher faculties each possessed its own special dean; but since they consisted of men who had graduated in arts, the oath of obedience which they had already taken to the rector was held to be binding even after they had become members or even graduates of a superior faculty. Thus it naturally came about that the rector ultimately was head not only of the Faculty of Arts, but of the whole University and his position and influence eclipsed those of the Chancellor who granted licences. The latter remained "le premier juge et censeur de la doctrine et mœurs des écoliers[2]," and the representative of the University in its dealings with outside bodies—especially the Holy See.

The University in course of time acquired many privileges some of which were due not to the Pope but to the king. Its students were exempt from certain taxes and from military service and offences committed by them were tried in special courts. Even more valuable was the University's right to have its own

---

[1] It had originally been the English nation and the inscription on its seal was S. NACIONIS ANGLICÆ. The change of name was made in 1436.

[2] Pasquier, *Recherches*, pp. 265 and 843.

messageries or postal service[1]. To each nation were attached certain officials called *messagers*. They were of two classes. The *petits messagers* were simply postmen who carried letters and parcels between students and their families and friends who lived in the district represented by the particular nation. These officials also undertook the transmission of supplies of money sent by provincial parents to their sons at the University of Paris. In the metropolis itself were various *grands messagers*. They were usually rich merchants or bankers and they administered a kind of post-office clearing-house, forming an intermediary between the students and those who were responsible for them, and controlling the activities of the *petits messagers*. This private postal service provided the University with a valuable income, and the privilege was therefore highly prized and tenaciously held; it depended on the Crown, and this fact helps to explain why the University, although so largely ecclesiastical in character, was consistently gallican and loyal—the "eldest daughter of the King of France."

Characteristic of the University of Paris was the college system. Originally most of the colleges had been little more than boarding-houses. Students in Paris in early times had often had difficulties in finding lodgings, and the founding of colleges had thus been a charitable work, due often to bishops or other notables, in order to furnish homes for poor scholars who were regarded as potential clergy. To judge by contemporary accounts, the buildings were as a rule dreary, the food unsatisfactory and the *régime* austere. It became a usual practice for the colleges to be conducted by masters who took their pupils who belonged to the Faculty of Arts to hear the public lectures which were given in the rue du Fouarre[2]. In the course of time it was found

[1] There are traces of this system elsewhere. *E.g.* Milton wrote a sonnet in honour of a Cambridge University carrier, and down to quite recent times common carriers at Oxford used to be licensed by the University.

[2] It was in the rue du Fouarre that Pantagruel "tint contre tous les regens, artiens, et orateurs, et les mist tous de cul." It has been said that the street took its name from the straw (*fouarre*) upon which the students sat when listening to lectures; but it seems more probable that originally a hay and straw market had been held here.

more convenient to give the arts lectures in the colleges themselves and thus they became assimilated in some measure at least to the constituent colleges of a modern university. The date of the change is not certain; but the rue du Fouarre had originally been shut off by a wooden barrier to prevent the through-passage of vehicles and to ensure quietness during lecture-time. The four nations used to keep this gate in repair at their common expense; but the last recorded instance of this being done dates from 1507[1], and this would seem to indicate that the custom of giving lectures in the colleges themselves had come into vogue by this time. But although the colleges were thus both halls of residence and places of instruction they never became the units of the social life of the University, as was the case at Oxford or Cambridge. Many of the Parisian colleges had been founded by public munificence or private benefaction for the natives of certain districts and might thus be restricted to students belonging to a particular nation. Again, the division of the University into Faculties bulked more largely at Paris than in the English universities. If students from more than one Faculty were comprised in the same college, they were grouped separately. At the College of Navarre, for example, each Faculty had its own hall and dormitories and so formed a kind of sub-college inside the larger foundation. While it is true, therefore, that the college system found its earliest home in Paris, it was complicated by the division of the University into Nations and Faculties.

At the end of the sixteenth century there were at Paris forty-three separate colleges. They were of two different kinds. The teaching arrangements of a college, including the staff and its work, as distinguished from the purely administrative side of the institution, were summed up by the term *exercice*. Thus the phrase *collège de plein exercice* came to mean an institution which had a full staff and provided all the ordinary classes of the Arts faculty—*i.e.* forms VI, V, IV, III, II, Rhetoric and Philosophy[2]. The full course in a

---

[1] See Crevier, *Hist. de l'Univ. de Paris*, v, 68.   [2] See note on p. 9.

college of this type extended over six years, corresponding roughly to the modern secondary school career, with the addition of a two years' study of philosophy. The curriculum in the Faculty of Arts led up to the degree of *maître-ès-arts*. But there were other colleges in which the *plein exercice* was not provided; in this case students followed special courses or were also allowed to attend lectures in the colleges which did provide it. At the head of the college, to whichever type it belonged, was a principal whose duties were largely administrative; he was assisted by an *économe,* a *sous-principal*, a *chapelain*, and other officials who can easily be paralleled in a modern Oxford college. The regents or *præceptores* were chiefly responsible for the instruction which was given. Like their modern representatives, they were badly paid; and it had therefore become customary for them to supplement their stipends by accepting gifts at stated times from their pupils; and this custom—as we shall see—had led to grave abuses.

The *boursiers*, or scholars for whose benefit the colleges had originally been founded, were of two kinds—the *petits* who were members of the Faculty of Arts and the *grands* who had obtained the master's degree and were now studying in a higher Faculty. Both alike were supposed to be in need of financial assistance. The latter seem to have enjoyed many privileges, but the lot of the *petit boursier* was a hard one; like the college servants they were subject to a strict authority—"parvos bursarios et omnes collegii famulos ad quodcumque iusserint paratissimos utique habento." The members of a college could be classified under various headings. The *convicteurs* or *pensionnaires* were boarding pupils who were put in the particular charge of the principal of the college. Like the commoners at a college at Oxford or Cambridge they were often really intruders into an institution which had originally been intended for poor students. The *caméristes* were parlour boarders; they were usually youths of wealthy parentage and were entrusted to a particular type of regent called a *pédagogue*. He lodged his pupils either in a special room in college, hired from the principal or allotted to him in lieu of salary, or else in a

private house outside the college precincts[1]. There were
also two types of external students who formed the greatest
part of the University; but beyond attendance at lectures
they seem to have been less connected with its life. The
younger were known as *martinets* or "swallows" and they
were usually in the charge of some responsible householder
who might or might not be a member of the University.
The *galoches* were older students who were not following
the regular curriculum for a degree, but who took elective
courses[2]. This class, as might have been expected, was the
least disciplined of all. In the *Satire Ménippée* the *galoches*
are classed with rogues, swindlers, debauchees and scullions
—"fripons, friponniers, juppins, galoches, marmitons et
autres sortes de gens malfaisants[3]." Crevier, the historian
of the University of Paris, says of them: "They were a kind
of bird-of-passage, who running from school to school and
from master to master used to try to gain degrees by fraud
without either real study, or decency of conduct or morals[4]."
For this reason after 1463 candidates for degrees were not
accepted unless they had followed regular courses and had
lived with some responsible person. There remained a fifth
class of students—that of the servants, like the sizars at
Cambridge or the servitors at Oxford. They were employed
by the college authorities[5] or privately by the *pédagogues*
who looked after *caméristes*; they picked up what education
they could amass in their spare time, but we can gather
that their lot was not a very enviable one.

   The statutes of the University contained several clauses
regulating dress. As in the Oxford *Statuta*, clothes of a
subfusc hue were prescribed. Regents and *pédagogues* wore
an academic gown and a square cap, and students were also

---

   [1] These *pédagogies* dated from about the fifteenth century when
paying students were admitted to colleges which had originally been
designed only for *boursiers*.
   [2] For these various classes of students see Pasquier, *Recherches*,
book IX, chap. CXVII.
   [3] p. 124.
   [4] *Hist. de l'Univ. de Paris*, IV, 281.
   [5] *E.g.* in 1557 the cook at the Collège d'Autun was a *petit
boursier*.

compelled to appear on all occasions in a similar costume[1]. At solemn functions graduates wore what in modern France would be called an *épitoge*—a kind of ornament on the left shoulder; while high officers of the University had the privilege of arraying themselves in very magnificent costumes; to the Rector, for example, was assigned a gorgeous gown of violet and ermine.

The academic year for the Faculty of Arts began on the first of October and continued till the end of August for the upper classes, and till the middle of September for the others. There were short breaks at Easter and at Whitsun and a number of saints'-days were also observed as holidays. The term between October and Easter was called *grand ordinaire*; that between Easter and the Long Vacation, *petit ordinaire*. The hours of work were long compared with those to which the present age is accustomed. According to the regulations of the Collège de Montaigu, dating from 1503, work began at 4.0 a.m. and lasted until the celebration of Mass at 6.0. This was followed by breakfast and at 8.0 a.m. instruction re-commenced and lasted till 11.0. After the mid-day meal work continued until 5.0 p.m. This brought a short respite, but there was another hour of study in the evening, making a total of eleven hours' work on an average every day; of these, six were spent in the class-room and five were devoted to *étude*—*i.e.* private study under supervision. On Saturdays a *vivâ voce* revision of the week's work was held; this exercise was known as a *sabbatine*; pupils who proved unsatisfactory in this ordeal were reported to the principal and punished—occasionally "virgae disciplinā."

The use of Latin, not only as a medium of instruction, but as the ordinary channel of conversation, was made obligatory upon all students and regents alike within the precincts of the college[2]. A knowledge of the language was required from those who entered the Faculty of Arts and for this reason elementary Latin formed part of the curriculum of the

[1] This regulation was re-enforced in Henri IV's Statutes, No. LXV.
[2] This was confirmed in an *ordonnance* of 1539 and again in Henri IV's Statutes (1600).

Little Schools. In the lower forms[1] of a college the necessary summary of Latin grammar was furnished by the barbaric rhymes of Despauter; in the *rhétorique* the works of Gerard Vossius were used. Among the authors studied we find Cicero, Quintilian, Virgil, Ovid, Horace, Tibullus and Plautus. Greek, as a rule, held a less important position in the colleges of the University; or rather, its importance tended to vary with varying conditions in the different colleges. One difficulty was that for some time Greek text-books were not easily procurable, though this handicap became much less severe as the sixteenth century progressed. Normally the study of Greek began in the IVth class. Henri de Mesmes, who was sent to the Collège de Bourgogne in 1542 and placed in the IIIrd class, was able at the end of eighteen months to recite Homer from end to end and to compose Greek verses without difficulty. He is quoted by Rollin[2] to illustrate the stress which the University of the sixteenth century laid on the study of Greek. But one may be permitted, perhaps, to doubt whether Henri de Mesmes's case was in the least typical. He himself tells us that he was sent to Paris in charge of a *précepteur*, Jean Maludan, who brought him on "par veilles & travaux incroyables"; and it is to this private "coaching" rather than to the Collège de Bourgogne that his proficiency in Greek was probably due. It seems true to say that in many of the colleges Greek took a place considerably inferior to that occupied by Latin—at any

---

[1] It will be convenient here to give a table showing the ordinary arrangement of classes in a college. Read from the bottom upwards:

Logicien ⎫
Physicien ⎭ (Philosophy—two years' course)
Iième (Rhetoric)
IIième (Humanity)
IIIième (1st Grammar)
IVième (2nd Grammar)
Vième
VIième

Here the pupil entered a college at the age of not less (and usually more) than nine. But some colleges supplied:

VIIième (Salle) ⎫ which were really a preparatory course
VIIIième (Pater) ⎭ and overlapped the *petites écoles*.

[2] *Traité des Études*, I, 180.

rate until the reforms at the end of the sixteenth century were accomplished; and at no time did it attain in the Faculty of Arts the position which it occupied at Port-Royal or in the Jesuit colleges[1].

The crown of the Arts course was a two years' study of philosophy. It was provided in the curriculum of the *collèges de plein exercice* and in order to qualify for the degree of *maître-ès-arts* it was necessary that the student should have followed such a course in this subject. The philosophy curriculum consisted mainly of a study of Aristotle. In the first year, after a course in *Prolegomena* (*i.e.* an introduction to the whole subject), Logic and Moral Philosophy were begun and were studied in the *Organon* and *Ethics* of Aristotle. Logic was taught largely by formal disputations in which syllogisms were advanced and rebutted, though the subject under discussion was often of a purely academic or quite profitless nature. In the second year of the course the text-books were Aristotle's *Physics* and *Metaphysics*, and a certain amount of mathematics also was taught. But throughout the sixteenth century, and even after the reforms of 1600, scholastic methods of teaching philosophy persisted in the University. Aristotle, still studied for the most part in unreliable Latin texts[2], remained the basis of the whole system, and few students were rash enough to venture beyond the bare letter of their text-books. The whole system was perpetuated and improvements were made difficult, because of the tendency to excessive centralisation which was perhaps the natural result of the consolidation of the monarchy in France. Reformers were not lacking even in the sixteenth and seventeenth centuries, and we shall have occasion more than once in this book to speak of them.

[1] Rollin says (*Traité des Études*, 1, 200) that formerly it was the custom of the colleges to limit the study of Greek to the mere writing of proses, and that this accounted for "l'aversion presque générale pour le Grec qui y régnoit autre fois."

[2] The real Aristotle was doubtless known by the early part of the sixteenth century; but the students of the Faculty of Arts (who were only elder boys) still used text-books and dictated notes in which scholastic methods were employed and there was little incentive to criticism or individual thought.

But the dead weight of tradition and the conservatism of vested interests made it extremely difficult for isolated individuals to effect any salutary change; and the sacrosanct character with which the Middle Ages had endued Aristotle rendered any would-be reformer at once open to the charge of heresy. The attitude of the University of Paris was imitated by all the other universities of France. No wonder then that men like Montaigne and Ramus could find little to praise in the philosophical teaching of the Faculty of Arts. It was not until the influence of Descartes began to be felt that improved methods of teaching philosophy penetrated into the schools of France; and even then it was at Port-Royal or in the Oratorian colleges that the change was first felt, and for long the University was still content to pursue its traditional methods.

When the pupil had passed through the philosophy course and had reached the age of eighteen or nineteen, he was ready to become a candidate for the *maîtrise-ès-arts*. The requirements for this degree varied from time to time; it normally included the passing of two examinations and the maintaining of a disputation upon some thesis chosen by the candidate himself; this ceremony was known as the *Quodlibetica*. Those who had passed successfully through these ordeals then applied to one of the Chancellors who conferred the licence to teach; but it was not until the newly-made licentiate had been incorporated into the society of masters and had entered upon the duties of his office that he finally became, with appropriate ceremonies, a full-fledged master of arts. Even so he would be no older than most of the boys who leave the sixth form of a modern public school and he would now be ready to embark upon what in our days would be regarded as the university course proper; he would be qualified to enter one of the higher faculties of law, theology, or medicine.

The inadequacy of the curriculum was a criticism justly levelled against the Faculty of Arts in the sixteenth century; but it was not the only criticism. As has been indicated, the statutes of many of the colleges of the University of Paris show quite clearly that the intention of the founders had been to provide gratuitous education for poor scholars, drawn usually from some particular district. The history of these institutions has something in common with that of some of the older public schools of this country. The original designs of founders and benefactors were sometimes forgotten, and wealthy young men were welcomed as fee-paying boarders. The only sources of revenue which most of the colleges possessed, in addition to the endowments and the *pension* of the paying students, were investments such as *rentes* on the Hôtel de Ville or possibly the income of ecclesiastical benefices. But there was often not enough to pay the regents and, as has been said, they were sometimes allowed to eke out their salaries by taking boarders; and rooms in college might even be allotted to them for this purpose, in part payment for their services. Still more galling to the poor student were the heavy expenses incidental to taking a degree and the periodic presents to the regents which custom had sanctioned. The annual fee for the philosophy course had been fixed by statute at 4–6 *écus*[1], but by the middle of the seventeenth century it had grown to 8 *écus* or more. The outlay incurred in taking the *maître-ès-arts* degree was 56 livres 13 sols, while in the higher faculties the charges were much heavier. To become a doctor of medicine involved fees to an extent of 881 livres 5 sols, while the doctorate in theology cost no less than 1002 livres. Three times a year it was customary for students in the Faculty of Arts to make presents to their regents. At the beginning of the year an *écu* was offered for the purchase of "les toiles qu'on attachoit aux fenêtres pour rompre le vent." Three days after the festival of St Remigius (*i.e.* on October 4th, at the beginning of the academic year) three or four *écus* were again due; these were stuck on the end of a candle of white wax and, thus tactfully concealed, were handed to the regent. But the greatest exaction of all was at the *landi* or *lendi*, to which frequent reference is made in contemporary accounts of the University of Paris. The name was given to a festival of St Denis[2], a time of unbridled festivity in the

[1] See Appendix A on coinage.

[2] It was an occasion for the holding of a market (*indictum*), whence the term *l'endit* which became *lendit* (cf. *l'en demain*). The fair began to fall into desuetude soon after 1556.

city and University alike; and it was customary on this
occasion for each student to place six or seven *écus* inside
a lemon which in turn was put into a glass and so presented
to the regent. Those who were too poor to make any offering
were held up to obloquy and received the title of *frippe-lendi*,
or "*lendi*-spoiler." A student's life entailed many expenses
of this kind; at every stage of his career, from his entrance
to his graduation, feasts and entertainments were expected,
and elaborate and expensive ceremonies were entailed, so
that it is obvious that the way of the poor scholar was
excessively hard and that reform was imperative.

The sixteenth century was a period of transition and unrest in France. The Wars of Religion and the ferment of new
ideas profoundly affected French life, and nowhere more
than at Paris where that life was at its intensest. The social
upheaval of the times is reflected in the history of the University during this period. The pages of Félibien or of Crevier[1]
are full of accounts of the riotous behaviour of members of
the University of Paris. "Ragging" of *béjaunes* or freshmen
was common, of course, and rowdiness in college was by
no means exceptional. We read, for example, of four
foundation scholars of the College of Beauvais who enlivened
a lecture on the Lives of the Saints by singing indecent songs
and afterwards assaulted the porter who was summoned in
order to correct them. But outside the colleges discipline
was even worse. Many of the students, as we have seen,
enjoyed considerable liberty and were but little subject to
authority. Numerous regulations were enacted and re-
enacted to forbid the carrying of arms and to restrict the
giving of lessons in fencing; but little effect resulted from
them. The delinquents, naturally, were not confined to the
Faculty of Arts; many were already graduates and had
entered upon a course in a higher faculty, and even the
regents themselves not infrequently took an active part in the
disturbances. But in order to give some general idea of the
environment which surrounded the pupil in the Faculty of
Arts it may not be out of place to describe a typical incident
of the period. As has been said, the *lendi* especially was a

[1] Refer Bibliography, pp. 302 ff.

time of almost unchecked licence. In 1554, for example, bands of students, headed by their own regents, marched round the country in the neighbourhood of Paris, carrying arms and making themselves objectionable, by night as well as by day, by beating drums and shouting. The Parlement de Paris, in view of this conduct, issued two *arrêts*[1]. By them all principals, regents, and pedagogues—*i.e.* all who were in any way responsible for students both inside and outside of the colleges—were forbidden to countenance these *lendi* revels. Moreover, the students themselves, "sur peine de la hart" (*i.e.* hanging), were forbidden to carry swords, sticks, or pistols, or to wear coats of mail. The *lieutenant-criminel* was instructed to visit houses where scholars lodged in order to search for arms; and principals and *pédagogues* were instructed to confiscate weapons found in the possession of students under their charge, and not to return them until their owners left the city at the end of term and went back to their own homes. Fencing masters were forbidden to settle in the *fauxbourgs* of Paris and innkeepers were not allowed to serve students after 7.0 p.m. in winter and 8.0 p.m. in summer.

These regulations—and others like them, for only part of the two *arrêts* has been described—served only to irritate the unruly element in the University. Disturbances continued, but they reached their height in 1557 when there occurred what Crevier calls "le plus triste orage dont jamais elle (*sc.* l'Université) ait été battue." At this period the Abbey of St Germain-des-Prés was surrounded by meadows among which was the famous Petit Pré-aux-Clercs[2]. This was a favourite resort of students. The authorities of the Abbey never admitted the right of members of the University to use the field and continual friction was the result[3]. The fields were also used sometimes for Protestant meetings and this was another cause of riots. Thus the neighbourhood

[1] They are dated June 14th and Aug. 10th, 1554; see Bréchillet-Jourdain, *Index*, MDCCCLVI, 365.
[2] Its site may roughly be represented by the area enclosed by the modern rues de Seine, Jacob, and Bonaparte.
[3] Fights between monastic and scholastic factions had taken place at least as early as 1192.

acquired an unsavoury reputation. On May 12th, 1557, a party of students who had intruded upon the Pré-aux-Clercs was fired upon from a neighbouring house and one of them —a young Breton of "good family"—was killed. The whole University rallied at this injury and in the resulting disorder three houses were burnt down by students, while the casualties on both sides were considerable. The Parlement thereupon ordered all college authorities to keep their students indoors, but the disturbances were continued by the *externes* over whom the colleges had no power. Eventually, one Baptiste Coquatre—"autrement dit Crococzou"—was sentenced to death and straightway suffered the "peine de la hart[1]." His fellow-students, burning to avenge him, displayed fiery placards on the college walls and maltreated *arquebusiers* who had been sent to restrain their violence. Meanwhile the Rector in great agitation had hurried to the king, saying that he had done his best to quell the tumult, but that regents and *pédagogues* all alike "complained that they could not be obeyed[2]." A week later the students killed a police-officer; whereat the king who by now was at La Fère-en-Tardenois wrote a forcible letter to the University enjoining upon the offenders "si rude et si violent punition que l'exemple sera de perdurable mémoire[3]." Ten deputies were nominated to interview him; in a humble address, in which he is entitled "prince benin et débonnaire," he is besought not to impute the disorders of "a few unbridled and seditious scholars" to the University, his "eldest daughter, sorely afflicted that she has not been able for all her efforts to remedy this by herself[4]." Henri II had already sent a body of some two hundred armed infantry to take up their position in the University quarter. Their orders were to prevent any member of the University from going to the Pré-aux-Clercs. At the same time students were commanded to take up their quarters in the colleges—*i.e.* to become *pensionnaires* for the time being if they were not already in

---

[1] See Bréchillet-Jourdain, *Index*, MDCCCLXXXIV, 369.
[2] Félibien, II, 1054.
[3] See Bréchillet-Jourdain, *Index*, MDCCCLXXXVII, 370.
[4] Crevier, VI, 39.

this category. Any other students were, by the same *ordonnance*, banished from Paris, so that the class of *externes*, whether *martinets* or *galoches* ceased temporarily to exist. The *lieutenant-civil* duly published the royal decree[1]; but in passing the Colleges of Narbonne, Bayeux, and Justice he was assailed with stones. Accordingly he effected an entrance into these colleges and haled off thirteen of their scholars to the Châtelet. The deputies who were still upon their mission to the king prevailed upon his majesty to be merciful, and a few days later the imprisoned students were set at liberty. But it was quite obvious that some real attempt must be made to remedy the disorders which continually troubled the life of the University. The king therefore appointed a commission which, after due deliberation and consultation with representatives of each faculty, issued a report. The chief result was an *arrêt* of the Parlement, dated July 26th, 1558[2]. Principals and regents were strictly forbidden henceforth to countenance the *lendi* revels or to take part in the riotous excursions of armed students into the surrounding country "comme ils avoient fait encore cette année-là, contre les arrests précedens de la cour[3]." This was an attempt to reform the manners of the University—not, be it noticed, its curriculum—and it seems to have been more successful than previous endeavours, for we do not again meet with any disturbance so serious as those which characterised the year 1557. But before a reform of University administration and of teaching methods could be effected much work had yet to be done.

Such then were the general conditions under which a student of the University of Paris lived during the greater part of the sixteenth century. We have described them at some length because they form the *mise en scène* of the career of one of the most eminent of French thinkers—Pierre de la Ramée or Petrus Ramus, to give his name its more familiar form. He saw clearly the abuses which were rife in the University of his day—the useless expenditure which

[1] It was dated from La Fère, May 24th, 1557
[2] See Bréchillet-Jourdain, *Index*, MCMIX, 372.
[3] Félibien, II, 1058.

rendered so difficult the way of the poor student, the idleness and ignorance and unworthiness of too many of the teachers, the barrenness of the curriculum in the Faculty of Arts and in the other faculties too. He was a true son of the Reform and of the Renaissance and his whole life was an unwearied fight against hide-bound conservatism in religion and education alike. He perished a martyr to his beliefs and it was but gradually that the reforms which he advocated were accomplished. But he is undoubtedly the most interesting figure that the history of French education during the sixteenth century has to show us and as such we propose to sketch his career against the general background which has already been drawn.

Ramus was born at the village of Cuth[1] in Picardy in the year 1515. His family was extremely poor although it was of noble descent; but wars and disturbances had impoverished it and Ramus's grandfather had been reduced to following the occupation of a charcoal-burner in order to gain a precarious livelihood. But from his earliest years Ramus showed a disposition towards learning, and in order to achieve his aim the only course open to him was to become a servant to a regent or *camériste* in one of the colleges of the University. Accordingly we find him making several attempts to gain such a position; his first endeavour was at the age of eight, which would be below the normal age of entry into the Faculty of Arts. At last, when he was twelve years old, Ramus gained his object; he became the personal servant of a *camériste* named De la Brosse, who belonged to the College of Navarre. The young aspirant entered upon an exceedingly strenuous career; during the day-time he was at the beck and call of his master, but he devoted no small part of the night to study. He worked through the ordinary Arts curriculum up to the rhetoric and then, since Navarre was a *collège de plein exercice*, he embarked upon the philosophy course. As has been said, this was concerned mainly with the works of Aristotle studied—so far, at any rate, as most of the students were concerned—with but little attempt at criticism or independent enquiry. Aristotle—or

---

[1] Other spellings are Cus, Cuz, Cuts, Cutz, Culz, Cut, Cuthe and Quut. The village no longer exists.

2

rather an unreliable Latin version of his works—had been
adopted whole-heartedly by the mediaeval Church and his
philosophy had therefore shared its dogmatic growth and
absolutist tendencies. What the Scriptures were to theology,
the works of Aristotle became to science and philosophy.
Each in its own domain was regarded as the inspired word,
the authority of which it was impious to call in question.
Aristotle was even styled the forerunner of Christ in the
Gentile world, as John the Baptist was in the Jewish world.
One is reminded of the philosopher who, according to
Rabelais, discovered the origin of the Mass in the *Metamorphoses* of Ovid. There is evidence that the customary
attitude towards Aristotle did not commend itself to some
of the more acute thinkers in the University at the period
when Ramus was an undergraduate[1]. The influence of
Erasmus—himself an old student of the Collège de Montaigu
—and the ferment of the Reform were among the causes for
this. But the academic authorities were unflinchingly loyal
in their allegiance to the Stagyrite. In 1534 the Faculty of
Arts definitely restated its position and asserted that "the
works of Aristotle are given as the standard and basis of all
philosophic enquiry[2]."

It is hardly surprising that a youth such as Ramus with
his singularly acute mind, his passionate desire for truth, his
intense application to study, and his freedom from the
trammels of inherited tradition, should have shown an
especial scepticism towards the Aristotelian dogma. His
aim was to discover realities, not to follow the prescription
of a former thinker, and he drew much of his inspiration
from the dialogues of Plato which enshrine the principles
of the Socratic method. Moreover, it now seems clear that
Ramus regarded the works of Aristotle, in the form in which
they were read in the University, as being to a large extent
spurious[3]. At any rate in the early stages of his career,
Ramus was of a somewhat rash and impulsive nature and
he did not shrink from the implications of the position to
which his meditations had led him. Accordingly when his

---

[1] He attended lectures given by Sturm and was profoundly im-
pressed by his teaching. See Preface to *Scholæ in Liberales Artes*.
[2] See Crevier, v, 266.   [3] See especially *Schol. Dialect.* pp. 26 and 117.

philosophy course was over and it became necessary for him to submit a subject for his *Quodlibetica*[1], he boldly proposed the theme: *Quaecumque ab Aristotele dicta essent commentitia esse*—that whatever has been said by Aristotle is false.

It is not easy for us to realise the effect that such a step would produce in the year 1536 and in the bosom of the University of Paris. It was comparable almost to a public denial of the sacrifice of the Mass. Ramus, though barely twenty-one years of age, had to dispute all day long with whomsoever should appear to defend the tutelary deity of scholastic philosophy; but he had an initial advantage in that the dispute had to be carried on according to the laws of formal logic and if his opponents adopted the usual plan of appealing to Aristotle as an authority for their statements, they would at once commit the fallacy of *petitio principii* or "begging the question." In the end, therefore, Ramus successfully sustained his thesis and could proceed in due course to the licence and the master's degree. But the matter could not be allowed to rest here. If Ramus were right, then the learned world, not merely of Paris but of the whole of Europe, must be wrong; for Ramus's challenge called in question the fundamental principles upon which the whole structure of knowledge was built. His action in putting forward his subject for disputation has not inaptly been compared to Luther's act when he nailed his theses to the church door at Wittenberg. Each alike cut to the root of conventional and traditional modes of thinking; each alike may perhaps be accused of couching his challenge in exaggerated language. But the reformer who does not overstate his case runs a risk of lacking an audience, and with Ramus there is abundant evidence that his youthful exuberance and self-assertiveness mellowed with age.

Contemporary judgments on Rámus's act varied considerably. To most observers he was merely a hot-headed revolutionary, eager for self-advertisement—"un génie hardi, amateur de la nouveauté, passioné pour la gloire." A certain professor Galland, who afterwards became Rector

---

[1] See *supra*, p. 11.

of the University, went so far as to call the young *maître-
ès-arts* a "parricide." But there was a progressive minority
who realised the value of Ramus's work and were prepared
to support him. He began teaching first at the Collège du
Mans and afterwards at the Collège Ave Maria or Huban.
In the latter institution, with the help of his life-long friend
Omer Talon, he started public lectures to which large
audiences were attracted. The whole trend of Ramus's
teaching was definitely in opposition to the Aristotelian
methods employed by the University, and thus he kept alight
the ardent hostility of the Peripatetic champions. But his
crowning act of heresy came in the year 1543 when he
published his Logic or *Dialecticæ Partitiones* and his *Aristotelicæ Animadversiones*. The latter was a bitter and un-
balanced attack on the ancient philosopher and could not
be passed over by a University which still officially adhered
to the mediaeval standpoint. Ramus was arraigned and
charged (like Socrates, whom he so warmly admired) with
being an enemy to religion and a corrupter of youth. The
first of these charges is an interesting commentary on the
extent to which the methods of the heathen philosopher
had been applied to the Christian religion in order to evolve
the mediaeval system of theology. A Royal Commission
was appointed and Ramus was adjudged to have acted
"rashly, arrogantly and impudently[1]." His books were
condemned and were publicly burnt in front of the Collège
de Cambrai. An attempt was even made to get the author
condemned to the gallows, but for the time being Ramus
escaped martyrdom in the cause of what he believed to be
the truth. As he said at the time: "Only the hemlock is
lacking."

A copy of the condemnation of Ramus was sent abroad
to all foreign universities, so that the University of Paris to
some extent saved its reputation in the eyes of learned
Europe. Ramus himself was forbidden to teach or lecture
on philosophy; but owing partly to the protection of Charles
of Lorraine, formerly a fellow-student of his and now a

[1] "Ramum temere, arroganter, et impudenter fecisse." See
Bréchillet-Jourdain, *Index*, MDCCLXXII, 354. The date is March, 1544.

cardinal, and partly to the fact that *philosophy* only was mentioned in the ban, Ramus was not silenced by being thus proscribed. Before long we find him lecturing on rhetoric and mathematics at the Collège Ave Maria. But a more influential post awaited him. Early in 1545[1] a plague broke out in Paris and most of the members of the University sought safety in flight. When the scare was past Ramus was asked to reorganise the Collège de Presles, in the capacity of principal. There he taught rhetoric and his friend Omer Talon assisted him by taking the course in philosophy. In 1547 Henri II came to the throne; his tutor had been Ramus's patron Charles of Lorraine, and to this cause we can trace the fact that the embargo laid upon Ramus teaching philosophy was at once removed; in fact, the *arrêt* of 1544 was entirely reversed.

Ramus made good use of his newly-recovered freedom. He republished his books which had been condemned and produced two new volumes in which Cicero and Quintilian were severely criticised[2]. Now these two authors held somewhat the same position with regard to the rhetoric course of the Faculty of Arts that Aristotle had in the teaching of philosophy. Once more the storm arose and conspicuous among the opponents of Ramus now appears Jacques Charpentier or Carpenterius, a teacher at the Collège de Boncour. This man became Ramus's life-long enemy and persecutor. The general attitude of the University also was definitely hostile to Ramus. His criticisms were too unsettling and there must have been an uneasy apprehension as to where his next attack might be delivered. In an entry in the Register of the Faculty of Medicine at this period Ramus is referred to as "universitatis hostem." As Crevier aptly remarks: "Ramus étoit de ces hommes qui ne sont point faits pour exciter des sentimens mediocres. La haine ou l'affection pour lui se portoient à l'excès[3]."

---

[1] Desmaze (p. 100) says 1544, but the date in the text is right. See Bréchillet-Jourdain, *Index*, MDCCLXXXVI, 355.

[2] *Brutinæ quæstiones in Oratorem Ciceronis* (1546) and *Rhetoricæ distinctiones in Quintilianum* (1549).

[3] V, 445.

But outside the University there were not wanting those who could realise the greatness of Ramus. The Collège Royal or Collège de France, which had been founded by François I, was quite independent of the University of Paris and it tended to be progressive, since it was less hampered by the traditional scholastic curriculum. There were professors of Greek, Hebrew, mathematics, philosophy, medicine, and rhetoric[1], each of whom received a salary from the king's own treasury and held the dignity of a royal councillor. Attendance at their lectures did not, of course, count towards the attaining of a degree in the University, but they were—and still are to-day—free to all students who cared to profit by them. It was to a chair in this royal foundation that Ramus was invited and he entered upon his new work in 1551. It is said that no less than two thousand auditors were present when, in his inaugural lecture, he set forth his views on Aristotelianism and on educational and university reform. The brilliance of his teaching did not decline, and in spite of minor vexations—such as the well-known controversy on the proper pronunciation of *Qu* in Latin—he continued to work with unabated vigour. In 1554 appeared a new edition of the *Institutiones Logicae* and it was followed by treatises on Arithmetic, Geometry, and Physics. As a matter of fact, the attention of Ramus had been given increasingly to the study of mathematics, and in 1559 he began a course of lectures on this subject at the Collège de France.

In July 1559 Henri II died; and this date marks the decline of Ramus's most flourishing period which had begun in 1551 when he was appointed to the Royal College. The various attacks which were made upon him by the Sorbonnists who pronounced "quisquis" *kiskis*, or by Galland who found fault with Ramus's method of expounding the classical orators, had been brought to nought. His credit with the University had also revived during this period, and his colleagues did not hesitate to use his favour with the king for their own advantage. Among the deputies who approached Henri II on the occasion of the disturbances in 1557[2] was Ramus, and it was largely owing to his good

[1] The number was afterwards increased.   [2] See *supra*, p. 15.

offices that the matter was settled satisfactorily. He also employed his influence to the advantage of the Collège de France by securing the payment to various professors of salaries which had become overdue. In the year 1557 a Royal Commission of which Ramus was a member had been held to enquire into the question of university reform. As might have been expected, this was a subject in which Ramus was keenly interested; but little seems to have resulted from the labours of the Commission. Ramus was not discouraged. He continued to give the subject his earnest attention and in 1562 published a scheme of his own entitled *Proœmium reformandæ Parisiensis Academiæ ad Regem*[1]. He points out that the number of teachers in the University has increased, while the number of students has remained stationary; the result has been an increase of fees and of incidental expenses which proves a heavy burden to a poor scholar. Some examples of the growth of university fees and of the expenses connected with various celebrations have already been given[2]. We can sympathise with Ramus's impatience when he sees all this frippery of banquets, candles, robes, and "bonnetz." In his clear-sighted search for truth and his single-hearted pursuit of knowledge, he would clear away all these trappings and abolish all university fees. The number of professors should be reduced and the chairs filled only by the best scholars and teachers that the University can produce. Ramus also pleads for a fuller teaching of mathematics, "qui sont les premiers des artz libéraulx, sans lesquelz toute l'autre philosophie est aveuglée[3]," and even of natural science without which there can be "nul usage ni expérience des choses." He would retain the three subjects of the *trivium*—grammar, rhetoric, and logic—in the first part of the Arts course, but after that he advocates putting mathematics "au premier honneur et degré," and following it up by a year's course in physics and ethics[4]. To put these

---

[1] A French version appeared at the same time with the title: *Avertissements sur la réformation de l'Université de Paris, au Roy*. It is quoted in Cimber and Danjou, *Archives Curieuses*, v, 117 ff.

[2] See *supra*, p. 12.   [3] *Op. cit.* p. 138.

[4] *Op. cit.* p. 123.

studies within the reach of every student in the Faculty of
Arts Ramus recommends the restoration of public lectures
such as had been given in former times in the rue du Fouarre.
The necessary funds for carrying out all these reforms may
be obtained from the disendowment of rich convents and
monasteries; addressing the king, but with a bitter side-
thrust at one of the abuses of his day, Ramus, in his
Prœmium, remarks: "The numerous religious houses of
Paris will count themselves most happy and highly honoured
to bear this expense, and will furnish it willingly and
promptly if only you, Sire, command them to do so[1]."

These and other fierce attacks upon the opulent and
indolent religious orders, large numbers of whom had their
houses in the University quarter in the southern part of
Paris, lead us to consider a new phase in the life of Ramus
and one which helps to explain why his period of comparative
prosperity came to an end soon after the death of Henri II.
By his attacks upon Aristotle and Cicero he had already
risked the enmity of those who had most influence in the
University; but he now brought upon himself the hostility
of the orthodox Church by espousing the cause of the reformed religion. As late as 1561 Ramus was outwardly a
conforming Catholic; but a spirit of criticism of the established religion was abroad and the University did not escape
its influence. In 1557, for instance, an *arrêt*[2] was passed by
the Parlement de Paris ordering all regents and *pédagogues*
to take the students who were under their charge to hear

---

[1] Ramus's recommendations have not yet lost their appositeness;
in fact the development of mathematics and natural science as
organised knowledge since his time gives added point to his remarks.
At Oxford the traditional course in philosophy is to this day based
on a study of classical literature. Yet it would seem—to say the
least—not unreasonable that mathematics or natural science should
form as suitable an introduction to philosophy as a study of linguistic
or poetry or classical historians and orators. Ramus complains that
a man "wholly ignorant of the sciences obtains the degree in philosophy," and the same criticism may be made of some of those who
to-day take the highest honours in the school of *Literæ Humaniores*.

[2] It is dated Oct. 21st. See Félibien, II, 1061. The decree was to be
enforced "sur peine de la hart et de confiscation de corps et de
biens."

Mass on Sundays and festivals. But Ramus was too honest
with himself and his neighbours to be deterred by legislation
from doing what he believed to be right. As has already
been seen, the Church had utilised what it conceived to be
the philosophy of Aristotle in order to build a framework
for Christian theology; an attack on Aristotle therefore
led on inevitably to an attitude of scepticism with regard to
the dogmas of the Catholic Church. But Ramus seems to
have been finally persuaded to break with the established
religion by the results of the Colloquy of Poissy. This
conference, which was held in September, 1561, was an
attempt to promote an understanding between the Catholic
party and the Huguenots who had already become a large
and influential section of the community[1]. But the doctrine
of the Real Presence proved an insuperable stumbling-block
and the conference broke down. The impossibility of reconciling the Protestantism of the Reformers with the
traditional Christianity of the Catholic Church became
apparent; and Ramus, for one, had no hesitation as to which
party he should join. His choice completely altered the
attitude of his old fellow-student and patron, Charles of
Lorraine. The Cardinal had been the chief champion of
Catholicism at the Colloquy and we can hardly be surprised
that he withdrew his support from one whom he believed to
have deliberately allied himself with the arch-enemies of the
Church. Thus Ramus's open adherence to the reformed religion meant much more than a mere change of opinion; it
involved forfeiting the favour of the king, with whom Charles
of Lorraine had great influence, and it rendered him more
than ever suspect in the eyes of the University. The students
of the Collège de Presles, following in religious as well as
in intellectual matters the Principal whom they had learned
to respect and to love, showed their Protestant zeal by
breaking into the college chapel and overthrowing the images
of saints. Such an incident could hardly be ignored, and the
enemies of Ramus eagerly took advantage of it. By a decree
of July 9th, 1562[2], all teachers in the University were

[1] See *infra*, p. 82.
[2] Bréchillet-Jourdain, *Index*, MCMLII, 380.

ordered to sign a profession of faith which was to be drawn up by the Faculty of Theology and which would leave no loophole for "la religion prétendue réformée." Under these circumstances Ramus could no longer continue to teach in the University, and he therefore retired to Fontainebleau, there to await a change of fortune.

The time was one of the utmost turmoil. The Wars of Religion, which were destined to deluge France with blood for thirty years, had begun. The whole country was split into two factions—the Huguenots, headed by Condé, and the Catholic party led by the Duc de Guise. The first act in this tragedy ended with the capture of Condé by Guise, followed by the murder of Guise himself by a Huguenot fanatic. In March, 1563, an unsatisfactory peace was effected, but it enabled Ramus to emerge from his seclusion at Fontainebleau and to return to his post at the Collège de Presles. There he resumed his lectures on philosophy and mathematics, refusing to accept the offer of an important professorship in the University of Bologna. But the horizon grew more and more threatening. Dark clouds of religious strife again began to gather, while the rise of the Jesuits, who had opened their Collège de Clermont in Paris in 1563, menaced not only the reformed religion but also the educational monopoly of the University. Moreover, the Cardinal of Lorraine, for reasons which have already been indicated, had withdrawn his support from Ramus and given it to Carpentarius. It was not long before the two antagonists were involved in another contest. In 1565 an incompetent person was appointed to the chair of mathematics at the Royal College. Realising his deficiencies, he sold his professorship to Carpentarius who was equally ignorant of the subject but is said to have remarked cynically that he could easily get it up within three months[1]. Ramus was jealous for the honour of this science and had no tinge of that contempt for non-literary studies which even yet is not quite extinct among those who profess the humanities. He therefore raised a vigorous protest against this scandalous transaction and appealed to the courts for redress[2]. Carpentarius was con-

[1] See Crevier, VI, 199.
[2] See Bréchillet-Jourdain, *Index*, MCMLXXXI, 385, and MCMXCVI, 386.

demned to prison and forced to recant, but in revenge he instigated a furious attack upon Ramus and attempts were even made on his life.

In 1567 the storm, which had been brewing since the hollow peace of Amboise, broke; and in the course of the ensuing civil war Paris was besieged by the Huguenot army. During this period Ramus took refuge in the Protestant camp[1], but at the peace of Longjumeau in March, 1568, he returned once more to the Collège de Presles. But the trend of events both within the University and in the larger world outside made it impossible for him to remain there, and Ramus sought and obtained permission from the king to travel in foreign countries until quieter times should return to his distracted motherland. He visited the Protestant districts of Germany and Switzerland. Everywhere he was hailed as one of the champions of the reformed religion and in Heidelberg he is said to have received communion in a Calvinistic church[2]. At the same time he was recognised as the greatest scholar that the University of Paris could show at this period; not inaptly he was hailed as the "French Plato." Several attempts were made to retain him as a professor at one of the Protestant universities of Germany; but, as in the case of the offer that had come from Bologna, he refused to abandon "son royaume de Presles."

His devotion to the University of Paris is the more remarkable in that he must have realised the danger of his position and the power of his enemies. Yet he still believed that the cause of educational reform would triumph amid all the political disturbances of the day. Before setting out on his travels in 1568 he had made a will[3] leaving practically all that he possessed to found a chair of mathematics (including arithmetic, geometry, music, optics, mechanics, astronomy and geography) in the Collège de France. Typical of the testator is the proviso that these subjects should be

---

[1] There is an *arrêt* of the Parlement de Paris, dated Jan. 29th, 1568, delegating the principalship of the Collège de Presles to M. Antoine Muldrat, bachelier en théologie, in place of M. Pierre de la Ramée, "absent pour cause de religion." [2] See Crevier, VI, 268.
[3] *Testamentum Petri Rami* (Paris, 1576); see also Bréchillet-Jourdain, *Index*, MMVIII, 387.

taught "non ad hominum opinionem sed ad logicam veri-
tatem[1]." The professorship was subsequently filled by some
of the most illustrious of French scientists and lasted until
the year 1732, when it lapsed through lack of funds. But
the royal foundation could offer nothing but persecution to
its benefactor and its most illustrious professor. The enemies
of Ramus were busy. Owing to the influence of the fanatical
Catholic party in the University, allied for the purpose with
the Society of Jesus, the Crown had been induced to issue
a decree forbidding anyone, who did not subscribe to the
orthodox religion, to hold a chair either in the University
itself or at the Collège de France. When therefore Ramus
returned from his travels he found the door shut in his face;
as a self-confessed Protestant, he could no longer be either
principal of the Collège de Presles or professor in the Royal
College. He appealed to the king, but in vain. He applied
for a professorship of philosophy at the University of Geneva,
the rector of which, Beza, had formerly been the Protestant
champion at the Colloquy of Poissy. But Beza replied that
there was no vacancy at Geneva and no funds wherewith
to establish a new chair; moreover that his University would
forego "ne tantillum quidem" of the teachings of Aristotle.
This answer was so discouraging that Ramus made no further
attempts in this direction; but at last a modification of the
obnoxious decree was obtained. Ramus was permitted to
return to the Collège de Presles, but at the same time he was
forbidden to *teach*[2]. Accordingly he betook himself to writing,
and from the year 1570 to his death in 1572 he laboured
incessantly with his pen.

Meanwhile the fierce party-strife between Huguenot and
Catholic grew more vigorous than ever and culminated in
the horrible butchery which began on St Bartholomew's
Day, 1572. It was on the third day of the massacre that a
band of assassins broke into the Collège de Presles where the
venerable principal awaited his end with a calm fortitude.

---

[1] *Testamentum*, p. 4.
[2] The college accounts are signed by Ramus for the years 1570
and 1571. He did not sign those for 1572, although they are dated
June 30th. See Desmaze, p. 102.

His body, mangled but not altogether lifeless, was hurled out of an upper window into the courtyard below. But his enemies were not content with their bloody revenge. With ghastly cynicism and in contemptuous reference to his profession, his corpse was flogged by students[1], egged on by regents who had hated Ramus; and finally it was dragged through the mud to be thrown into the Seine. The causes of his death were doubtless his unconcealed attachment to Protestantism and his spirit of reform which, when applied to the existing institutions of the University, seemed to imply a criticism of his fellow-teachers there. But it has been established, almost beyond a doubt[2], that the prime instigator of the murder was Carpentarius who for long had regarded Ramus with bitter hostility. It would seem then that Carpentarius, like so many other participators in the massacre, profited by an outburst of popular fury against the Protestants in general to rid himself of a particular Protestant against whom he had a private enmity.

In Ramus perished the greatest French thinker of the sixteenth century. He inevitably invites contrast with his contemporary Montaigne. Both were in a sense free-thinkers; but while the essayist is a cynical, half-contemptuous Pyrrhonist, who deliberately chose as his motto the words: "Que sçais-je?", Ramus is a serious and earnest seeker after truth, who waged a life-long battle against uncritical dogmatism, and who laid down his life rather than compromise with what he believed to be false. His career is a remarkable parallel with that of Socrates, for whom he always had the warmest admiration. Ramus was essentially a critic and a reformer and he applied his reforms to almost every branch of knowledge; but he remained an academic writer and his influence therefore, outside university circles, was small. The charming essays of Montaigne, although the work of a man of less profound character, did far more to spread abroad a spirit of free inquiry and to break the spell of tradition, than did all the weighty volumes of the professorial Ramus; the fact being that the essayist was a popular, and the

[1] "Ils le frappèrent d'escourgés au mépris de sa profession."
[2] See Waddington, p. 270.

university teacher an academic, philosopher. At the same time Ramus was not a mere theorist who inculcated principles which he had not already tested in practice. All that he advocates is the outcome of deep experience and the reformed methods in education which he recommended had already been tried and proved efficient. His position at the Collège de Presles and the Collège de France gave him ample opportunity for testing his theories, and therefore in matters educational, he is not an armchair critic like Montaigne or Rabelais—or so many other writers since who have aired their views on the subject. For all these reasons Ramus must always be an outstanding figure in the history alike of educational thought and of educational practice. It is incumbent upon us, therefore, to estimate shortly the value of his reforms.

At a time when far too much stress was still laid upon authority—whether of Aristotle in philosophy or of the Church in religion—Ramus steadfastly upheld the supremacy of reason. He strenuously opposes any coercive dogma, in whatever realm of human knowledge it is applied. "Nulla auctoritas rationis, sed ratio auctoritatis regina dominaque esse debet[1]." The human mind must be unfettered in its pursuit of truth; "libertatem animi excelsam, amabilem, gloriosam; servitutem autem caducam, detestabilem, odiosam semper esse duxi[2]." In this spirit he proposes to treat all the arts and sciences *more Socratico*, brushing aside the petty quibbles and trivial subtleties of a degenerate scholasticism. This method, he says, was that employed by Plato and Aristotle, by Hippocrates and Galen, by Virgil and Homer, by Cicero and Demosthenes. Ramus's attempt to make all knowledge his province may have resulted in a certain shallowness of treatment in some of the branches of learning with which he deals; and this reproach has often been levelled against him. But this does not detract from the value of his method itself. He is indeed the direct forerunner of Descartes and Bacon and, in fact, of all thinkers since who have applied inductive and critical methods to philosophy and science alike.

[1] *Scholæ Math.* iii, 78.   [2] *Dialecticæ Partitiones*, p. 3.

In applying his system to the processes of education Ramus distinguishes three steps to which he gives the names of Nature, System, and Practice. Under the first heading comes a study of the actual subject matter of the science or art concerned. In "grammar," for example, it would be the actual words of the classical authors themselves; in logic, the actual operations of the human mind. The right attitude is one of original research, not of complacent deference to authority. This operation is followed by System—the sifting and arrangement of the material that has already been acquired. But the process does not stop here; the knowledge gained must be applied to some useful end—it must be put into Practice. "Ç'a esté toute mon estude," Ramus says, "d'oster du chemin des artz libéraux les espines, les cailloux, et tous empeschements et retardements des esprits, de faire la voye plaine et droicte pour parvenir plus aisément, non-seulement à l'intelligence mais à la pratique et à l'usage des artz libéraux[1]." This insistence on the practical application of knowledge is characteristic of Ramus and earned for him among his contemporaries the nickname of *usuarius*— "the utilitarian."

Let us now examine how the method of Ramus was applied to the curriculum of the Faculty of Arts. It had come down from the Middle Ages and was divided into the traditional Trivium and Quadrivium. The former comprised "grammar" (*i.e.* the classical languages), rhetoric, and dialectic or logic; while the latter dealt with arithmetic, geometry, astronomy and music. But it was the Trivium which occupied the student in the Faculty of Arts during the greater part of his seven or eight year course. Music—or rather the theory of this subject—had by the time of Ramus practically disappeared from the curriculum, and the mathematical subjects were studied in an *a priori* fashion from such text-books as the *Physica* and *Meteorica* of Aristotle. The most vital part of the whole system was the study of grammar and dialectic, and it is here therefore that the reforms of Ramus were of greatest importance.

The first years of a boy's career in one of the colleges of

[1] *Remonstrance au Conseil privé*, p. 21.

the University were spent in mastering the classical languages
—especially Latin. To aid him in this task he used the
Grammar of Ælius Donatus which had been written in the
fourth century and, with elaborations and commentaries,
was still being used in the sixteenth; or, perhaps, he studied
the *Doctrinale* of Alexander de Villa Dei, which was written
in Latin hexameters and had been published about the year
1200[1]. Both these books in the time of Ramus were giving
place to the *Grammatica* of the Fleming Van Pauteren or
Despauter; this volume also was written in barbarous Latin
verse and it attained a wide popularity on the continent[2].
All these books alike exhibit a complexity which must
inevitably have beset the early stages of learning Latin with
"espines et cailloux." Exceptions, irregularities and rarities
appear as conspicuously as the normal declensions and the
commonest words, and the authors have evidently not
realised, with Quintilian, that there are some things of which
a grammarian ought to be ignorant. When we turn to
Ramus's own Latin Grammar[3] we find a most marked contrast with the *Doctrinale* or the *Grammatica* of Despauter.
True, the treatise which aims at teaching Latin is still written
in Latin; but the brambles and stones which beset the
traveller's path have been cleared away and the grammar
has been simplified to an astonishing extent. Ramus defines
grammar as "ars bene loquendi—id autem est Latinis
latine[4]." He classifies nouns under four declensions—two of
"parisyllables" and two of "imparisyllables"; and the
verbs are classified into two conjugations with the future in
"*-bo*" and two with the future in "*-am*." Ramus proceeds
to treat of the rules for agreement in the case of nouns and
of verbs, and he concludes his treatise with a section on
syntax. To a modern reader the book is remarkable because
it is the first of its kind which, if translated into English,
would bear any resemblance to the average Latin primer

[1] For details as to these two books consult Adamson, *Short History*,
pp. 14–15 and 68–71.
[2] For details see Barnard, *Little Schools of Port-Royal*, pp. 126–128.
[3] *Grammaticæ Latinæ, Libri IV* (Paris, 1559).
[4] *Op. cit.* p. 5.

used in the schools of to-day. The verses of Alexander de Villa Dei or of Despauter and the turgid prose of the Donats, with their exhaustive lists and their complicated classification, are utterly foreign to the modern conception of a text-book designed for school use.

Ramus recommends a three-years' course in "grammar" and under this head he would include Greek as well as Latin. True to his general method, he would have the rules learnt largely through illustrations drawn from the best classical writers and he believes that the study of authors should begin as soon as possible.

The pupil who has passed through the "grammar" course will be ready to embark upon the study of rhetoric—"ars bene dicendi," as Ramus defines it. He restricts this subject to mere forms of speech and would not deal at this stage with the underlying mental processes. Of greater value, therefore, are his reforms in the next stage of the curriculum—the study of logic or dialectic—"ars bene disserendi." As has already been indicated, the staple of this course throughout Europe for some centuries past had been an arid and un-critical study of Aristotle's *Organon*, with mediaeval com-mentaries; the aim of the process being to enable the pupil to take part in syllogistic disputations. Ramus would clear away all this formal parroting and study the actual processes of the laws of thought. But instead of concentrating his attention on the operations of his own mind, as did Descartes, he is still so far fettered by mediaeval tradition that he naturally turns to classical authors for guidance. He collects examples of various mental processes as illustrated in the writings of the Greek and Latin poets, orators and historians[1]; then he applies his process of System and classifies them. "Pour avoir le vray loz(*i.e.* lois) de la logique," he says, "n'est pas assez de sçavoir caqueter en l'eschole des reigles d'icelle, mais il les fault pratiquer ès poëtes, orateurs, philosophes, c'est-a-dire en toute espèce d'esprits[2]." At the same time

---

[1] The title of Ramus's chair at the Collège de France was that of "eloquence and philosophy." It was in his lectures here that he applied the principles described in the text. Refer also to *De Studiis Eloquentiæ ac Philosophiæ coniungendis Oratio* (1546).

[2] *Dialectique*, p. 137.

Ramus was not in bondage to his classical authorities; he collected and classified their methods of reasoning, but he did not neglect to examine them in the light of his own reason, and he had no exaggerated respect for Plato or for Cicero. He can look beyond his authors to the truth itself.

Of Ramus's reforms in what remained of the mediaeval Quadrivium little need be said. As has been pointed out above[1], he was an earnest student of mathematics and bequeathed his fortune to found a chair of this subject at the Collège de France. He would include the higher and applied branches of the science, and here again he does his best to investigate actualities rather than to take statements on trust. In dealing with natural phenomena, however, he is less consistently true to his own method. He is often content to appeal to classical works (as, for example, the *Georgics*) rather than to actual observation. It is at this point that one begins to realise the vastness of the task which Ramus had set himself and to wonder not that he left certain things undone, but that he managed successfully to apply his method to so large a part of the entire field of human knowledge.

No estimate of Ramus's importance in the history of education would be complete did it not take into account his services to his native language. In the sixteenth century Latin was the medium of conversation and instruction in the schools and universities not only of France but of all western Europe. It was regarded as the only tongue in which a book could be written in order to render it of permanent value. Erasmus despised the vernaculars; at Sturm's school at Strasbourg to speak in one's native tongue was expiated "non nisi plagis." Even Montaigne considered that his Essays were destined "à peu d'hommes et à peu d'années" because they were written in French. Here we cannot do more than refer briefly to this subject[2]; but the rise of the vernacular literatures was bound to affect the position which spoken and written Latin held in the educational system of Europe. Ramus was one of the first of the

---

[1] See *supra*, pp. 22 and 27.

[2] I have dealt with it at greater length in *The Little Schools of Port-Royal*, pp. 107–113.

French reformers who attempted to make their native tongue replace Latin as the language of scholars. His *Dialectic*, to which reference has already been made, was written in French, and in this respect at least—if in no others—it paved the way for the Port-Royal *Logic* which appeared more than a century later. Even more interesting is Ramus's Grammar of the French language in which he anticipates the modern movement in favour of a simplified spelling. This book takes the form of a dialogue between a "précepteur" and his pupil, and the text is given in parallel columns; on one side appears the ordinary French of the period and on the other the equivalent in the system of spelling advocated by Ramus. The volume is prefaced by a scheme explaining the symbols which the author adopts. They number some thirty in all and are classified as *voyelles, demivoyelles liquides, demivoyelles fermes,* and *muettes;* in addition there are eight diphthongs. The treatment of the subject matter of the book is closely parallel to that adopted in Ramus's Latin Grammar; it need not detain us, for the chief interest of the work for the modern reader lies in the system of spelling adopted. The following excerpt[1] will serve to give an idea of it. The "précepteur" is speaking (Ramus's equivalent of this passage in ordinary contemporary spelling is given in the right-hand column):

Or juſkęs iſi ję vɤs e deklarę leʹs Rudimens dę notre langę Franſoeʒ̧ leʹfkeʹlz (komę j'eʃpeʹrę) ſęront amendes pętit a pętit, akrus e ωgmentes par l'etudę e dilijenſę deʹs bons e ſavans eʃpris Franſeʹos, ki ſ' adonęront dę plus eʹn plus a orner e embeʹlir lɤr patrię, nõ ſɵlęment par teʹlz enſeŋęmens, meʹs par notablęs exemplęs e vre uzaję, lękeʹl vɤs ſęra propoze bęωkɤp plus pɤr bien parler e kɤçer par ekrit, kę tɤtęs leʹs reʹglęs dę gramerę kę l'on pɤrroet in- venter.	Or iusques icy ie vous ay de- claire les Rudimens de nostre langueFrancoyse,lesquels(comme iespere) seront amendez petit a petit, accreus & augmentez par lestude & diligence des bons & scavans esprits Francoys, qui sa- donnerõt de plus en plus a aorner & embellir leur patrie, non seul- lemẽt par tels enseignements, maisparnotables exemples & vray vsaige, lequel vous sera propose beaucoup plus pour biẽ parler & coucher par escript, que toutes les reigles de grammaire que lon pourroit inuenter.

[1] *Grammaire* (1587), pp. 221–2. The earliest edition of this book, in which the scheme of spelling differs slightly from that adopted here, appeared in 1562.

It is, of course, difficult for us to know exactly the standard pronunciation of French (if there was such a thing) at the time when Ramus wrote; but through the kindness of M. Paul Passy and on his authority, I am enabled to give the following transcript, in modern phonetic symbols, of the passage quoted above, showing how probably Ramus would have pronounced it in the sixteenth century[1]:

ɔːr ʒyskəz isi ʒə vuz e dɛklare lɛ(z) rydimɛ̃n(z) də notrə lɑ̃ŋgə frɑ̃nsŏɛːzə, lɛ(s)kɛl(s) komə ʒɛspɛr(ə) sərõnt amɛ̃nde(s) pətit a pəti(t), akry(z) ɛ ɔːgmɛ̃nte(s) par lɛtyd ɛ diliʒɛ̃nsə dɛ(z) bõnz ɛ savɑ̃nz ɛspris frɑ̃nsŏɛs, ki sadonərõnt də plyz ɛ̃mplys a orner ɛ ɛ̃mbɛlir lœr patriə, nõ sœləmɛ̃nt par tɛlz ɛ̃nsɛɲəmɛ̃ns, mɛ(s) par notabləz ɛgzɛ̃mpləs ɛ vre yzaʒə, ləkɛl vus səra propoze bŏɔːkup plys pur bĩen parler e kuʃer par ɛkrit, kə tutə(z) lɛ(z) rɛglə(z) də gramɛrə kə l õm purrŏɛt ĩnvɛ̃nter.

It'is possible that the spelling advocated by Ramus may not have been intended to be strictly phonetic; it may have been merely an attempt to simplify the current orthography, but it had to take into account the fact—for example— that there is normally no difference in pronunciation between the singular and plural of a French noun. Still the experiment is not without its value and its interest in view of subsequent developments; and it serves also to illustrate the versatility and reforming zeal of its inventer. Crevier, with a half sarcastic touch, remarks that Ramus was so fond of reforms that he even invented a simplified spelling[2]. The *Grammaire* certainly ran through many editions, but there is no evidence that Ramus's improved alphabet was ever adopted. There are perhaps insuperable obstacles— even in these enlightened days—which hinder the adoption to any great extent of even the best conceived schemes of spelling reform.

Ramus's claim to greatness rests upon more important

---

[1] Ramus had a slight provincial accent. Cf. "Ie recognois de jour à autre plusieurs traicts de vostre picard." Pasquier, *Lettres*, Bk III, No. 4. [2] See VI, 269.

services to the cause of education. He struck a powerful
blow to free human thought from the bondage to which it
had gradually become enslaved during the Middle Ages. He
looked back to the example of classical antiquity, just as in
religion he recoiled from what he regarded as the slavery of
mediaeval Catholicism, and wished to return to the freedom
of the early days of Christianity. He maintains an untram-
melled and rationalising spirit, and resists the tyranny of
authority wherever he finds it. The burden of Calvinism is
almost as distasteful to him as the burden of Catholicism;
and in religious matters he seems to have inclined towards
the views advocated by Zwingli. In his educational method
he adopts a definitely modern standpoint; he would clear
away all possible difficulties from the learner's path and
would advance always from what is easy to what is more
difficult. This is the keynote of all his educational treatises
and he sets an example which was extensively followed in the
century after that in which he lived.

Ramus is indeed the forerunner of Descartes and of the
Port-Royalists. His reforms spread widely, particularly in
Protestant countries, and his system received the name of
"Ramism." Even in the conservative and Catholic kingdom
of Spain the grammarian Sanctius, at Salamanca, based his
work on the *Grammatica* of Ramus. In England the University of Oxford imitated her sister of Paris in condemning
the doctrines of Ramus. In 1574, for example, a student
named Barebone was degraded for having proposed to
attack the philosophy of Aristotle. But at Cambridge and
at the Scottish Universities Ramism found many supporters.
Milton, himself a Cambridge man, published in 1672 a
treatise on Logic which was an abridgment of the *Dialectic*
of Ramus[1]. Yet it remains true that the services which

[1] It is entitled *Artis logicæ plenior institutio ad Petri Rami methodum
concinnata*. The following is a quotation from the Preface: "Quan-
quam philosophorum multi, suopte ingenio freti, contempsisse artem
logicam dicuntur, eorum tamen qui vel sibi vel aliis propter ingenium
aut iudicium natura minus acre ac perspicax utilissimam esse sibique
diligenter excolendam iudicarunt, optime est de ea meritus, ut ego
quidem eum Sidneio nostro sentio, Petrus Ramus."

Ramus rendered to the cause of educational progress have
been largely forgotten. He paved the way for other men who
entered into his labours and to whom posterity has awarded
the fame. Ramus lived at a period which in some respects
might almost be considered as still part of the "Dark Ages";
scholasticism, valuable as it had once been, had degenerated into barren formalism; it had played its part and
had now to give place to a new and more effective system.
Ramus was one of the greatest of those who heralded the
new era. He belongs essentially to modern times because of
his spirit of reform and his passion for liberty. He was
entirely devoted to the interests of knowledge and progress.
In an age when party and sectarian strife wasted the land
and filled life with turmoil and danger, he pursued as best
he could his peaceful avocation as a scholar and a teacher;
and yet with an absolute fearlessness and a whole-hearted
devotion to the truth, as he conceived it, he was ready to
sacrifice wealth, comfort, even life itself. Addressing those
who should come after him, he once said: "I am happy to
think that if I have been tossed by the tempest, if I have had
to encounter so many reefs, my troubles will at any rate have
served to make the course easier and safer for you." The
subsequent history of human thought, not only in France
but in every country to which western civilisation has
penetrated, proves that not in vain did Ramus make his
valiant stand for truth and lay down his life in her cause.

CHAPTER II

ELEMENTARY EDUCATION AND THE EDU-
CATION OF GIRLS—ANNE DE XAINCTONGE

I N France under the *ancien régime* the education of girls
plays a far less important part than that of boys. This
phenomenon is, of course, not confined either to this particular period or to France alone, for only within quite recent
times has the principle been generally admitted that girls
are entitled to as complete an education as that which is
permitted to their brothers. But although the Middle Ages
had neglected the education of girls, the Renaissance brought
the question into prominence. In the fifteenth century the
humanists of Italy—at any rate in such towns as Florence
or Ferrara—had admitted the right of women to a higher
education such as was possible for men; though even so this
privilege was confined to women of the governing class. In
the sixteenth and seventeenth centuries also there were not
wanting those who, like Vives, Erasmus, Mulcaster, and
Fénelon, pleaded for a deeper and more widespread education for the future mothers of the race; but few even of such
advanced thinkers as these were prepared to carry the instruction of girls to the degree that was prescribed for boys.
Men were ready to admire learning in a lady of high rank
such as Lady Jane Grey or Marguerite d'Angoulême, or in
the daughters of some famous scholar, such as Pirkheimer
of Nuremberg. But there was always a very general hesitation to extend opportunities for education of an advanced
type to daughters of the people. This does not mean that
the education of girls was entirely neglected; but it does
imply that it was normally of a quite rudimentary kind.
It comprised reading, writing, domestic accomplishments,
and possibly arithmetic as far as what Mrs Malaprop would
term "a supercilious knowledge in accounts." A girl who,
like Margaret More, could read Greek, Latin, and Hebrew,

was a *rara avis*; and because such instances were unusual
there is perhaps a tendency to emphasise them when they
do occur. An account of the education of girls in France (or
indeed elsewhere) during the period under discussion is
therefore a description of what would now be called elementary education; and we must deal with the whole subject
a little more widely in order to ascertain what exactly was
the type of education which was available for the great
majority of girls in France from the latter part of the
sixteenth century almost down to the Revolution. The
schools to which they might be sent were of three types—
the *petites écoles* or little schools, the charity schools, and
the schools attached to convents. We will consider each of
these in turn.

The "little schools" were in origin designed to provide a
free elementary education. An *ordonnance* of 1560 even lays
it down that "parents are forced, under penalty of fine, to
send their children of both sexes to school[1]." Sixteen years
later the États de Blois considered a proposal to levy a
contribution upon ecclesiastical revenues for the maintenance of a schoolmaster in every town and village, to give
gratuitous instruction to children in the "Christian religion,
other necessary branches of knowledge, and good manners."
In 1598, again—the year of the Edict of Nantes—a law of
Henri IV re-enacts the command that parents are to send
their children, whether boys or girls, to school. Nothing
could be more explicit than these regulations; but there
is plenty of evidence to show that it was found impossible
to enforce compulsory elementary education. The difficulties
were many; sufficient funds to finance such a project were
not available; the public opinion of the day held the office
of elementary teacher in low esteem; there was no widespread desire on the part of the parents of the poorer classes
to avail themselves of an education for their children even
when it was offered free of cost.

At the same time a real attempt was made to staff these
little schools and so to render them efficient. The masters
or mistresses (*maîtres* or *maîtresses d'école*) who taught in

---

[1] See Desmaze, *Pièces justificatives*, p. 187.

them were licensed by an official who was attached to the
cathedral in each diocese. He was known as the Scholaster[1]
and his position was one of considerable dignity. He combined his office with that of Precentor, and his connection
with teaching dated from the time when in each diocese the
Precentor was also master of a choir-school attached to the
cathedral. The Scholaster, as the representative of the
Bishop[2], licensed teachers of both sexes[3] and he was responsible for all the "little schools" in his diocese. As part of
his duty he had to visit and inspect each school twice a year.
The teaching licence was renewable annually and the
Scholaster reserved to himself the right of cancelling it or
withholding it if he thought fit. At Paris in the early part
of the seventeenth century there were apparently as many
as seventy little schools, although only twenty of them were
for girl-pupils; but by the end of the century the number had
risen to 167 and in the year 1736 there were no less than
91 *maîtres d'école* and 170 *maîtresses d'école*, all of whom
held the Scholaster's licence and, in probably every case,
had charge of a separate school.

The masters and mistresses of the Parisian little schools
formed a close gild or *confrairie*. They used to meet each year
on May 6th at the Precentor's office where they renewed the
oath which they had taken on receiving their licence. It
included promises to catechise their pupils on Thursdays

[1] His title appears in French as *scholastique, écolâtre, capiscol,* and
maîtrescol; and in Latin as *scholasticus* and *scholiarcha*. He sometimes
delegated his duties to an *intendant* who was usually known as
recteur or *grand maître des écoles*.

[2] The same system obtained in England. Cf. *B. C. P. Constitutions
and Canons Ecclesiastical,* § 77. "*None to teach School without Licence*:
No man shall teach either in publick school or private house, but
such as shall be allowed by the Bishop of the diocese, or Ordinary of
the place, under his hand and seal, being found meet as well for his
learning and dexterity in teaching, as for sober and honest conversation, and also for right understanding of God's true religion;
and also except he shall first subscribe to the first and third Articles
aforementioned simply, and to the two first clauses of the second
article." This was not formally abolished until 1870.

[3] For a copy of the licence granted to a *maîtresse d'école* see
Appendix D.

and Saturdays, to keep the peace among themselves, to refrain from inveigling assistant-teachers (*submoniteurs*) from neighbouring schools, to notify any change of address to the Scholaster, never to set up a school nearer than twenty houses to another school, and other clauses of a similar type. There remains to us a speech made by a certain M. Sonnet to a conference of teachers from little schools who had been convened by Claude Joly (1607–1700), the most celebrated of all the Parisian scholasters. "You are recognised, ladies and gentlemen," says the orator, "you are established by the Precentor of the Church of Paris, not only to teach children reading, writing, arithmetic, the church service, and grammar[1], but also to teach them the catechism and to give them instruction in Christian doctrine. ...Take care that the children do not bring evil, heretical, or immoral books to school; examine well the books by which you teach children to read....Teach them to obey their fathers and mothers, their masters and mistresses, their superiors and everyone else. Remember that you yourselves must teach poor children free of charge, as well as the others ...love them tenderly; treat them kindly; correct them wisely and without passion....Warn your boys—and especially your girls—against vanity, luxury, pride, vain adornments, bare necks and bosoms and shoulders and arms, curled and powdered hair. Teach them Christian humility and modesty."

The mention of heretical and undesirable books in the speech of the good M. Sonnet is one among many indications of a matter which was greatly exercising the educational and ecclesiastical authorities of the time. France was still recovering from the Wars of Religion, and the progress of the Counter-Reformation was making itself widely felt. As Adamson points out, there is evidence that in France men "were beginning to feel the need...for a more widely extended elementary school system[2]." The Church, which had control of education, recognised that the school, more than any other institution, was the most effective instrument for

---

[1] *I.e.* the elements of Latin.
[2] *Pioneers of Modern Education*, p. 199.

combating the heresies of the Reformers; this is one of the
reasons at any rate for the revival of an interest in elementary
education at this period. But, as is shown in Chapter III of
this book, the adherents of Calvin realised the propagandist
power of the school no less than did their opponents; and
the Church set itself to meet this danger. As early as 1552
an *arrêt* of the Parlement de Paris forbids anyone who is
suspected of Protestant leanings to teach "sur peine d'amende
arbitraire et de prison et de punition corporelle." Two years
later a similar edict renewed the prohibition against unlicensed schools where "evil and pernicious doctrine" is
taught. In 1570 Pierre de Gondy, Bishop of Paris, issued a
mandement to the same effect. But, for reasons explained
elsewhere, it is during the reign of Louis XIV that the
danger offered to Catholicism by the unlicensed or unorthodox
little school is most energetically combatted. As during the
earlier Wars of Religion, the Huguenots, when they were
prevented from carrying on little schools of their own in the
chief towns in France, resorted to *écoles buissonières*, held
in the woods or in the open country near the city. "Playing
truant" by attending such schools was made a punishable
offence. Still the practice went on and it was not unknown
for unlicensed little schools to be opened within the bounds
of Paris itself. In 1677, for example, the Rector of the
University complains that "gens sans caractère et sans
autorité" have attempted to open schools; while in 1678
a certain Dutchman named Van der Enden, who is referred
to as "ce buissonier," was accused of having opened an
unlicensed school in which the Koran *inter alia* was studied;
and he paid the penalty for such temerity with his life. The
persecution of such teachers at this period was part of an
attempt to kill out all non-Catholic schools[1].

In default then of Huguenot little schools, children of
Protestant parents were compelled to attend Roman
Catholic schools. In some cases the *maîtres* or *maîtresses*
d'école refused to take heretical pupils; but they were
ordered to do so on the condition referred to by M. Sonnet—
"that their pupils do not bring any bad catechisms or other
books suspected of heresy"; further, they were commanded

[1] See *infra*, pp. 104–105.

to teach such children "the ordinary catechism" and certain prescribed prayers in both French and Latin, "in the same way as Catholic children, teaching them with the same kindness and gentleness." After the Revocation of the Edict of Nantes, two laws were passed to the effect that children of both sexes belonging to the Reformed religion should attend Catholic schools; while those who had passed the age of fourteen were compelled to undergo special instruction on Sundays and festivals. In many places there were no schools available for this work, though the inhabitants of each locality were ordered to pay 150 livres *per annum* for the stipend of a *maître d'école* and 100 livres for that of a schoolmistress. It cannot be said that this legislation was very effective; but it proves that the proselytising value of education was clearly realised and it helps to explain why so great importance was always attached to the licensing of the schoolmaster or schoolmistress, even though their work were of an elementary kind and lay among children of the poorest class.

The *maître* or *maîtresse d'école*, on receiving the licence to teach, undertook to put up a board or sign at the door or window of the little school. The following was the prescribed inscription: "Ceans on tient petites écoles." [Then followed the name of the master or mistress who kept the school, and the words] "qui enseigne à la jeunesse le service[1], à lire, écrire et former les lettres, la grammaire, l'arithmétique, et le calcul, tant au jet qu'à la plume [2], et prend des pension-

---

[1] *Sc. divin.*

[2] *Le calcul au jet* was performed with *jetons* or counters of ivory or metal. They were of different kinds, representing units, tens, and hundreds. If * stands for a unit-counter, o for a ten-counter and § for a hundred-counter the number 762 would be arranged thus: §§§§§§§
If two numbers were to be added, the units, tens, and   oooooo
hundreds in each group would be added separately; for   **
example: 531   +   754
             §§§§§   §§§§§§§ = 12 hundreds ⎫
             ooo   ooooo   = 8 tens   ⎬ *i.e.* 1285
             *   ****   = 5 units   ⎭

If necessary counters could be carried to a higher series; *e.g.* 13 units = 10 + 3—*i.e.* 1 ten-counter + 3 unit-counters. *Le calcul à la plume* was the ordinary method of calculation performed with pen and paper.

naires[1]." It was forbidden under pain of fine to add anything to this or to exhibit specimens of handwriting by way
of advertisement. The teacher who kept the school was
further required to reside on the premises and to teach in
person unless he had an assistant who was authorised by the
Scholaster. The books used in the little schools included a
Life of the Saints, selections from the *Imitation*, and a
catechism by the controversial theologian Bellarmin; elementary Latin was also studied. Masters and mistresses
were strictly forbidden under pain of a heavy fine to allow
their pupils to take part in public shows, on horseback or
with music or "en habits dissolus." But the children of the
little schools were not without their festivals when they
played their part before the public. At Paris, for example,
on the feast of St Nicholas (December 6th), like the boys of
Eton, they chose their boy-bishop and made a solemn
procession through the streets of the city. This annual
festivity was abolished about 1725. On Shrove Tuesday,
again, a "king" was chosen and the children escorted him
in triumph about the streets singing an uncouth rhyme:

> "Vive en France
> Et son alliance.
> Vive France
> Et son roi aussi[2]."

Beside the *maîtres* and *maîtresses d'école* who were licensed
by the Scholaster, there was another type of teacher—the
writing masters or *maîtres écrivains*. They belonged to a
corporation which had been authorised by Charles IX in
1570 to give expert advice on suspected forgery and to
teach writing, spelling, and elementary arithmetic. To these
subjects, as has already been indicated, the *maîtres d'école*
by the terms of their licence were allowed to add elementary
Latin ("grammar"), church singing, and the explanation
of the catechism and the divine offices. Thus in theory the
work of the two types of teacher was clearly limited, but in

---

[1] See Bréchillet-Jourdain, *Hist.* p. 215 (*arrêt* of July 2nd, 1661);
and also *Index*, pp. 410, 411 (*arrêt* of April 22nd, 1600).

[2] What the first line means is uncertain. Perhaps it is a corruption
of "Vive enfance."

practice there was continual friction. The *maître écrivain* was supposed to use printed books only for teaching spelling and not for teaching reading; should he confound this somewhat subtle distinction he rendered himself liable to a visit from a *commissaire au Châtelet*. The *maître d'école*, on the other hand, was not allowed to teach writing from a copy of more than three lines long if it had been written by some person other than himself; transgression of this regulation was punishable by a fine.

In addition to the competition offered by the writing schools, there were sometimes financial difficulties to embarrass the teachers in the little schools. It was the custom to devote the revenues of a prebend in every cathedral or collegiate church to the support of masters or mistresses; but as a rule they benefited only the cities in which the church was situated. In 1698, as we have seen, when the State had assumed some of the burden which had formerly been borne by the Church, a *rétribution* of 100 or 150 livres a year was levied as a kind of education rate on parishes for the maintenance of a teacher. But for many years past the problem of financing the little schools had been a pressing one. There are many decrees and resolutions of Church Councils dealing with the situation. Typical are those of the Council of Evreux (1576) which order that, if sufficient money is not forthcoming to maintain little schools, patrons of churches, hospitals, *léproseries*, and religious societies, shall be instructed as to the claims which the cause of education has upon their generosity. Parish priests were also instructed to invite the faithful, when they made their wills, to remember the needs of these schools. Even so it proved in many cases difficult and even more often impossible to finance the little schools from these sources alone, and the *maîtres* and *maîtresses d'école* were driven to recoup themselves in some other way. Although they were still under bond to teach the children of the poor "gratuitement et sans salaire," it became a common practice to take additional paying pupils[1] and to take *pensionnaires* who

---

[1] The oath taken by a candidate who received a licence to teach in a little school, included a promise not to teach pupils who still owed fees to a former master.

paid extra for board and lodging. The same tendency is shown not only in the case of the colleges of the University of Paris but also in that of many of the schools of old foundation in this country. Some of the *maîtres d'école* added to their income by acting as *pédagogues*[1] to members of the colleges of the local university. Moreover there was a continual tendency on the part of the little schools to venture beyond their prescribed curriculum and to make incursions into that of the Faculty of Arts of the University —*i.e.* to give a secondary education. By 1673 the activities of the little schools in this direction were so marked that they are said to have made the colleges of the University of Paris "almost deserted"; and in 1675 the University presented a *Requeste au roy contre les petites escholes*[2] in which Louis XIV is besought to forbid *maîtres d'école* to teach anything beyond the subjects to which they were confined, and to make it a punishable offence for children to be kept at a little school after the age of nine.

At the same time the teaching personnel of the little schools at times left much to be desired, though this was less true of Paris than of the provinces. A picture of a little school by Adrien van Ostade, dating from 1662 and preserved in the Louvre, shows a few children being taught in an ill-furnished kitchen by a man of rough and uncultured appearance; and these conditions must often have been realised. Teaching licences were given, we are told, to eating-house keepers, to hair-dressers, to showmen, "and even to lacqueys." This meant that many children who had passed through a little school might come to the colleges of the University very badly prepared. The colleges therefore were sometimes constrained to repel the attack which the little schools had made upon their province, by carrying the war into the enemy's country. They invaded the domain of primary education. Preparatory departments were opened; forms VII and VIII (usually known as *Salle* and *Pater*) were set up below the ordinary course of the Faculty of Arts; and

---

[1] See *supra*, p. 6.
[2] See Bréchillet-Jourdain, *Pièces justificatives*, CXXXI, 104.

régents abécédaires were appointed[1]. The problem is precisely the same as that which we have to face to-day. The upper forms of the elementary school tend to overlap the lower forms of the secondary school, though the course of instruction in the two cases is not exactly the same; many of the public schools have had to form preparatory departments for boys who are not fitted to enter at once upon the ordinary school course. With us the confusion rages almost unchecked and is realised to the full only by those who suffer from its effects; in France in the sixteenth and seventeenth centuries there was at any rate a definite system and efforts were frequently made to enforce it.

The question of the education of girls has led to a discussion of elementary education in general because the system of *petites écoles* legislated for boys and girls alike, and women as well as men were eligible for the licence to teach. But there was a unanimous feeling on the part of the ecclesiastical authorities against mixed schools. Masters also were forbidden to receive girl pupils and mistresses to teach boys. There is a long series of ecclesiastical statutes, episcopal mandates, and parliamentary *arrêts* all enforcing this principle. "Take great care," says Maître Martin Sonnet, whose address to "messieurs les maistres et maistresses d'écoles de la ville cité université faubourgs et banlieue de Paris" has already been quoted, "Take great care never to have in your schools children of both sexes. There are no longer children, there is no longer innocence. Wickedness has grown to such a pitch that children of five, six or seven years know more about it at the present day than persons of thirty or forty did in the old days." But the fulminations of the authorities could not entirely prevent poverty-stricken masters and mistresses from supplementing their salaries by taking children of the opposite sex. This difficulty arose much less in Paris and the other large towns of France because there was a considerable population upon which to draw for pupils; but in the smaller towns and villages it became a real problem and a concession was sometimes made

---

[1] Cf. the preparatory or "petty schools" which were sometimes attached to English grammar schools.

to the exigencies of the situation by allowing masters to teach
little girls who were less than nine years old.

Although the little schools were supposed to afford a free
education to the children of the poor they were not of
themselves sufficient to supply fully the demands that were
made upon them. They were numerous in the north and
east of France and it is said that in Alsace and Franche-
Comté every parish had its own *petite école*; but in the south
and centre of the country and in Brittany they were much
fewer. To supplement the little schools therefore there arose
a demand for charity-schools, independent of the scholaster,
ttached to each parish and put in charge of the parish-
priest. As early as 1526 the Council of Chartres had decreed
that "every parish, if it is possible, shall have free-schools
to which children can go and that at least there be a priest
or clerk sufficiently well-educated to teach the children the
Lord's Prayer, the Creed, and the other things which are
contained in the *Alphabet*[1]." The Council of Tours, held in
the same year, made a similar recommendation. These
parishional charity schools were inspected from time to time
by the rural-dean, and we can believe that within their very
circumscribed limits they were usually efficient. As a rule
they had their full complement of pupils, and often afforded
the only bulwark against a proletariat sunk in utter ignorance. Charity-schools were founded not only by parishes
but also by religious orders and by private individuals. There
was, for example, a school attached to the Hôpital de la
Trinité in the rue Saint-Denis; it was designed for destitute
children who were taught a manual trade in addition to
reading, writing, and arithmetic. Somewhat similar was the
school founded under the will of Henri de Joyeuse in 1588
and attached to the monastery of the Minimes in the rue
Saint-Honoré. It is interesting also to note that an educational institution of such widespread activity at the present
day as that of the Christian Brothers, founded by St Jean-
Baptiste de la Salle in 1684, owed its origin to the custom of
setting up parishional charity-schools which were free from

[1] *I.e.* an elementary reading book.

3

the control alike of the scholaster and of the municipal authorities.

It must be reiterated that in the whole system of elementary education which has been described girls were catered for as well as boys; though the opportunities afforded to girls were often less numerous. For the daughters of noble families a governess or private tutor was usually provided; but for those girls who were not educated at home or in the *petites écoles* or charity-schools there remained the teaching facilities offered by the convent. From the earliest times communities of women had been accustomed to take a few *pensionnaires*—usually girls of noble birth or relatives of the nuns. The teaching of these children was too often regarded as a form of penance, suitable for self-mortification; and the school itself was designed largely as a *pépinière* from which vacancies in the community could be filled. This aim was reflected in the curriculum. It included a modicum of reading and writing, enough arithmetic to enable a girl to keep simple accounts or to understand the table for finding Easter; together with a large amount of instruction in morals and doctrine. The convent schools of the Middle Ages had reached their highest stage of development at about the period of the Crusades; the reasons for this were similar, to some extent, to those which explain the fact that the parents of many pupils in our modern boarding-schools are serving in various capacities in India or the colonies. But several causes had co-operated to bring about a gradual deterioration, until the Counter-Reformation gave a new importance to conventual schools and greatly developed this type of educational institution. As Adamson says: "One of the striking facts of ecclesiastical history after the great separation of the sixteenth century is the rapid multiplication of religious communities, of societies of women more particularly....The majority of these new communities were either corporations of teachers or of persons otherwise especially interested in children[1]." It may be added that many of these communities of women—as, for example, the Visitandines—were devoted to the care of the sick; but

[1] *Pioneers of Modern Education*, p. 197.

there were other orders—the Ursulines, for instance—which
aimed at combining this work with that of teaching girls.
As a rule it was difficult for such communities to offer
instruction gratuitously to all comers; and consequently it
was customary to charge fees and to cater for girls of the
class which could afford to pay them. Yet there were not
wanting those orders which gave education free of cost and
by so doing helped the parishional charity-schools to discharge their function. The best known among these communities are the Angelicals, the Piaristes, the Filles de la
Croix, the Filles de la Pénitence, the order of La Présenta-
tion de Notre-Dame—and many another, the name of
which appears frequently in the pages of French educational
history.

A less-renowned, but hardly less important and less
interesting, community was that which was founded by the
Venerable Anne de Xainctonge and attached to the Ursuline
Order. Her system combined most of the good points which
characterised the various types of school which were available for girls at this period and which have already been
described; and for that reason a more detailed account of
it would seem to have some value. The schools which owed
their origin to Anne de Xainctonge were staffed by a
religious community and they were essentially religious in
outlook and aim; but the teaching sisters in this case were
not bound by the vow of enclosure and were therefore not
cloistered within the walls of a convent; their primary aim
was not to recruit the ranks of their society but to train girls
for the duties of life in the "world." Their ambition was to
afford for girls, within the limits prescribed by their sex and
the public opinion of the day, an education comparable to
that given to boys by the Society of Jesus. Like the charity-
schools, therefore, their institutions charged no fees and catered
primarily for the poor. The curriculum was similar to that of
the little school for girls, but the teachers were not coarse and
ill-educated as were some of the *maîtresses d'école*; they were
women of breeding and culture who did not teach for the
sake of gain, but had given up all that the world had to offer
them in order to embrace an occupation which was despised

by their contemporaries. Thus their methods of teaching, compared with those in vogue in other contemporary girls' schools, were intelligent and progressive; while the moral influence exerted by a staff of devoted women of good education and deep religious earnestness must have been an asset which any school of that or any other period might well envy.

Anne de Xainctonge, the foundress of the Order which we now have to consider, was born at Dijon on November 21st, 1567. She came of a well-to-do family belonging to the class known as *gens de robe*; her father was a prominent member of the local Parlement. From him Anne inherited a strength of character and a tenacity of purpose which were much in evidence throughout her career. Her mother—as is not unusually the case with the wife of a masterful man—was of a calm, submissive, and patient nature, and these characteristics also reappeared in her daughter. Thus Anne de Xainctonge presents us with that somewhat rare phenomenon of a woman who is at once strong and gentle; she always had a clear vision of her object and a steadfast determination in the pursuit of it; and with all this went a complete submission to the claims of what she considered to be her duty and an absolute negation of self. When a woman of this type devotes her life to the cause of education, the story of her career can hardly fail to be of interest and inspiration to those who still carry on the work of the teacher.

Although the progress of the Reformation and the troubles of the League were spreading discord and dissension not merely between the various towns and districts of France but even between members of the same families, the De Xainctonges remained steadfast in their allegiance to the Roman Church; and thus Anne's earliest years were spent in an atmosphere of faith which was not affected by the storms which raged outside. From her childhood she evinced a marked religious bent; "it was clear that God was instructing her inwardly at the same time as her father and mother were doing this outwardly." But besides this she was eager to impart what she had learned to others who had not

ANNE DE XAINCTONGE

(1567–1621)

had the same opportunities as herself. "As soon as she had
begun to learn the catechism and to read," says one of the
historians of her life[1], "she was seized with a great desire
to teach the servants what she knew and to tell them what
she had read." Her education was carried on at home—
an indication of the lack of suitable schools for girls. Her
father gave her religious instruction and taught her the
rudiments of Latin; in this task he was aided by a Jesuit
priest—Jean-Antoine de Villars—who became Anne's confessor and acquired a considerable influence over her. Nor
were practical matters neglected, for she soon became expert
at all kinds of domestic work and throughout her life she
showed how highly she valued this factor in the training of
girls.

The house in Dijon in which the De Xainctonge family
lived was situated at the corner of what are now the rue
Chabot-Charny and rue Petit-Potet. When Anne was fourteen
years old, a Jesuit college was opened in Dijon; it owed its
origin to the munificence of Odinet Godran, president of the
Parlement. The site chosen for the new school lay immediately
opposite the Hôtel de Xainctonge; the building still exists
and part of it is now used as an *école primaire*. To one who,
like Anne, had already shown a natural aptitude for teaching,
the work of the Jesuit college was a source of never-failing
interest; she watched from her window with unflagging
attention the routine of the class-room and the boys at their
play. One day her confessor, Gentil[2], coming upon her as she
was looking at the busy scene, asked her what she thought of
"tout ce fracas." "Sir," she replied, "I am struck with the
good fortune of those schoolmasters and I envy them because
they employ their natural abilities to instruct boys in piety
and to make of them true Christians....But when I turn to
pupils of my own sex I find that hitherto they have been
very unfortunate in that no one has undertaken to bring
them up piously as you do with boys[3]." As a matter of fact,

---

[1] Orset, p. 4; see also Mourath, p. 14.
[2] De Villars had left Dijon and Gentil succeeded him as Anne's
"director."
[3] Orset, p. 98.

the benefactor of the Jesuit college, Odinet Godran, had in
his will left a sum of money for the founding of a girls'
school also; but—as was so often the case—it was found
impossible to staff such an institution, and there is no
evidence that this part of the testament was ever put
into effect. In the whole city of Dijon there were—if we may
believe Anne herself[1]—only three or four "little schools" open
to girls and in them, as we have seen, the teaching was of
a most elementary kind.

The lesson was not lost on Anne and from this time
forward she consecrated her life to the education of the
poor and ignorant of her own sex; to that end she "prayed
God fervently to help her to form a community of women
devoted to educating young girls and inculcating in them
virtue and good manners as well as the arts and sciences
suitable to their sex[2]." In the fulness of time her prayer
was answered, but in her path lay many difficulties which
had to be encountered and overcome. Her first step was
to form a class of "les plus fortes têtes"—poor and unedu-
cated females of all ages who had not even enough knowledge
to profit by the catechism taught by the clergy in church.
Anne's father had been desirous of arranging a marriage for
her; but when she announced her unwillingness "to be
united to any creature," he obviously recognised that the
tendencies which she was already showing towards the
religious life were signs of a true vocation and, with more
wisdom than he evinced on subsequent occasions, M. de
Xainctonge acquiesced in the choice which his daughter
had made. Mme de Xainctonge was quite content to follow
her husband's lead and Anne was even given some tepid
encouragement also by the ecclesiastical advisers whom she
consulted. The latter had a strong bias against teaching
being carried on by women who did not belong to a properly
constituted and enclosed religious order; and they quoted
St Paul's strictures upon the behaviour of females in church.
But Anne refused to be discouraged; her courteous common-
sense supplied a cogent answer to every objection. She
adopted a nun-like costume and began to study popular

---

[1] See Arens, p. 38.   [2] Mourath, p. 168.

works on religion, that thus she might be the better fitted to instruct others. She also visited hospitals in order to care for and instruct the sick, and she obtained entry into a little school where she taught reading and explained the simple text-books that were used.

It is a little difficult for us, living under conditions so different, to realise the scandal that Anne's actions created among the social circle in which she lived. In a provincial French town of the sixteenth century it was an unheard of thing that the daughter of a prominent and prosperous lawyer, a member of the local Parlement, should dress herself like a nun and ape the office of nurse and schoolmistress. Had she enrolled herself in one of the regular religious orders which consecrated themselves to such work, no comment would have been made. But for an isolated individual—an unmarried daughter of a well-known family—to disregard custom and convention in so startling a manner, provoked considerable comment. She was accused of excessive and ostentatious devotion; her parents were too easy-going or had forgotten the dignity of their position; her Jesuit confessor had either lost his influence or else was responsible for her vagaries. But Anne's own conduct in school and hospital soon furnished sufficient answer to her detractors. By degrees the storm passed over, and although Anne doubtless continued to be regarded as extremely eccentric by the young ladies of her acquaintance, the purity of her motives at any rate was no longer challenged.

Meanwhile the troubles brought by the Wars of Religion were at their height; even after Henri IV's conversion the Duc de Mayenne and his Leaguers still held out for a time in Burgundy. But at length the strife died down and M. de Xainctonge, recognising his daughter's vocation and seeing that it was now possible of fulfilment, gave his consent to Anne's project and promised to support it financially. But this concession had hardly been granted when another obstacle presented itself. The Society of Jesus, on whose schools Anne modelled her proposed institution and from whose ranks she had chosen her advisers, was in 1595 banished from France. Though this expulsion was not

altogether complete so far as certain parts of the country
were concerned, the college at Dijon, at any rate, was
entirely broken up. Some twenty-five miles from Dijon
lay Dôle, the frontier town of Franche-Comté which at this
period was an appanage of the crown of Spain. Between the
two cities there existed a deep-seated jealousy and dislike;
differences in customs, history, and political allegiance helped
to keep the breach open. But since Dôle lay outside France
and under the dominion of His Most Catholic Majesty, the
King of Spain, the town had never wavered in its devotion
to Holy Church. It now presented a welcome haven of
refuge for the expelled Jesuits from Dijon. When therefore
Anne also avowed that by divine revelation she had been
called to begin her ministry of teaching in the foreign city
of Dôle, we may recognise—without in the least questioning
the sincerity of her statement—that there were reasons for
this step which come more directly within the purview of
an account such as that which we have to give. Her proposed course of action inevitably courted opposition. M. de
Xainctonge who, as a good Dijonnais, prided himself on his
loyalty to the French crown, was among those who believed
that the Jesuits had been responsible for Châtel's attempt
upon the life of Henri IV; and as a member of the Parlement
de Bourgogne he had recorded his vote in favour of their
expulsion as "corrupters of youth, disturbers of the public
peace, and enemies to the King and the State." But the
aim of Anne's life was to provide for girls an education
modelled so far as was possible on that which the Society
of Jesus gave to the pupils in its colleges. Can we wonder
then that M. de Xainctonge's half-grudging consent to his
daughter's unconventional scheme is now changed into
bitter and furious opposition? He flatly forbade her to
leave her native city, and his passionate and obstinate
nature was henceforth the greatest obstacle which Anne
had to encounter in her attempt to realise her plans. But in
spite of her father's anger and the contempt and suspicion
which her association with the Jesuits had re-awakened
among her friends[1], Anne would not abandon the vocation

[1] In a letter to her confessor Gentil she says: "Depuis votre

to which she felt God had called her and she persisted that
her life's work lay not in her own town of Dijon but in the
foreign and rival city of Dôle. So the months passed and
Anne waited, bearing her persecutions and disappointments
with exemplary patience. But at last her prayers were
answered and a way was opened to her. The party passions
excited by the Wars of Religion had not yet died down. M. de
Xainctonge, although a zealous Catholic, was, as we have
seen, a supporter of Henri IV and, knowing Anne's fidelity
to the Society of Jesus, he suspected her of sympathising
secretly with the League. In an outburst of ill-temper he
upbraided her for the attitude which she had assumed and
cried: "As for you, Mademoiselle, be assured, you can leave
my house when you will and go to the Spaniards, since you
hold their opinions."

Anne promptly took her father at his word and made the
most of her advantage. Accompanied by a female servant,
she left her home the same night without informing any of
her family of her intention. The two women lost themselves
in the dark and dangerous streets of the town, and the
break of day found them still searching for the city-gate.
But at last they passed safely out into the country where they
were met by an elderly *procureur*, or attorney—an old friend
of the De Xainctonge family to whom Anne had confided
her plan and who had promised to aid her. It is worth while
to make some attempt to realise the courage and determination required for such a venture. At the age of just 29[1] Anne,
who had never before travelled further than to a village in
the near neighbourhood of Dijon where the De Xainctonges
had some property, embarked almost alone upon a journey
which led along unknown roads to a foreign city where she
had few friends to welcome her. Even in these days of female
emancipation an adventure of this kind would be—to say
the least—an unusual one. But in the case of Anne such
conduct was utterly at variance with the traditions of her

éloignement, je suis en un estrange décri, et si les pensées de Dieu
sont comme celles des hommes, le malheur de votre ordre est beaucoup moindre que le mien."
[1] Anne left home on November 29th, 1596.

class and the conventions of contemporary society. Moreover, the roads were particularly dangerous at this period because the countryside was infested with discharged soldiery. But Anne's faith in her mission as a teacher and her trust in God nerved her to throw over the trammels of convention, to face danger and hardship, and in the end to triumph over every obstacle.

The journey occupied a day and a half, the night being spent in an inn at St Jean-de-Losne. The *procureur*, having seen his charges safely arrived at Dôle, returned home without delay. Anne's first care was to enquire for her Jesuit friends from Dijon, but she learnt that they had already moved on elsewhere. Disappointed but not daunted, she obtained an interview with the Rector of the Jesuit College at Dôle. She gave him an account of herself and unfolded her plans, calling herself "fille de la Société de Jésus, autant qu'on peut l'être." The Rector welcomed her, seeing in her proposals an answer to a project which had already been exercising the thoughts of several high-born ladies of Dôle. They had recently been making a *novena*, or nine days of prayer, to obtain a leader for the work of instructing girls and women of the poorer classes; and the appearance of Anne seemed not unnaturally to be a direct answer to their prayers. Anne's joy was unbounded and the Jesuit Rector followed up his kindly reception of her by securing for her a lodging in the town. Dôle appeared in truth to be the land of promise. Anne quickly began preparations for her work; every morning and evening she visited the sick at the hospital of Saint-Jacques, and she also obtained permission to assist a somewhat rough and ignorant *maîtresse d'école* called Suzanne Renard[1]. Anne's cheerful and gentle methods—so unlike those hitherto in use in the school—soon won the hearts of the thirty pupils who attended it, and for a while all seemed to be going well. At the same time Anne got

[1] She is described as "femme vertueuse, mais de caractère difficile et dur" (Mourath, p. 41). "Par n'importe quelle cause elle se mettait en colère et déchargeait tout son fiel sur sa vertueuse compagne" (*ibid*. p. 42). Elsewhere she is described as "un dogue aboyant sans cesse."

into touch with the ladies who had celebrated the *novena* and one of them—Claudine de Boisset—became deeply attached to her; but for the others the test was too hard and all alike made "the great refusal." They would pray for the work of education among the poor and would even contribute towards its maintenance, but they could not bring themselves to sacrifice position and prospects by devoting themselves personally to it.

Meanwhile M. de Xainctonge had repented of his hasty words and had recourse to every form of persecution in order to induce Anne to return to Dijon. He first sent her "une lettre foudroyante"; then, finding this ineffective, he sought to prejudice against his daughter the Jesuit Rector and the widow with whom Anne was lodging. Not content with this, he called the terrors of the law to his aid and persuaded the Parlement de Bourgogne to send a formal plaint to the Parlement de Dôle. As feeling between the two provinces at this time ran even higher than usual, it was not difficult to instigate a persecution against the rebellious daughter. She became suspect, and an "isolement absolu" was decreed against her. It was rumoured that she was a spy and she was insulted in the streets. At last her maid deserted her and she was turned out of doors by her hostess; but the latter's daughter-in-law offered Anne a refuge in a garret which formed her home for the next four years.

Such experiences might well have daunted the bravest heart and induced Anne to resign her project of forming a teaching community. But hers was the faith that can remove mountains and no privation or persecution was strong enough to weaken her purpose. She continued to teach in Suzanne Renard's little school, although for this she received no salary; but she was aided by Claudine de Boisset and by remittances secretly sent to her by her mother; these scanty sources of income she supplemented by doing needlework after school-hours in her draughty and rat-infested garret. There was no thought of returning to the comforts of her father's house at Dijon. Anne preferred to stay on at Dôle, in which town she believed that her mission lay, and she regarded the trials which she was undergoing as a cross which she was called upon to endure. She evidently realised that her experience in the *petite école* was for her a novitiate for the new teaching order which she hoped to found, and she was able at the same time to work out the plans for her proposed institute.

One of the chief obstacles which she had to overcome was the very general prejudice in favour of the principle of "enclosure" for women who embraced the religious life. It was considered unbecoming for communities of women to be free from the restraints of the cloister and to be able to lead an active life in the midst·of the world. But Anne recognised fully that if her teaching work were to benefit the children of the poor, it must be taken to them; and that her sisters, like the friars of old, must imitate their Lord and His Apostles by going out into the world to seek and to save that which was lost. What Anne proposed therefore was a community somewhat on the lines of the Flemish *Béguinages*, although her religious were to renounce private property and their vows were to be perpetual. But her schemes were too unusual to win official approval, and to the opposition of the ecclesiastical authorities were added renewed persecutions on the part of M. de Xainctonge. He drew up a formal *mémoire* on her conduct and laid it before a council composed of the chief lawyers and ecclesiastics of Dijon; he also sent copies of it to the authorities at Dôle and elsewhere. Still regarding the Jesuits as ultimately responsible for Anne's defection, he demanded that they should cease to hold communication with her and he induced the Parlement de Bourgogne to support him by a threat that the Jesuits should not be allowed to re-establish themselves in Dijon if they refused to do as he wished. The storm which had resulted in the banishment of the Society of Jesus from France was by this time blowing over, and the community—not unnaturally—was anxious to take up its interrupted work once more. The people of Dijon had felt the lack caused by the cessation of the educational labours of the Jesuits and were eager to have the Collège de Godran re-opened. Some children from the town had even been sent out of the country to Jesuit colleges in Lorraine or the

Franche-Comté, so great was the attraction which they
exerted. Thus public opinion was bound to be divided on
the point which M. de Xainctonge had raised. But the
Jesuits preferred to take no risks. Anne was proving a
somewhat embarrassing *protégée* and so they disavowed
responsibility for her and her projects. Looking at the
situation from an impartial standpoint, we can perhaps
understand and sympathise with both parties; but for Anne
the blow was a very hard one. She had declared herself to
be a "daughter of the Society of Jesus," and to be thrown
over by those whom she followed was the severest test of
her faith in herself and her mission which she had yet
experienced. Still, with that divine obstinacy which helped
her to surmount every obstacle, she refused to lose heart.
If the Jesuits were unwilling to direct her she would take
a confessor from no other order; and since she could not
communicate without first receiving absolution, she would
abstain from the sacred Food, which was so infinitely
precious to her, until the ban was withdrawn. When Anne's
decision was made known the old scandals at once blazed up.
Why did she not obey her father? Why did she fly in the
face of all custom and authority? Why did she not join a
cloistered community? Why did she obstinately refuse to
take a confessor from one of the numerous other orders?
But Anne, strong in her sense of duty, went on her way undismayed and continued to teach in Suzanne Renard's
petite école. At last her opportunity came. When the Jesuits
were re-admitted to Dijon M. de Xainctonge made his peace
with the Père de Villars who had influenced Anne so profoundly at the beginning of her career. This meant that
Anne was now able to return to the Jesuits at Dôle for a
director and the "grand jeûne," as the historians of her life
often call this period of abstention from the Holy Communion,
came at last to an end.

But the strain had been a severe one and Anne's health
broke down. News of her serious illness reached M. de
Xainctonge; he hastened to Dôle and a reconciliation
between father and daughter took place. Before he returned
home he exacted a promise from Anne that she would visit

Dijon to see her mother who was in failing health. About
two months later Anne left Dôle and was warmly welcomed
at her native town. But when some weeks had elapsed and
she proposed to go back to her work at Dôle, her father
strongly opposed the step. Once more he had recourse to the
machinery of the law. He convoked four ecclesiastics, none
of them Jesuits, who with himself as chairman formed a
council to catechise Anne and to give a formal pronouncement on her conduct. The old topics of non-cloistration,
St Paul's views on the office of women in the Church, and
Anne's refusal to take a confessor outside the Society of
Jesus, were again debated; but Anne answered all the charges
with such skill and sincerity that she completely turned the
tables against her father. A report, entirely in her favour,
was issued in which it was laid down that "as to the education of girls which she proposes to undertake, it is certainly
a despised occupation in the eyes of the world, but it is as
clear as day that the call to so humble yet useful a work
comes from the Spirit of God Who, loving humility, rejects
the proud and gives His grace to the humble[1]." Nothing
daunted, M. de Xainctonge addressed his complaint to the
Jesuits themselves with whom he had made peace. A commission of three Jesuit fathers was appointed to examine
Anne; but again she answered every objection so appositely
that judgment was once more given in her favour. M. de
Xainctonge was worsted, but, like his daughter, he was of
the type that may be beaten but never realises it. He had
recourse to means which were more effective with Anne
even than ecclesiastical pronouncements. Madame de
Xainctonge was still in bad health[2], and it was easy to
suggest to Anne that her illness had been aggravated by her
daughter's absence and neglect. This was a fearful charge
to make and Anne's heart was riven asunder. Her love for
her mother urged her to give up her work and stay in Dijon,
but what she believed to be God's will commanded her to
return to Dôle. Terrible as the choice was, there remained

[1] Mourath, p. 62.
[2] As a matter of fact the seriousness of her illness was much
exaggerated and she outlived her daughter by many years.

for Anne only one possible decision; "qui amat patrem aut matrem supra me, non est me dignus." She was willing to stay with her mother for a while, but sooner or later she must go back to take up her interrupted life-work. Her parents began at last to appreciate the reality of her vocation; coming once more into close touch with their daughter, they realised better than ever before the strength of her character. They decided no longer to oppose her designs and henceforth she was free from opposition from this quarter.

Anne was now at liberty to return to Dôle. During her absence its inhabitants had also begun at last to see her true worth and to recognise the value of the work which she had been carrying on and of the projects which she had in view. She was welcomed especially by Claudine de Boisset and her friends who had interested themselves in the education of the poor. Anne's "extraordinary virtues and devotion," we read, "attracted to her the hearts of the ladies and young women of Dôle, as the magnet attracts iron[1]." It now seemed possible at last to put into practice the project upon which Anne had meditated for so many years. As has already been pointed out, a large number of teaching orders of women had made their appearance in France at this period, and their remarkable success proved the necessity and the importance of their work. Conspicuous among these orders were the Ursulines who had begun their work in Italy in 1537. They were introduced into France in the last decade of the sixteenth century and were already carrying on a valuable teaching work in the southern part of the kingdom. The mother-house was at Avignon. Anne therefore obtained a copy of the constitutions of this Order and decided to adapt them to the needs of her proposed community "as far as they could, for the time being, be suited to her design." Thus the Society which Anne founded was connected with the Ursuline Order and her nuns have ever since been known as "Dames de Ste-Ursule[2]." But it is obvious that she did not contemplate a complete adhesion

[1] Mourath, p. 33.
[2] Or simply *Ursules*. The ordinary name for the nuns of St. Ursula was *Ursulines*.

to all the rules and constitutions of the Order as established at Avignon. "They were made use of and observed," says Mourath[1], "but only until others more suitable and more specially adapted to the new Institution could be drawn up." It is obvious that one of the chief sources of Anne's inspiration was the organisation of the Jesuit colleges, and that she followed, *longo intervallo*, their *Ratio Studiorum*. In fact, Orset, one of the earliest biographers of Anne de Xainctonge, whose work is based on the memoirs of De Villars, Anne's confessor, definitely says in reference to the rules of the new Order: "I can tell them to my reader in a few words if I say that they were formed on those of the Company of Jesus[2]."

Thus the various obstacles which lay in Anne's path were, one by one, overcome. Early in 1606 the Bishop of Lausanne, who was a suffragan of the see of Besançon, authorised the nascent congregation and even approved of the principle of non-enclosure. It was more difficult to obtain the necessary sanction of the Parlement of the Franche-Comté; but by persistence and good fortune even this was obtained and on the 16th of June, 1606, the Society, consisting of Anne and six companions, started its existence in a house which had hitherto been used as a restaurant. The new community was a "company of women, consecrated to God by the three vows of poverty, chastity, and obedience, united together and making a society by the vow of stability, devoted to education[3]." They formulated their objects as follows: "to instruct girls, servants, and poor women in the principles of religion and the way of living according to these principles; and in order to do this the more effectively and to make them the more disposed to receive our instruction, we shall teach them reading, writing, domestic work, and in a word everything which girls ought to know in order to be useful in a family; and we shall teach them the great art of working out their salvation by performing properly the most trivial duties of their station[4]." Anne's aim, therefore, was that of all earnest teachers in every age—

---

[1] p. 68.   [2] Orset, p. 412.
[3] Orset, p. 410.   [4] Orset, pp. 388–9.

to produce good citizens; and though she worked, as did almost all educationists of her day in France, along the lines prescribed by the established religion, yet she did not aim chiefly at training aspirants to the religious life. She wished to educate girls to be good wives and mothers who, in performing the duties of the home, would sanctify themselves no less than did their sisters who entered convents. For this work she and her companions would take no recompense from their pupils; their reward was to be "the penny at the end of the day." The expenses of Anne's institution would be met out of the private means of the Sisters themselves[1], or by legacies and benefactions from private individuals or municipalities.

The Ursuline school at Dôle rapidly developed and won public recognition. A chapel for the community was built and it was also found necessary to erect larger buildings for the school. In public religious processions the girls of the "dévotes sœurs de Sainte-Ursule" appeared on an equal footing with the pupils of the Society of Jesus. Parents from neighbouring towns became anxious to enter their daughters as *pensionnaires* and, after considerable heart-searchings, Anne decided that such pupils might be taken if fees were paid to cover expenses of board and lodging[2]; but no attempt was allowed to make profit and no charge was made for tuition. As the school grew bigger there was no room for more *pensionnaires* and girls who came from a distance were sometimes boarded out with widows and other persons of unimpeachable respectability. Such pupils were known as *pensionnaires du dehors*. All this meant that, although the school had been intended primarily for the children of the poor, it was no longer confined to them. "A number of girls, big and small, rich and poor, came eagerly to profit by the inestimable advantages of a good education[3]"; and as no class distinctions or changes of curriculum were made for the different types of girl, it is obvious that Anne's

[1] Claudine de Boisset gave all her fortune to the Institution and has always been regarded as its "fondatrice temporelle."
[2] This fee was fixed at 10 pistoles *per annum*. See Appendix A.
[3] Binet, p. 79.

school must have had a democratising influence of unusual value.

The fame of the Ursulines of Dôle soon spread abroad and other municipalities began to ask for daughter houses. The later part of Anne's life, from 1615 to the beginning of her final illness towards the end of 1619, was spent mainly in journeys in connection with this work. In seven successive years (1615–1621) Ursuline teaching communities, founded direct from Dôle, were established in Vesoul, Besançon, Arbois, Saint-Hippolyte-sur-le-Doubs, Porrentruy, Gray, and Thonon; and although these houses were confined to the Franche-Comté and the adjacent parts of Switzerland, the influence of Anne's community was not confined to these districts: But the foundress herself was destined to see only the beginnings of her work. The hardships, physical and mental, which she had endured ever since she first left Dijon, had undermined her constitution, though they had never weakened her indomitable spirit; but she now lay seriously ill. For twenty-one months she endured almost continual physical suffering with exemplary patience. As she lay on her death-bed it was announced that the famous Père Cotton, the Jesuit confessor of Louis XIII, was passing through Dôle and had expressed a wish to see Anne de Xainctonge, of whom he had heard so much. In spite of her illness she consented to receive him. After the interview the Jesuit, in saying farewell to Anne's companions, remarked: "You will be great saints if you are true daughters of that great soul!" And it is said that on his return to Court, when asked what was the most extraordinary and interesting thing he had met with on his travels, Cotton answered "La Mère de Xainctonge[1]." At last her release from suffering came. On June 6th, 1621, she was stricken with apoplexy and expired two days later without recovering consciousness. Her body was buried in the school chapel, but the only remaining trace of her tomb is a simple slab, bearing her name, which until recently was preserved by the Ursuline Community at Dôle. In 1900 she was declared

[1] Arnoulx, p. 351.

Venerable by Pope Leo XIII and the process for her beati-
fication, at the time of writing, is still slowly in progress.

   The whole history of education can show few pioneers
worthy to be compared with Anne de Xainctonge in whole-
hearted devotion to the work of the teacher and in unswerving
patience in facing and overcoming difficulties. She began
her work, friendless and alone, in an alien and often hostile
city; destitute of funds, opposed by parental, ecclesiastical
and civil authority, she was strong in nothing save her
unwavering trust in God and her steadfast belief that in
His strength she would achieve her ideal. She lived to see
her Community established and flourishing, and the proud
mother of seven daughter houses. After her death the work
did not flag. It was hindered from time to time by wars and
civil disturbances, but even the Revolution did not succeed
in destroying it entirely. The Community was definitely
re-established in Dôle in 1802. Twelve years later a nun
who had been professed at Dôle in 1788, established a
daughter house at Tours. From this was founded a community in England, which, after a preliminary sojourn in
Suffolk, was established at Oxford in 1890; and to this some
more of the community from Tours was transferred upon
the passing of the Congregations Act in 1904[1], though some
also went to Belgium. England thus has the honour of giving
shelter to a community of Ursulines which is the direct de-
scendant of the original foundation of Anne de Xainctonge.

   There remains for us to give some account of the actual
working and organisation of the schools which owed their
origin to Anne de Xainctonge. The "façon d'instruire" of
the foundress herself is summarised for us by Orset[2]. She
had a cheerful way with children although she never forgot
the seriousness which befits a task of such solemn importance;
she did not allow faults to pass unchecked, but instead of
railing at the delinquent and using "paroles d'impatience

---

[1] The Community has a house in St Giles, to which is attached a
hostel for women-undergraduates who are registered as members of
the Society of Home Students; there is also a country-house in
connection with the Convent on Boar's Hill.

[2] pp. 301–2.

et d'aigreur," she was always kindly in manner and used
to give certain indulgences to such of her pupils as did well;
and finally she always reminded her girls, in work or play
alike, of their duty to God and thus won over some who were
originally "petites brutes." In short, by gentle methods
she inculcated moral responsibility; and this was a very
real advance upon the practice of the average *petite école*
of her time. She took the utmost pains that those who
assisted her should be inspired with her own ideals. The
companions of her order were not chosen because of the
magnitude of their dowries; they were carefully selected
and trained with a view to their future career. Not only
were they to be able to give instruction in reading, writing,
arithmetic, and church-singing, but they were expected to
be expert at all kinds of needlework and some even specialised
on illuminating, the making of wax flowers, and similar
arts with an ecclesiastical bias. Many of them came from
"good families" and were well qualified to teach their pupils
the rules of polite behaviour, upon which great stress was
laid. The chief mistress or *préfectrice des classes* had "practically the same duties as the prefect in a college (*i.e.* of the
Society of Jesus), but she was not exempt from teaching,
although she was not attached to any particular class[1]."
She was ultimately responsible both for the staff and for the
pupils; she placed new girls in the forms most suited to
their age and capabilities, and she drew up the time-table;
she inspected the teaching, held periodical examinations,
enquired into cases of absence, ensured that discipline in
class was kept, and made a weekly report on both classes
and teachers to the Superior of the Community. All these
regulations are signs of a well-organised school, and in this
respect Anne's institution was far superior to the average
convent-school of the period. We can easily trace the influence of the Jesuit model. The mistresses were directed
to pay special attention to moral instruction[2], to pray for

[1] Orset, p. 440.

[2] Cf. Orset, p. 485: "Nous ne donnons aucune instruction pure-
ment temporelle, car tout ce que nous faisons ne tend qu'à enseigner
les choses de la religion et cette distinction chez nous n'a point de
lieu."

their pupils and to set them a good example. Anger and favouritism were condemned as the teacher's gravest faults, and corporal punishment was absolutely forbidden.

The school itself was divided into classes—a scheme imitated from the Jesuits. Several of these forms had separate rooms instead of being taken in a common schoolroom, as was the contemporary custom. Of the six classes the lowest (VI) comprised little girls of six or seven who had not yet learned their alphabet. They were instructed in the rudiments of religion and were taught to spell, the *Pater*, *Ave*, and *Credo* being used as texts for this purpose. Stress was laid on politeness and the little girls were told not to forget to say "bonjour aux parents et à la compagnie." In the next class (V) the emphasis was still on "modestie chrétienne et civilité humaine." Reading was continued and for this purpose the seven penitential psalms were employed. Two or three words were spelt out at a time and frequent revisions ensured that the whole was clearly known and understood. In this class simple needlework was begun—"of the kind that parents desire and according to the capacity and rank of the pupils." When a girl could spell and read competently she was promoted to the IVth form. Here frequent questioning was employed in order to test the memory; and as an aid to the development of her powers of expression, the pupil was made to reproduce orally what she had been taught, "selon sa petite capacité." The manual work at this stage consisted chiefly of knitting and hemming. In the IIIrd form, which comprised girls aged about nine or ten, writing was first begun. Reading and spelling were continued and for this purpose children were asked to bring to school old manuscript deeds. Most families of the period had a store of such documents and the deciphering of these, under proper supervision, must have added considerably to the interest of the reading lesson. This method of teaching reading in the Ursuline schools lasted—so it is said—until as late as 1842. Particular care was always taken to ensure good pronunciation and a thorough understanding of whatever was read. In form II writing and reading were continued and written compositions were at last attempted.

Religious instruction dealt chiefly with the explanation of
the Church offices. In the last year of the course the pupils,
who by this time had reached the age of 11 or 12, were
introduced to the rules of arithmetic and "the application
of them which a woman can make in the upkeep of a household. There were even lessons on elementary "cosmo-
graphy," astronomy, and drawing; while the needlework
at this stage included embroidery and the cutting-out and
making of garments. Nor was the curriculum necessarily
limited to these subjects. According to Anne's regulations
her pupils were to be taught "whatever is useful for a girl
to know." Naturally the content of a girl's education in the
twentieth century differs from that which would have been
deemed suitable in the seventeenth; and thus it has been
found easy to adapt the type of instruction given by the
"Ursules" to the conditions imposed by a particular place
or period. At the present day they prepare their pupils for
public tests such as the Local and Matriculation examinations, as well as for musical certificates and diplomas. But
the influence of the foundress is still evident in the important place assigned to needlework, the lowness of the
fees, and the continual emphasis on moral and religious
education.

In Anne's school there were only two and a half hours of
teaching in the morning and two hours in the afternoon,
but during the whole year there was only a fortnight's holiday,
given in October. The sisters and their *pensionnaires* rose
early to recite the office of the Blessed Virgin and to hear
Mass which was said in the school chapel. After breakfast
at 7.30 a.m. the day-girls arrived and school-work went on
until 10.0 when the *externes* returned to their homes. The
boarders dined and spent an hour in recreation. Afternoon
school began at 2.0 and lasted till 4.0. Time not occupied
in school was consecrated to prayer, to study, and to various
forms of needlework and other manual arts. Although the
sisters were not cloistered, they were instructed always to
go abroad in pairs—never singly—a custom which is still
very general among communities of women. The costume
worn by the earliest members of the Society was that

adopted by widows at Dôle; it is illustrated in the portrait of Anne de Xainctonge. Its object was not to suggest melancholy and sadness;—"pestes de la dévotion," as Anne calls them—but to render its wearers as inconspicuous as possible in the streets. The care of the sick, which Anne had intended to form part of the work of her Institution, had eventually to be given up owing to the rapid development of the educational activities of the Community[1]. Thus it is probable that, in spite of the absence of vows of cloistration, the majority of the teaching sisters would rarely have occasion to leave the houses to which they were attached.

Judged from a modern standpoint, Anne's schools may seem to have little to render them worthy of attention; but in the light of the contemporary education of girls, such as was described in the first part of this chapter, they mark an important step on the road of progress. They were designed for the poor, and throughout it was the poor who benefited chiefly by them; but, as we have seen, they were not closed to the children of well-to-do parents. The daughter of "people of quality" learnt to become proficient at needle-work and domestic arts, and in rubbing shoulders with her less fortunate sisters she must have gained some inkling, at any rate, of the ultimate insignificance of those class distinctions which bulked so largely in France under the *ancien régime*. But the daughters of the poor also gained something which the *petite école* could rarely offer them. The cultured and refined companions of Anne's Society instilled into their pupils habits of courtesy and consideration, and in all reading lessons the greatest pains were taken to drill pupils in a proper pronunciation of their mother-tongue. Thus the girl who had entered Anne's school at the age of six and left it at about twelve or thirteen was extremely well equipped for the part in life which she was called upon to play. She could read, write, cipher, sew, embroider and draw. She had learnt to express herself clearly and in good French and to give an account of what she knew. She had

[1] The definitely educational aim of the Society is illustrated in the old couplet: "Tant qu'Ursule tu seras—En classe tu iras."

acquired the graces which good manners can give; and she had gained a thorough and intelligent knowledge of the tenets of her religion. Anne's schools—so far as they went— are well worthy of comparison with Madame de Maintenon's institution at Saint-Cyr which many years later was founded under the royal aegis and for the benefit of girls of a favoured class. At Saint-Cyr the pupils stayed sometimes till the age of twenty, for they were drawn from a stratum of society where this was possible; but in Anne's school the leaving age was twelve. If we bear in mind this inevitable limitation it would seem true to say that there was no girls' school in Europe during the three hundred years which elapsed after the founding of Anne de Xainctonge's Institute where a more real and efficient education was given. The story of Anne's unwavering faith in her vocation and of her gradual triumph over difficulties render her story full of encouragement to those who have still to pursue the some- times tedious and always arduous task of the teacher; while the thoroughness of her methods, the soundness of her curriculum, and her single-hearted devotion to the cause of her own sex entitle her to a high place among the pioneers of education not merely in France alone but throughout the civilised world.

CHAPTER III

HUGUENOT EDUCATION

THE Protestant party in France from its very beginnings down to the Revocation of the Edict of Nantes displayed a conspicuous and unfaltering determination to provide for its youth a system of education based upon its special religious tenets. Even when persecution was at its height, when worship was proscribed and ministers were banished, when funds were ebbing and teachers were few, the French Protestants never lost their interest in the work of education and their belief in its unique importance to their cause. Such a belief was in fact a corollary of the "religion prétendue reformée." Protestantism at any rate opened the Bible to the layman and preached, if it did not practise, the right of private judgment. Seekers after truth whose own interpretation of the inspired Scriptures led them to conclusions contrary to those of official Protestantism might run as much risk of censure and persecution as did heretics who ventured to question the teachings of the Holy Roman Church. But the fact remains that the reformed religion implied an extension of education to all and sundry, since the knowledge of salvation was to be a personal discovery and not something given by prescription. At the same time the existence of definitely Protestant schools was a vital necessity for the supply of fit persons to serve in the ministry of the reformed Church. Thus it was inevitable that the founding and maintenance of schools should be an integral and essential part of the work of the Huguenots. To sketch the origin and growth of those schools and to estimate the importance of their work will form the subject of the present chapter.

In its early stages the Reformation in France aimed at improving the Church from within and was not a conscious

attempt to form a schism. At this period the movement is
closely related to the Renaissance. The introduction of
printing popularised the Bible. Already, between the years
1457 and 1517—*i.e.* before the influence of Luther had begun
to be felt—it is computed that over four hundred different
editions of the Bible, or of parts of it, had been printed in
France; and although these were almost without exception
Latin versions, the turn of the vernaculars was soon to come.
Lefèvre d'Étaples, known also as Faber Stapulensis, a teacher
of mathematics in the University of Paris, published a
New Testament in French as early as 1523; and this was
closely followed by translations of the Psalms and the other
books of the Old Testament. It was inevitable that, when
once the Bible became generally accessible, comparisons
should be made between the doctrines preached or the
standards of conduct set by the representatives of the orthodox Church, and the teachings which apparently were inculcated by the Scriptures. Thus the movement was given
a powerful impetus and some kind of official sanction was
lent to it by Marguerite, sister of François I, who showed
herself an enthusiastic protectress of the reform party. But
the theologians of the Sorbonne remained fierce champions
of orthodoxy[1] and after the disaster of Pavia, when François
became a prisoner in the hands of Charles V, there was a
reaction against heresy. A campaign of persecution broke
out in Paris, and in the provinces many reformers went to
the stake. François I, on returning to France, took up a
vacillating attitude, but deprecated violent measures; he
even wished to invite the German reformer Melanchthon
to Paris to become head of the newly-formed Collège
de France; but negotiations to this end broke down. The
Protestants by acts of vandalism and by coarse attacks on
the Mass exasperated public opinion against their party.
The king also, towards the end of his life, reacted definitely
to the side of the orthodox Church and attempted to stamp
out heresy by ordinances of pitiless severity. After resisting

[1] Cf. "...quæ vinculis, censuris, imo ignibus et flammis coercendo,
potius sit quam ratione convincendo." See Gerdes, *Historia Refor-
nationis*, IV, 6.

for some time he consented, in a moment of weakness, to authorise the massacre of the Vaudois, of whom a French historian has said: "Never in history have there appeared victims more innocent or assassins more infamous[1]."

Hitherto the Reformation in France owed its distinctive doctrines to Luther; but we must now turn aside to consider one who was destined to give French Protestantism the character which it henceforth maintained and who by his counsel profoundly influenced the course of the movement. Jean Calvin or Cauvin, a Frenchman by birth, had studied at Orleans, Bourges and Paris, and had shown great promise of winning for himself a high place among the humanists of his day. His first work was a commentary on the *De Clementia* of Seneca, but the study of theology, rather than that of classical literature, soon claimed his chief interest. He had early been attracted by the reformed doctrines and in 1534, at the age of 25, had deemed it prudent to go into exile at Basle. There he wrote his *Institutio Christianæ Religionis*, a text-book of Protestant doctrine, in which the dogmas of predestination and election were set out in all their grim unattractiveness. In 1536 he became professor of theology at Geneva and began to teach an advanced type of Protestantism which differed even more violently from orthodox Catholicism than did the teachings of Luther. Calvin was soon expelled from Geneva, but upon a change of government in 1541 he returned and gradually built up the rigid tyrannical theocracy which will always be associated with his name. He showed himself quite as narrow and intolerant as any of his Catholic opponents had ever been and, as Lord Acton points out[2], nothing more unlike liberty could be found than the State of Geneva when Calvin was the most important man there. But since Calvin became also the controlling influence over the reformed religion in France, the Protestant schools which rapidly took root all over that country were moulded upon the pattern of the educational institutions which he set up in Geneva. We must pause

[1] A detailed account of these persecutions is given in Baird, *Rise of the Huguenots in France*, ch. VII.
[2] *Lectures on Modern History*, p. 134.

therefore to ask what was the work which Calvin did for the cause of education.

He lays it down clearly that "the liberal arts and good training are aids to a full knowledge of the Word," and that schools and colleges are therefore necessary to maintain a supply of persons fit to serve God in Church or State. Calvin's system provided a unified scheme of elementary, secondary, and university education. It is with the second of these that we are chiefly concerned. There was a general tendency to discourage independent *petites écoles* and to attach them as lower forms to *collèges*; and the question of what to-day would be called "higher education" hardly comes within the scope of this book. Thus it is Calvin's secondary school at Geneva, which became the model for similar schools in France, which must now be described. This institution[1] was opened in June, 1559, with a total membership of 600 pupils and under the direction of Theodore Beza—himself an eminent reformer. On Monday, Tuesday, Thursday, and Friday, lessons began at 6.0 a.m. if it were summer, or at 7.0 a.m. in winter. Work continued until 9.0, breakfast—normally a hunk of dry bread—often being eaten during the course of a lesson. At 9.0 a.m. all the pupils returned to their homes. They were without exception *externes*, though some whose parents did not live in Geneva, lodged with families in the city. After the mid-day meal, school began once more. From 11 to 12 there was a singing lesson. The children were taught to sing the psalms and hymns that thus they might lead the praise of the church services, and instruction in singing for this purpose became a feature also of the Protestant schools in France. Lessons continued till 4.0 p.m. when all the forms assembled in the hall, or *salle basse*, to hear admonitions and notices from the rector.

It was customary in the early days of Calvinistic Pro-testantism to hold public worship on Wednesday mornings. On this day therefore the pupils went to church in charge of their regents. Names were checked to discover possible

[1] The building still exists and is used as a school. It stands in the Promenade St Antoine, not far from the Cathedral.

JEAN CALVIN
(1509–1564)

defaulters, and boys who proved "nonchalants à écouter la parole de Dieu" were duly punished. After service there was an interval for dinner and the afternoon was taken up with "questions" or disputes, which were supposed to exercise the mind and improve the power of speaking— important accomplishments for those who might one day have to preach the gospel or argue in defence of the reformed religion. From 12 to 3 the boys were allowed to play in the school court, and this was followed by an hour either of oratorical exercises or of written composition. Saturday morning was a holiday, but during the afternoon instruction was given in the catechism. It is interesting, in passing, to remark that the custom of having only half a day of schoolwork on Wednesday and Saturday has remained fairly general in Protestant countries, while it is not customary elsewhere; it is true, of course, that lessons are given nowadays in the morning of these half-holidays and not, as was customary at Geneva and in the Huguenot schools, during the afternoon.

Sunday at Geneva must have been for children a day of even greater gloom than it has ever been in Presbyterian Scotland. The whole day was devoted "à ouir et à méditer et à recorder les sermons." Services were held in the morning, afternoon, and evening, and at all of them attendance was compulsory. The pupils were afterwards catechised by their regents on the subject of the preacher's remarks.

The *Collège* at Geneva contained eight forms. In the two lowest—those corresponding to the *petite école* of the French system—children of five or six learnt the elements of reading and spelling. The next three classes were occupied mainly with grammatical work in Latin, but Greek was also begun. Forms III and II were the "humanities" in which Latin and Greek poets and historians were studied; while the highest class—the Rhetoric—specialised on Cicero and Demosthenes. In short, the curriculum did not differ appreciably from that of any other secondary school of the period. Promotions were decided on the results of a Latin essay, the subject of which was set to the whole school each April and at which every one worked to the best of his ability.

4

Prizes were awarded to successful pupils. Prior to 1616 these had taken the form of money awards varying from 1 florin 3 sous in the first form to 5 sous in the eighth; but after that date all rewards were given in the form of medals. The promotions were solemnly announced in public at a prize distribution held each year in St Peter's Church; and as this occasion was the only festival allowed by the Genevan sumptuary laws, it became the annual national feast-day of the community. It was by no means assured that a boy got his remove more or less automatically at the end of each school-year. There remains on record, for example, the case of a boy who in 1573, at the age of $7\frac{1}{2}$, was in form V. Three years later he was still in the IVth. Over two years later he was in form III and finally reached the IInd where he stayed for two years. It was possible to be specially promoted at the half-year in October; but this was for the benefit of boys who had already spent over a year in one form. What is now called a "double remove" seems to have been unknown.

From the *collège* (or *schola privata*) the pupil could proceed to a five years' course in the university (*schola publica*). The two institutions were closely connected and together were known as an *académie* or *école*, the *collège* sometimes being distinguished by the appelation *basse école*. A similar nomenclature was afterwards adopted in the French Huguenot universities which had a secondary school dependent upon them; though in this case the term *grande école* is often used instead of *académie*. The teachers in the Genevan university were called *professeurs* while those who taught the boys in the school were simple regents. The school itself was supervised by a principal whose Latin title was *Ludi-magister*. There is abundant evidence that at Geneva and generally throughout the Huguenot schools of France also, the greatest care was exercised that teachers should be men of real ability and sound knowledge, as well as of irreproachable character.

During the reign of Henri II who succeeded François in 1547 the persecution of "Lutheranism" had been revived with great vigour. Accounts of Protestant worship were spread abroad which remind one of the descriptions of Christian rites which the popular imagination made current in the days of the Roman Empire. Followers of the reformed religion were accused of eating human flesh and of practising all kinds of debauchery[1]. But the influence which Calvin exerted from Geneva was already beginning to take effect. Protestant literature was disseminated all over France by pedlars and the Edict of Chateaubriand (1551) proved powerless to stem the tide. In 1555 the first Protestant church in Paris was opened and this example was followed by many provincial towns. As yet there were practically no institutions inside France at which a candidate for the Protestant ministry could receive training; but a supply of pastors was maintained from Calvin's *académie* at Geneva, which has already been described, and from institutions of a similar character which had been founded at Neuchâtel and Lausanne. "Send us wood," said Calvin in one of his letters to the reformed Church of France, "and we will make arrows." Persecutions did not avail to check the spread of Protestantism. From his headquarters at Geneva Calvin did not cease by his letters to encourage and instruct those of the new faith in France; he also induced the Protestant cantons of Switzerland to intercede with Henri on behalf of their persecuted French co-religionists; but they met with a rebuff and did not venture to press the matter further.

In 1559—the year of the foundation of Calvin's school at Geneva—the Peace of Cateau-Cambrésis was signed. For the time being it ended the struggle between the House of France and the House of Austria. But France was not destined to enjoy peace. The fires which had been kindled for the martyrdom of the Protestants soon spread until the whole kingdom was involved in the conflagration. The civil war which began with the massacre at Vassy in 1562 and ended with the Edict of Nantes was doubtless complicated by political considerations; but for long it remained to a large extent a struggle between a Catholic majority and a not insignificant nor inconsiderable Protestant minority.

[1] See Claude Haton, *Mémoires*, I, 48–51, *et passim*.

The struggle was bitter; but at hardly any period during the thirty years that it lasted did the Huguenots slacken their efforts in the cause of education.

It was in 1559 also that the isolated Protestant churches, as a measure of self-defence and under the instructions of Calvin, first organised themselves into a united body. The first synod of the reformed Church met at Paris in this year and henceforward, in spite of difficulties, a meeting of this kind was held at more or less regular intervals[1]. Questions of education and the administration of Huguenot schools naturally formed a considerable part of the matters debated on these occasions; and it is upon the still extant reports of these synods that the present chapter is largely based. When the first synod of Paris met there were already 72 reformed churches in France, and by the year 1561 this number had increased to no less than 2150. Nor was the movement now confined to "les gens mécaniques," who had chiefly been attracted by the Lutheran doctrines when Protestantism first made its appearance in France. Members of noble families—nay even of the royal house[2]—were declared adherents of the new faith; and it was this fact that gave the Reformation in France a political significance and helped to cause the Wars of Religion.

The first educational institution in France to be profoundly influenced by the reformed doctrines had been the college of Nîmes in Provence. It had been founded in 1539, at the urgent request of the magistrates of the town, by François I with the co-operation of his sister, Marguerite of Navarre. The college supplied courses for boys between the ages of five and fifteen, and was supplemented by a university with one faculty only—that of philosophy—which provided a further course for students who stayed on until the age of twenty. The organisation of this institution, therefore, was much like that which was adopted later by Calvin at Geneva. In both cases we can trace the

[1] See list of National Synods in Appendix F.
[2] Before the death of Henri II in 1559 Antoine de Bourbon (who became king of Navarre by his marriage with Jeanne d'Albret) and his brother, the Prince de Condé, were already Protestants.

influence of Sturm's school at Strasbourg which had an
advanced course following on from the highest form of
the *Gymnasium* proper. The first principal of the college
at Nîmes was a certain Claude Baduel who had studied at
Wittenberg and was a personal friend of Melanchthon. Thus
it was naturally the Lutheran type of Protestantism which
first took root at Nîmes; but with the spread of Calvinism
in France it soon changed its character and, in spite of many
vicissitudes, became one of the largest and most flourishing
Huguenot colleges. It drew its scholars not only from all
parts of France but even from Holland and Germany.

But it is in the last few decades of the sixteenth century
and under the ægis of Calvin that Protestant schools begin
to multiply in France. Many of them were founded by
municipalities and maintained partly by grants, partly from
pupils' fees, and after the Edict of Nantes partly by subsidies
from the national synods. But in some cases a local *seigneur*
who had embraced Protestantism would open a school on
his estates for the education of his co-religionists. One of the
first colleges to be founded in France upon the model of
Calvin's school at Geneva was that of Châtillon-sur-Loing.
It owed its origin to the munificence of Admiral Coligny[1].
There were indeed at this time powerful influences at work
for the cause of moderation and tolerance. Catherine de
Médicis, the queen-regent, seconded by her chancellor
Michel de l'Hôpital, was anxious in the interests of her son,
the boy-king Charles IX, and of the kingdom over which
he would soon have to rule, to establish peace between the
Catholic and Calvinist parties. A meeting of orthodox

---

[1] Cf. "He thought the institution of schooles, and the well training
up of yong children, to be the singular benefite of God. This he
termed the seedleape of the Churche, and the Nurcerie of godlinesse.
Affirming that the want of learning had cast a mist, not only uppon
the Common Weale but also uppon Religion....And therefore he
founded a schoole in a pleasant and wholesome place hard by the
Shattilion house, and when he had finished the building of it, at his
great cost he maintained many children and yoong men there, and
many lerned *Hebricians, Grecians,* and *Latinistes* too reade those
languages too them." Golding, *Lyfe of Iasper Colignie*: no paging;
quotation is three pages from end of book.

bishops and of Huguenot pastors was arranged—the well-known Colloquy of Poissy (September, 1561); and although no agreement was reached, yet at the beginning of the next year there was passed the Edict of January—a kind of Five Mile Act by which Huguenots were allowed freedom of public worship in the outskirts of towns and in the country. But with the French Protestants the existence of an organised church usually implied the existence also of a primary school; and it would seem a fair inference that the passing of the Edict would imply the growth of "little schools" attached to separate churches. As Baird says[1]: "Not a city, not a town or village, was conquered by the 'new doctrines,' but a Protestant school followed closely upon the newly instituted church and the teacher was esteemed a scarcely less essential officer in the ecclesiastical polity than the preacher of the gospel himself." We know very little as to the details of the growth of these primary schools, and in tracing the rise of the Huguenot colleges in the latter part of the sixteenth century we may run the risk of overlooking what was being done at the same time for Protestant elementary education. Yet there is evidence that the activity was considerable. As early as 1560 it was observed that in many parts of France "the children were learning religion only in the catechism brought from Geneva and all knew it by heart[2]." In addition to this Protestant catechism the subjects taught in the Huguenot "little schools" included reading, writing, elementary arithmetic, and singing. As a rule a school of this kind was supported by the local congregation or by the *seigneur* on whose estate it was situated, if he were a Protestant. If the school were a small one children of both sexes might be educated together. In some places where the Huguenots were in power[3] elementary education was not only free but compulsory, and parents who omitted to send their children to school were liable to a fine. The problem of staffing the Huguenot "little

[1] *The Huguenots and Henry of Navarre*, II, 474.
[2] De Villars, Lieutenant-Governor of Languedoc, letter to the Guises; see Baird, *Rise of the Huguenots*, I, 429.
[3] This was the case, for example, at Castres in Languedoc.

schools" sometimes proved a difficult one. Often the local minister undertook the duties of headmaster and was assisted by ex-pupils; but the latter had first to be licensed by the local consistory which thus took the place of the Catholic *écolâtre*.

The Edict of January, although it aided the spread of Huguenot education, did not satisfy either side. A month after its promulgation an attack was made by the Duc de Guise on a party of unarmed Calvinists who were worshipping in a building at Vassy in Champagne. This was the signal for civil war and for about a year hostilities were carried on by the two parties. Both sides appealed to foreign powers for help; the Huguenots received money and troops from Elizabeth of England, while their adversaries looked to Philip II of Spain. This overture to a series of wars, which lasted in all for more than thirty years, was terminated by the Edict of Amboise (1563) which was framed on the lines of the Edict of January, but was somewhat less favourable to the Protestant party. None the less it secured for France four years of peace and for the Huguenots in particular considerable freedom of public worship; and thus in addition to the growth of Protestant "little schools" it is precisely at this juncture that we find the foundation of several colleges or secondary schools designed largely for the training of future ministers.

With the rapid spread of Protestantism in France it seemed that it would soon become impossible for the educational institutions of Geneva and other Swiss towns to cope with the increasing demand for clergy. At the time of the Colloquy of Poissy it was estimated that from four to six thousand pastors were needed for the Huguenot congregations which had sprung up in all parts of France. It was essential therefore that the country should not be content to depend upon foreign aid in a matter of so vital importance, and the provision of adequate facilities for secondary and university education at once engaged the attention of the Huguenot party. In February, 1562, the church at Orleans had announced its intention of setting up a school for the training of those who might one day become

ministers[1]; but owing to the outbreak of civil war—the
letter in which the plan is outlined was dated the day before
the massacre of Vassy occurred—the project never took
effect. A college at Vendôme, however, dates from 1562 and
by 1571 it was already of sufficient importance to possess a
professor of Hebrew[2]. In 1563 was founded the college of
Metz which, although outside French territory, was definitely
a product of French Protestantism and of the inspiration of
Calvin. It differed from all the other Huguenot colleges and
from their prototype at Geneva in that it made provision
for the reception of boarders. In 1566 another Protestant
secondary school was opened at Orthez in Béarn; it owed
its origin to the public spirit of Jeanne d'Albret, mother of
Henri IV.

By 1567 the two factions were at blows again; but the
Protestants, although they suffered severe reverses at Jarnac
and Moncontour, were by no means crushed. The Peace of
St Germain in 1570 renewed the Edict of Amboise and gave
the combatants two years' breathing space. The Huguenots
seized the opportunity to found colleges at La Rochelle and
at Montargis[3] in the province of Berry. It seems probable
also that the college of Vitré in Brittany dates from about
this time. But a terrible blow was about to fall upon the
Huguenots. Catherine de Medicis, jealous of the influence
which the Admiral Coligny had gained over her son Charles
IX, precipitated the massacre of St Bartholomew. On the
festival of this saint—August 24th, 1572—the Protestant
leaders, as well as many of the rank and file, were butchered
under circumstances of revolting brutality. The murder of
the aged Ramus, which has been described in Chapter I, is
a typical incident of the massacre[4]. But the Protestant

---

[1] See *Letter* from the Church of Orleans to the "Venerable Company," in Gaberel, I, 110, *pièces justificatives*.

[2] There are several examples of Huguenot colleges which at some time or other in their career could boast a teacher of Hebrew (*e.g.* Châtillon); but there is no indication that this language formed part of the regular curriculum in Huguenot schools.

[3] It is possible that Montargis may be of earlier date than this.

[4] Although the Bartholomew massacre is perhaps the most hideous crime in the whole of French history, it is worth while to remember

party, though scotched, was by no means killed. The Huguenots of the provinces, with courage born of despair, took up arms and held out at La Rochelle with so much success that the king, Charles IX, was forced to come to terms with them. Once more, then, there is a respite; and in this same year, 1573, a Huguenot college, due to the munificence of Ludovic, count of Nassau, was founded at Orange[1]. In 1575 a similar institution was opened at Sedan; while from the following year dates a Huguenot secondary school at Castres, near Toulouse, where a flourishing Protestant "little school" was already in existence.

In 1578 was held the synod of Sainte-Foy—the first to meet after the massacre of St Bartholomew. The times still looked black for the Protestant party. The extreme Catholics had already formed a Holy League to preserve the orthodox religion and to safeguard the interests of the country which, they believed, were being betrayed by the king. The Edict of Beaulieu (1576), which had accorded unparalleled concessions to the Huguenots, had been challenged by the States General assembled at Blois; and a demand was made that all exercise of the Protestant religion, whether public or private, should be forbidden. Thus Catholic and Huguenot were already at each other's throat once more; yet even so the synod of Sainte-Foy definitely laid it down that "the

for the sake of fairness that the Huguenots were capable of atrocities as well as their Catholic adversaries. In 1567 a number of Catholics were massacred at Nîmes and the bodies of dead and dying alike thrown down a well which was hastily filled up with earth. In 1569 Coligny himself butchered in cold blood 260 Catholic peasants at the castle of La Chapelle-Faucher in Périgord. Priests who fell into the hands of the Huguenots were sometimes tortured with indescribable barbarity. This brutal disregard for human life is not the mark of any one party. The law of the land still visited offences with the most horrible penalties; the counterfeiter of coin, for example, was punished by being boiled alive. In short, the mediaeval standpoint, typified by the Nuremberg Maiden or the *Auto da Fé* of the Inquisition, had not yet been abandoned.

[1] Both Orange and Sedan were at this time outside French territory. Ludovic was a brother of William the Silent. He had fought against Alva and taken part in the battles of Jarnac and Moncontour. Walsingham, the English ambassador, calls him "the rarest gentleman which I have talked withal since I came to France."

deputies from the provinces will be ordered to instruct and exhort the aforesaid provinces to find means to provide schools in which the aforesaid youth may be educated and made fit one day to serve the Church of God[1]."

None the less there is a distinct slackening of educational activity after the synod of Sainte-Foy. The last and most bitter stages of the wars of religion had been reached. Foreign potentates still lend their aid to the conflicting parties. In France itself new complications arise. The death in 1584 of the Duc d'Anjou (formerly Duc d'Alençon), who had headed the moderate party among the Catholics, left as heir to the throne a Protestant prince—Henri of Navarre. The Holy League at once made a treaty with Philip of Spain "for the defence and preservation of the Catholic religion and the extirpation of all heresies." More than this, the association was strong enough to negotiate on equal terms with the king of France himself—Henri III—and to demand that the Calvinist religion should be suppressed throughout his realm. This was the signal for renewed civil war. The Duc de Guise, the hero of the extreme Catholic party and leader of the League, had achieved great popularity and his influence in Paris particularly was far greater than that of the king himself. In desperation Henri III effected the assassination of his rival; "à présent je suis roi" he wrote just after the murder had been committed. But the Leaguers were furious and Paris broke out into open insurrection. Henri was forced to make a reconciliation with Henri of Navarre, the Protestant leader, and the two joined forces and marched against Paris, the headquarters of the League. In the midst of these tumults a fanatical monk, eager to take revenge upon the king who had betrayed Catholicism, stabbed Henri III under pretence of giving a letter to him. One of the king's last acts was to recognise Henri of Navarre as his rightful successor. The new king's position as leader of the Calvinists was fraught with difficulty, but by skill and moderation he subdued his enemies and made himself master of Paris. But he realised that if he were to be in truth king of France, to give his

[1] Aymon, I, 126 and 127.

distracted country peace once more, and to free her from foreign interference, it could only be by becoming a Catholic. His abjuration of Protestantism, therefore, was at once a politic and a patriotic act; and although he changed his religion he did not abandon those who still remained faithful to it.

In spite of the difficulties created by this period of civil strife the Protestant party had not abandoned its interest in education. The political assembly of La Rochelle in 1588 had made plans for the foundation of an academy in that city, adding to the existing college a university with faculties of theology and the humanities. Forty-six students drawn from the various provinces were to be admitted, and the necessary funds were to be provided by confiscated Roman ecclesiastical revenues. This scheme was never realised, but so soon as the Wars of Religion had finally died down the Huguenots founded the colleges of Saumur (1596) and Montauban (1597), both of which quickly took an important place among Calvinist schools. They owed their origin in part at any rate to a proposal contained in the Ordinance of Mantes, dating from 1593, whereby Protestants were to be guaranteed the right to educate their children in their own schools and to erect colleges for the instruction of youth wherever the need might arise. But by the Edict of Nantes, promulgated in 1598, the Huguenots were granted full liberty of conscience and the right of public worship almost everywhere in the kingdom. At the same time all their civil disabilities were removed; their right to hold national and provincial synods was formally recognised and they became qualified to hold any public office. The Edict had important educational implications. It laid down that no student should be debarred from any university, college, or school on the grounds of his belonging to the reformed religion[1]. This permission of itself might have contented the Huguenot party but little, had not the Edict also provided that Protestant schools might be opened freely in all cities and places where the public exercise of the reformed religion was permitted, and that Huguenot fathers, either during

[1] § XXII.

their lifetime or by will after death, might arrange for the education of their children exactly as they wished[1].

We have seen that during a period of thirty years, when the Huguenots were struggling for their very existence, they had displayed as much determination and high spirit in providing schools for their children as in vindicating their religious beliefs upon the field of battle. It follows therefore that when the Edict of Nantes ushered in an era of peace under the benign rule of a well-disposed sovereign, the efforts of the Huguenot party on behalf of education became more vigorous than ever. In 1595 the Jesuits, who had already proved themselves most formidable opponents of the Calvinist party, had been banished from France as "corrupters of youth, disturbers of the public peace, and enemies of the King and State." It was by means of their free schools that the Jesuits had carried on much of their work of propaganda and already, during the Wars of Religion, it was not unknown for Huguenot parents to send their children to these Catholic schools. Naturally the Calvinist authorities regarded this as a most serious tendency. The synod of Sainte-Foy, held in 1578, had issued the following manifesto: "Fathers and Mothers are exhorted to be exceeding careful in instructing their children which are the seed and nursery of the Church, and they shall be most bitterly censured who send them to the schools of Priests, Jesuits, and Nuns; as also the Gentry shall be reproved who place them pages or domesticks in the Houses of Lords or Noblemen of the contrary religion[2]." The definite permission accorded by the Edict of Nantes that Protestant schools might be provided and that there should be no embargo upon the sending of Calvinist children to them, coupled with the temporary eclipse of the Society of Jesus[3], gave the Huguenots an opportunity to extend their educational work and they did not fail to profit by it.

In 1596 the fourteenth national synod had been held at Saumur. Amongst the resolutions which were passed on this occasion appears the following: "On the subject of

---

[1] § xxxvii and § xxxviii.　　　　　[2] Quick, i, 119.
[3] It was re-admitted to France in 1603.

scholars it has been found advisable to instruct each of the Provinces to endeavour to found a college, and all of them together to found at least two academies. To this end the locality alike of the Colleges and of the Academies shall be chosen for the future by the Provinces. The present Synod has decided that this town of Saumur is suitable as a site for a college and for an academy when God makes this possible; for this reason we have besought the Governor of this place to continue the goodwill which he has shown in this matter, and each member of the assembly is asked to exhort to the same end those of his own province[1]." This resolution makes clear the general intention of the Huguenot party as to the provision of secondary and higher education. Each of the sixteen provinces into which France had been divided for the purposes of the Protestant Church, was to have, so far as possible, its own college—*i.e.* secondary school; and there were to be at least two of these which, like Calvin's educational institution at Geneva, possessed a university course following directly from that of the secondary school. As a matter of fact, the actual provision that was eventually made exceeded the scheme originally laid down by the fourteenth national synod. In all, thirty-five Huguenot schools[2] were founded after the Genevan prototype, and although Provence apparently never possessed a college, yet in some of the provinces several were opened. Berry, Xaintonge, and Dauphiné, for example, each had three, while Anjou could boast of four. The number of the academies, which were designed chiefly for the professional training of Huguenot ministers, in time far surpassed the original two proposed at the Saumur assembly. Inside France alone no less than six are found—at Nîmes, Orthez, Montpellier, Montauban, Saumur, and Die; while many French Calvinist students also continued their studies at Orange, Sedan, and Montbéliard, at Strasbourg, and especially at Geneva[3]. By 1607 when the eighteenth national

---

[1] Aymon, I, 197.   [2] See Appendix G.
[3] At the time of the Edict of Nantes there were 400 "*proposants*" or candidates for the ministry. See Gregorio Leti, *Vie d'Elizabeth*, II, 418.

synod was held at La Rochelle, there were already inside France sufficient facilities for the training of Protestant theological students, so that it was possible to decree that candidates for the ministry should no longer go abroad for their professional training—unless it were to Geneva—without the express permission of the synod of their own province[1].

The synod of 1596 had laid down a definite plan of action and the Huguenots at once proceeded to carry it out by opening colleges in important towns where educational facilities of this kind had not yet been provided. Reference has already been made to the foundation of a school at Saumur in 1596 and at Montauban in the following year. It seems probable that in 1597, or perhaps slightly earlier, a college was opened at Loudun. But the question of finance was still a difficult one. When a college was provided by the munificence of a Protestant noble—as was the case, for example, at Châtillon, Montargis, Sedan, Orthez, and Orange—funds were usually allocated by the founder for the expenses of maintenance. Where the school was provided by a municipality—and this was a more usual condition after the Edict of Nantes—the problem was more acute. Sometimes a special tax—as for example on salt—was imposed to cover educational expenditure, or the local synods tried to raise contributions from the faithful, who were often too poor to make any effectual response. But with the Edict of Nantes this difficulty was to some extent and for the time being solved. By the terms of this decree a grant of 43,300 écus was allotted from public funds to the Protestant Church. Of this sum the synod of Montpellier, held in the same year as that in which the Edict was passed, appropriated one-thirteenth for the upkeep of the academies; and in the reports of the following four national synods held during the reign of Henri IV there are frequent references to sums voted for the support or foundation of colleges from "les deniers octroiés aux Églises de ce Roiaume par la liberalité du Roi[2]." At the sixteenth synod held at Gergeau

---

[1] Aymon, I, 312.

[2] They were usually known as *deniers de la liberalité*.

in 1601 it was enacted that "the Provinces at their provincial synods, when making the distribution of the sums granted by the King, which shall be apportioned to them, shall found schools[1]." It was also laid down that the academies at Montpellier, Saumur, Montauban, Nîmes, and Sedan should be supported from this same source.

In 1604 was founded the academy of Die in Dauphiné. It was to be "un collège aux lettres humaines et arts libéraux" and to have a principal and a sufficient number of regents and other officials as should be necessary "for the instruction of youth in all branches of knowledge and good morals." The local synod voted a sum towards the foundation of the college on condition that it should be employed "for the instruction of the aforesaid youth, not only in good letters but also in the knowledge of religion according to the doctrine of the reformed churches." The municipality of Die also contributed a grant.

Thanks to the researches of M. Arnaud, a Protestant minister of Die, we have some detailed information as to the organisation of this Huguenot school at Die. Too often we have to be content with a mere catalogue of names, but in this case we can see the institution at work. It is interesting to note in almost every respect the influence of the prototype—Calvin's academy at Geneva. At Die there was a university, in which the faculties were not sharply differentiated, and a *basse école* or secondary school. In the former there were four professors—one for Hebrew, one for theology, and two for philosophy; while the latter had seven forms, each with its regent, like any other contemporary college. The whole institution was controlled by a council of governors. The rector of the academy was its president and the four professors of the university together with the principal[2] of the *basse école* were *ex officio* members; but they were assisted by six other persons not concerned professionally with educational work, but distinguished in the

[1] Aymon, I, 251.
[2] In some Huguenot academies the principal of the college was also a professor of philosophy in the university, and was in charge of a two years' course leading up to the *maîtrise*.

life of the municipality. It is with the organisation of the
basse école or college that we are primarily concerned. The
regents, in accordance with a canon of the reformed Church[1],
were required to subscribe to a confession of the Calvinistic
faith, and none might be admitted to office without the
consent of the local consistory. Each regent taught for five
hours daily and was instructed to appear always in a long
black robe[2]. In each class the pupils were subdivided into
groups of ten, each headed by its *dizanier* whose duties were
similar to those assigned to the *decurio* in the schools of the
Society of Jesus. As at Geneva, promotions from one form
to the next were possible twice a year; they were made
on Easter Monday and on September 1st. Examinations
were held at the end of the summer term and the month
of September was a holiday. The boys—as was usual in
Huguenot schools—were given frequent practice in declamation and in the higher forms there were monthly
discussions on subjects appointed by the regent. Religious
instruction was imparted by the Calvinist catechism[3] and
by devotional exercises which played a large part in the
school routine. The pupils were compelled to attend public
worship on Sundays and Wednesdays. Swearing, card-
playing, and the frequenting of taverns were forbidden under
severe penalties; and although there were no boarders at
Die and all pupils either lived with their parents or lodged
in the town, they were not allowed under any pretext
whatever to venture out of doors after nightfall. Offences
against school discipline were punished by the use of the
cane, and in serious cases, by expulsion. If a boy showed up
unsatisfactory work he was merely detained after school
hours and made to do his task again.

The programme of studies was in outline as follows: The

---

[1] See Quick, p. xxvi.

[2] At Saumur the annual salary was 400 livres for the regent of
form I; 300 for II; 250 for III; 210 for IV and V.

[3] A regulation made at the twenty-fourth national synod (Charenton, 1623) enacted that "all regents shall read to their pupils every
Saturday a passage from the big catechism, in French, Latin, or Greek,
according to their capacity, and shall make them learn it by heart and
explain it to them in a familiar manner." See Aymon, II, 249.

seventh form, which was really a *petite école,* learnt reading
in Latin and French. The sixth specialised in writing, but
also learnt the Greek characters. In the fifth class the
rudiments of Latin grammar were acquired from Despauter
and Cato's *Disticha de Moribus*—a favourite school-book in
the Middle Ages. Ability to converse in this language was
fostered by a study of the Colloquies of Corderius and Vives
or in the *Sacred Dialogues* of Sébastien Châteillon, who had
been a Protestant schoolmaster of Geneva. According to a
rule of the school, Latin conversation was compulsory for
all pupils in the upper classes. On reaching the fourth form
the pupil was set to read Ovid, Terence, and Cicero's Letters.
Latin grammar was continued and Latin composition begun.
It was in this form also that the pupil commenced to study
Greek. In the third class the boys perfected their knowledge
of Latin and Greek grammar and read Virgil, Hesiod,
Xenophon, and the *De Officiis* of Cicero. They also occupied
themselves with composition both in Greek and Latin.
Verse composition was first attempted in the second form,
though prose themes in both Greek and Latin were not
neglected. The authors studied at this stage included Caesar,
Cicero, Florus, Isocrates, Homer (*Iliad*), and Virgil (*Georgics*).
The top form or Rhetoric, as was customary elsewhere,
specialised in the study of the classical orators and in the
art of declamation. Cicero's *De Oratore* was taken as the
text-book. In Greek the plays of the great tragic poets
were read.

This ended the work of the secondary school proper and
the pupil who wished to follow it up by a course in philosophy
would do so in the higher school or university. There, at the
end of two years and after a study of Logic, Ethics, and
Metaphysics, a candidate could obtain the degree of *maître-
ès-arts*[1], or—if he followed a more prolonged and wider
course of instruction—the baccalaureate or doctorate in

[1] By a resolution (Art. VIII) of the nineteenth national synod (Saint-
Maixent, 1609) it was laid down that students in philosophy should
undergo a strict examination at the end of their two years' course
and that no *lettres de maîtrise* should be granted to such as were
inefficient. See Aymon, I, 377, and Quick, p. 331.

philosophy. At the same time the study of philosophy in most of the Huguenot academies tended always to be subordinated to that of theology. The synod of Alais (1620) expressed doubts as to the value of metaphysics and ordered professors of this subject to treat it invariably in accordance with the principles of the true religion. Protestantism, in fact, no less than Catholicism, had to face the possibility that an independent search for truth might be dangerous to orthodoxy. Eleven years later, at the synod of Charenton, it was decided that metaphysics should be entirely banished from the curriculum "because for a long time past it has been entirely corrupted by the false subtleties of the Roman Church[1]."

The school at Die seems to have won an immediate success. As in all Huguenot colleges, a fee was paid for tuition, but there were a few scholarships for the children of needy parents and for boys who intended to enter the ministry[2]. In 1610 there were already 134 pupils in the *basse école*; but for reasons that we shall shortly have to investigate, it is probable that this number was never equalled again after that year.

In 1605, the year after the foundation of the *académie* of Die, another Huguenot school was opened at Privas, a neighbouring town; but its career was a short one. The poorer provinces were already finding it difficult to carry out the provisions of the fourteenth national synod (Saumur, 1596). To supplement the royal *deniers* considerable sums were needed for the foundation and upkeep of colleges, and in many cases the faithful were not able to fulfil the demands which were made. Among the resolutions, therefore, of the eighteenth national synod (La Rochelle, 1607) we find one to the effect that the richer churches should be exhorted to aid the poorer ones in the maintenance of their schools. At

[1] Aymon, I, 510.
[2] "The fifth penny" of all Huguenot charities was set aside for the maintenance of poor scholars who were candidates for the ministry. See Quick, p. xxvii and p. 66. The eleventh synod (La Rochelle, 1581) also enjoined every *colloque* to maintain at least one poor scholar during his training for the ministry.

the same synod it is recorded that "the deputies of divers provinces moving that there might be particular colleges erected in their respective provinces for the educating of youth in the humanities before they were sent to the universities, this Assembly grants them their request[1]." Sums of 100 *écus* were allotted to each of eleven provinces for the erection of colleges, and the deputies from each were charged to submit to the next national synod an account of how the money had been employed. The amounts assigned seem very inadequate and one is not greatly surprised to find that the scheme proved unworkable; as a matter of fact the money was probably devoted to the foundation or maintenance not of colleges but of "little schools."

None the less in 1609 a college was opened at Gergeau, or Jargeau, in Berry. It owed its existence to the munificence of the Duc de Sully, the finance minister of Henri IV. At the nineteenth synod, held in the same year, this illustrious benefactor is formally thanked for his services to education and a sum of 500 *écus* is set aside from the royal grant for the upkeep of the school at Gergeau. Permission was also given for the foundation of a college at Bergerac. In this case the demand came from the municipality, and the necessity of a Protestant school in this town was emphasised by the fact that the Society of Jesus, re-admitted to France in 1603, had already opened a college the excellence of which was tempting Huguenot parents of Bergerac to send their sons to it as pupils. From the year 1609, also, dates the college at Clermont-sur-Beauvoisis, the only Huguenot school in the province of L'Ile de France. It began work with three regents, one of whom numbered music among the subjects which he taught. This school had a short and chequered career and had completely disappeared by 1631.

Henri IV perished under the dagger of Ravaillac in 1610, and with his death the *floruit* period of Huguenot education in France comes to an end. A writer on the history of the town of Loudun[2], in discussing the Huguenot colleges and referring more particularly to those of Montauban, Saumur,

[1] Quick, p. 275.
[2] Dumoustier de la Fond (1778), p. 93.

La Rochelle, and Sedan, says: "These institutions were most flourishing; they were already (1610) at the head of the most learned in Europe. But their strict regulations disgusted many youths who were studying philosophy, owing to the rule which rendered them liable to the discipline of the cane." It may be noted that this same discipline was in vogue at this period in the colleges of the University of Paris; but it is obvious that, whatever its drawbacks, Huguenot education had become a real power in France. Its importance was destined soon to wane. The dates of the foundation of some of the Huguenot colleges are doubtful or even unknown, but it is almost certain that all thirty-five of them had come into existence before 1610 and that after the death of Henri IV no more Protestant secondary schools were opened. Not only so, but the existence of such institutions as were already at work now became precarious. Some came to a premature end; others dragged on an existence which can best be described as "intermittent"; and few continued an unbroken career from the early days of the reform down to the year 1685 when the Revocation of the Edict of Nantes gave the final blow to the Huguenot schools of France. It is the history of this decline that we have now to trace.

The new king, Louis XIII, was a boy of nine and the regency was in the hands of his mother, Marie de Médicis. One of the first acts of the new reign was a confirmation of the Edict of Nantes, but the benevolent policy of Henri IV towards the Huguenots was not continued. Sully, who had been the late king's chief minister and to whom the re-organisation of France during his reign is largely due, was soon dismissed and the confidence of the queen-mother given to an Italian upstart named Concini. At the same time, the Protestants themselves were to a great extent responsible for the change in the official attitude towards them. Marie de Médicis was prepared to tolerate Calvinism, "being persuaded by past experience that violence had served only to increase the number of those who had left the Church instead of teaching them how to enter it." But she had opened negotiations with Spain whereby Louis should marry a Spanish princess. The Huguenots viewed with alarm this alliance with the chief Catholic nation in Europe which had so often aided their enemies, the Leaguers, during the Wars of Religion. As a measure of defence, therefore, they organised themselves once more into a state within a state. At an assembly held at Saumur they set up what was virtually a Protestant republic inside a Catholic monarchy. In 1617 the machine was put into motion. In that year the Catholic religion was reintroduced into Béarn and ecclesiastical revenues which had been sequestered were ordered to be returned to their former owners. This command, after considerable resistance, was enforced with the aid of an army; whereupon a general assembly, held at La Rochelle, issued a declaration of independence, and raised troops which were put under the command of the Duc de Rohan who some years previously had stirred up a Protestant revolt in the Cevennes. Montauban, held by the Huguenots, successfully withstood a siege, but Louis carried on the campaign so vigorously that the Protestants were soon ready to make peace. In 1622, therefore, the Edict of Nantes was once more renewed, but Protestant political assemblies were forbidden and the Huguenots were not allowed to hold any fortified places except La Rochelle and Montauban.

If then the religion of the Huguenots was still tolerated their political power was already on the wane. This is reflected in their educational work. Not only does the renewal of party strife make difficult the peaceful work of the school, but the lack of teachers and of money are serious hindrances. At the period of which we are speaking there were some thirty-five colleges and a considerable number of "little schools" under Huguenot control. This meant that a constant supply of trained teachers had to be maintained and it was from the secondary schools that the supply was chiefly drawn. But there was always an even more insistent claim—that of supplying candidates for the ministry. The shortage of teachers had been less acute—though by no means unknown—during the earlier Wars of Religion because there were fewer schools, and during the time of Henri IV because the Huguenots enjoyed peace and considerable power. But throughout the reign of Louis XIII we can trace a growing need for teachers and expedients of various kinds have to be tried in order to meet it. Sometimes a local minister has the principalship of a college added to his duties, but more often teachers are imported from Scotland, Holland, or French Switzerland—all three Calvinist countries—to fill up the gaps. This tendency is illustrated by many of the lists of masters in Huguenot secondary schools during the seventeenth century. At Saumur, for example, we find Robertson and Cameron, Tressel and Hendricks, among a number of French surnames. The employment of foreigners was facilitated by the fact that Latin was the teaching medium at any rate in the upper forms of every Huguenot college.

With the gradual disappearance of the *deniers du roi*[1] finance became an even more perplexing problem. In the report of almost every national synod henceforth the question intrudes itself with growing insistency. At the synod of Privas (1612) it is laid down that the existing number of colleges shall not be increased; and the number of the professors in each academy and the stipends payable to each are strictly regulated[2]. At the next synod, held in 1614, an attempt was made to evade the rule which prohibited the foundation of new colleges, and a request was considered from a certain Sieur Joli, pastor of the church at Millau, a Calvinist stronghold in the south, suggesting that a school should be erected in that town; but the demand was refused on the grounds that no funds were available. In 1617, at the synod of Vitré, it was decided that inspectors should be appointed to visit the colleges "in order to see if the public are profiting and if the masters do their duty[3]." To this end two pastors, "taken out of those churches whereunto the universities (*i.e. académies*) do belong," were

---

[1] Even during the reign of Henri IV these payments had been made very irregularly and they were entirely suppressed about 1630.

[2] A professor of theology at Saumur, for instance, received 700 livres; his colleagues who taught Hebrew, Greek, or philosophy each received 400 livres *per annum*.

[3] Quick, p. 514.

chosen and they were instructed to report to the next national synod to be held at Alais.

Meanwhile a new figure had appeared upon the stage of French history. Armand du Plessis, Duc de Richelieu, had succeeded Concini as adviser to the queen-mother. In 1616, at the age of 31, he was already minister for war; by 1622 he had received a cardinal's hat and soon afterwards became the controlling influence in the State. He held very extreme theories as to the nature of the royal power. For him kings were the "living image of God and the royal majesty second only to the divine." Such views profoundly affected his attitude towards the Huguenots. In his own memoirs he has outlined for us his policy in regard to them. Addressing the king Louis XIII, he says: "When your Majesty resolved not only to admit me to your councils but also to give me a large share in your confidence, I can say with truth that the Huguenots shared the state with you.... I promised your Majesty that I would devote all my energies and all the authority which you were pleased to give me to ruining the Huguenot party[1]." Richelieu was as good as his word. In 1625 the Protestants, led by the Duc de Rohan and his brother Soubise, were already in revolt. The stronghold—one might almost say the capital—of the Calvinist "republic" was La Rochelle. Richelieu laid siege to the place; but for the time being he was not strong enough to effect his object and a truce was signed. Two years later the struggle recommenced. The Rochellais, reinforced by a fleet under the incapable Duke of Buckingham, made a spirited and desperate resistance, but at the end of fourteen months they were constrained by famine to open their gates to the Cardinal's army. There were no reprisals, but La Rochelle was treated as a conquered city and its fortifications were demolished. Montauban and the other Protestant cities which had revolted made their submission, and in June, 1629, the "Grâce d'Alais" marked the termination of the last of the Wars of Religion. The title of this peace is significant. No longer does the king treat with organised Protestantism on terms of equality; he

[1] *Succincte Narration—Mémoires*, IX, 331.

regards the Huguenots as conquered rebels to whom pardon is granted. Henceforward there is no longer a strong separate political party within the State, and the unity of France under a despotic monarchy becomes possible. To ensure this, the special privileges accorded to the Protestants by the Edict of Nantes are withdrawn; for example, they no longer enjoy the right to hold fortified cities or to convene general assemblies for political purposes. But it is as a political organisation, and not as a religious body, that Richelieu desires to "ruin the Huguenot party." Complete freedom of worship and civil equality with Catholics are conceded to adherents of the reformed faith; and in spite of opposition from the extreme Catholic party Richelieu, in an age when religious toleration was unknown outside France, observed scrupulously throughout his career the terms of the "Grâce d'Alais."

If the reign of Henri IV had seen French Protestantism in its prime, that of Louis XIII was at any rate a period of toleration. But the work of the Huguenot schools was carried on under increasing difficulties. In 1617 the deputies from Basse Guyenne had reported to the national synod at Vitré that they could scarcely maintain the colleges of that province. At the synod of Alais in 1620 a debate arose as to whether economies could be effected by reducing the number of academies already in existence. The same question was discussed at considerable length in the next synod (Charenton, 1623); but it was decided that no steps should be taken for the time being. As a measure of economy, however, the same assembly decreed that in future no appointments should be made to professorships of Greek, this language being "de peu d'utilité." It is noticeable also, as a sign of the times, that the grant made to the *académie* of Saumur, which in 1617 had amounted to 5190 livres, is now reduced to 4100 livres. The same tale of poverty is revealed in the reports of the assembly at Castres (1626) and at Charenton (1631). Meanwhile some of the Huguenot colleges had already been compelled to shut down. Niort disappears by 1620 and Clermont-sur-Beauvoisis by 1631. The cause is not merely lack of funds, although this was always a most serious matter, but also—as we have already noticed—the competition of Jesuit schools[1]. The latter gave a free secondary education of singular excellence; and it is hardly surprising that Huguenot parents, whose convictions as to the reformed religion were not very firm, should be tempted to send their sons to a flourishing and efficient institution where no fees were payable, in preference to a struggling and ill-equipped school which was in continual need of subsidies. Nor was the Society of Jesus the only competitor. The full tide of the Counter-Reformation was now flowing. Oratorian schools were springing up in many towns and their work was ably seconded by that of other teaching orders. The situation therefore was becoming serious for the Huguenot party if they were to retain control of the education of their children, the hope of their cause.

Since the year 1559, when the Huguenot churches were first organised into a united body, the national synod had been convened at frequent intervals. At first it met almost every year, but soon it was found sufficient to hold the synod once every two or three years. After the "Grâce d'Alais" the intervals become much greater. The twenty-sixth synod, held at Charenton in 1631, is followed by that of Alençon six years later. Eight years then elapse before the twenty-eighth synod—that of Charenton—in 1645; while for the twenty-ninth synod (Loudun, 1659) we have to wait no less than fourteen years. At Alençon the needs of education took a prominent place among the subjects of discussion. Deputies from Montauban and Saumur complain that subsidies due from certain congregations in their respective provinces have not been paid; and a solemn exhortation is issued by the synod to the defaulters. Even more significant is the fervent appeal[2] issued to "toutes les Églises, tous les Seigneurs, tous les Gentils-hommes et toutes les Personnes en particulier." They are exhorted "to prefer the service of God, the glory of His holy name, and

---

[1] During the reign of Louis XIII Jesuit colleges were set up in the following towns where there were already Huguenot schools: Die, Castres, Nîmes, Montpellier, Montauban, Sedan.

[2] Quoted in Aymon, II, 583.

the establishment of order in His house, to all human
considerations, consecrating to His divine majesty, each
according to his ability, their voluntary offerings; and to
share among them the necessary expenses for the upkeep of
academies and colleges, using in this exercise a pious charity."
It was ordained that this touching manifesto should be read
in all Huguenot churches; but there is little indication that
any adequate response was made to it. The burdens which
the reign of Louis XIV was destined to bring upon the
Huguenots and the renewed persecutions which they were
soon to endure rendered the proper maintenance of their
educational work wellnigh impossible.

Richelieu died in December, 1642, and Louis XIII survived
him by only six months. The new king, Louis XIV, was a
boy of five, and once more the regency was in the hands of
a queen-mother—Anne of Austria. The work of Richelieu
was continued by Mazarin, whose attitude towards the
Huguenots did not differ appreciably from that of his
predecessor. The early years of the reign were marked by
the civil wars known as the Fronde; but ever since the
"Grâce d'Alais" the Protestants had acted as loyal subjects
and they took no part in these disturbances. Mazarin himself
said: "The little flock browses on poisonous herbage, but it
keeps to itself." He realised the wisdom of a policy of
toleration and in 1652 solemnly renewed the agreement that
no interference should be made with the Huguenots' liberty
of worship. With the death of the minister in 1661 the
situation is profoundly changed. Louis XIV now begins his
personal rule. His chief aim is to be absolute monarch of a
united kingdom, and unity of religion is regarded by him as
an indispensable factor in the evolution of such a nation.
The old political maxim "une foi, une loi, un roi" is now
rigorously enforced. In his memoirs Louis XIV explicitly
records the policy which he adopted at this period towards
his Protestant subjects. "I thought," he says, "that the
best way of gradually stamping them out was, firstly, not to
subject them to any rigours and to continue what they had
obtained from my predecessors, but to make no concessions
whatever beyond that, and to restrict the exercise of these

within the narrowest limits which justice and decency could
allow. As to favours which depended upon myself alone, I
decided (and I have pretty strictly observed this since) to
grant them none at all, in order to make them reflect from
time to time—of their own accord and not through violence
—whether it were with good reason that they deprived
themselves voluntarily of advantages which they might have
enjoyed in common with the rest of my subjects[1]." This
narrow and illiberal policy had already been voiced by the
Royal Commissioner in his speech at the twenty-ninth
national synod (Loudun, 1659). He had called attention, for
example, to the fact that Huguenot ministers were wont to
excommunicate parents who sent their children to Catholic
schools and to censure in their published writings those who
were converted. This was stated to be a breach of the Edict
of Nantes and as such was strictly forbidden[2].

It can hardly be said that Louis XIV kept within the
limits of his tolerant, if not very generous, policy. It is true
that Colbert, who reorganised the financial and economic
resources of the kingdom, regarded the Huguenots with
favour because many of them were industrious and skilful
workmen. Even so, the position of the Protestants in France
had become a very difficult one. It was not merely that the
king regarded the existence of a schismatic body within
his dominions as a menace to absolutism; there was at the
same time an unsleeping hatred of the reformed religion on
the part of the national Church of France. Barely a month
after the death of Mazarin the French clergy formulated a
demand that commissioners should be sent out to discover
whether any Protestant churches had been opened since the
Edict of Nantes; for they claimed that this decree permitted
Huguenot worship only in those places where it existed
when the Edict was passed. Louis acceded to their request,
and as a result a number of Protestant churches were pulled
down. With them disappeared numerous Huguenot "little
schools." Nor were the elementary schools alone involved.
Several colleges were forced to close. Nîmes had already shut

---

[1] *Mémoires*, II, 456.   [2] See Quick, p. 509.

down in 1644 and its buildings had been taken over by the
Society of Jesus. The synod of Charenton (1645) was called
upon to consider appeals for help from several colleges which
were in difficulties; while at the following synod (Loudun,
1659) it was found necessary to prohibit professors and
regents, whose salaries were in arrears, from asking for gifts
from their pupils, in addition to the ordinary school fees.
Moreover, the discipline and *moral* of some of the academies,
owing to the disordered conditions prevailing, were becoming relaxed. Complaints are made as to the behaviour of
students; they have been guilty of wearing long hair, of
adorning themselves with ribbons and silk gloves, of frequenting female society and of being seen in taverns. Such
worldly practices are strongly censured by the synod. Those
who offend in this manner are to be expelled and the rest
are exhorted to "perfume the House of God betimes with
the sweet odours of an early religious conversation[1]."

The beginning of the personal rule of Louis XIV initiates
the final stage in the decline of Huguenot educational
activity. In 1661 the college of Montauban closed its doors.
For some years past it had been sharing a building with the
Society of Jesus; but this naturally proved an impossible
arrangement. In 1662 the school at Pont-de-Vesle in
Burgundy was suppressed. In the following year the college
at Anduze, one of the oldest of Huguenot schools, came to
an end and was transformed into a Catholic *petite école*. By
this time a system of semi-persecution, based on the
narrowest possible interpretation of the Edict of Nantes,
was already in vogue. By an edict of 1663 fathers who had
married Huguenot wives were forbidden to send their
children to Protestant schools. An *arrêt* of 1665 forces a
mother to give up her son who at the mature age of ten has
abjured the reformed religion; and he is forthwith despatched
to the Oratorian college at Vendôme, there to be educated
at his parent's expense. In 1670 schoolmasters in Huguenot
"little schools" were forbidden to teach any subjects beyond
reading, writing, and arithmetic, on the ground that the
Edict of Nantes did not specify what exactly might be

---

[1] Quick, p. 574.

taught in Protestant schools. Distinctive religious teaching
—the essential characteristic of Huguenot education—was
thus suppressed. It was also decreed that only one "little
school" might be permitted in each town where Huguenot
worship existed; that it must be close to the Protestant
temple—a regulation which made it necessary for some pupils
to walk long distances to and from school; that not more
than twelve pupils might be drawn from outside localities
in addition to those who lived in the town itself; that no
boarders might be taken[1]; that not more than one master
should be allowed to teach in each school. Such were the
petty interpretations which were set upon the terms of the
Edict of Nantes and such was the spirit in which Louis XIV,
influenced by the opponents of Protestantism, carried out
the plan of campaign upon which he had resolved. The
regulations, frivolous as they were, were severely enforced
with the aid of the local clergy and the Huguenot primary
schools were effectually ruined.

By this time Protestant emigrations from France were
already taking place. Numbers of Huguenots had crossed
into England[2] or Holland, and the cause of those who
remained behind was correspondingly weakened. After the
Peace of Nimeguen in 1678, when Louis reached the summit
of his glory, his policy towards the reformed religion took
on a more sinister aspect. The influence of Colbert was now
waning while that of Madame de Maintenon[3] and Père la
Chaise increased. False estimates of the power and intentions of the Huguenot party were dinned continually into
the king's ears, until he saw in the "little flock" a malignant
and powerful foe to absolutism. But the days of Huguenot
political power had ended with the "Grâce d'Alais," and by
now the Protestants were neither highly organised nor
politically dangerous. Yet the persecution of them grew

---

[1] The minister was permitted to have not more than two boarders;
the *maître d'école* none at all.

[2] An account of some Protestant refugee schoolmasters is given in
Foster Watson's *Religious Refugees and English Education*, pp. 150 ff.

[3] In 1681 she writes: "The king is beginning to think seriously of
his salvation and that of his subjects. If God preserves him to us,
there will no longer be more than one religion in his kingdom."

daily in intensity. In 1681 it was decided that children of
Huguenot parentage might renounce their religion as early
as the age of seven—"at which they are capable of reason
and of choice in so important a matter as that of their own
salvation[1]." On the strength of this edict many children
were torn from their homes and sent to Catholic schools;
while the cost of their education there was levied on the
Huguenot parents. When Protestants endeavoured to avoid
the penalties and dangers thus put upon them by sending
their children to schools in countries outside France, the
practice was strictly forbidden by law.

Savage as were these measures, steps even more drastic
were taken to stamp out heresy. By the system of *dra-
gonnades* large numbers of harmless Protestants were
terrorised by the brutalities of a savage soldiery into verbal
abjuration of the reformed religion. Innumerable conver-
sions were reported, but there still remained many *obstinés*
who clung faithfully to the teachings of Calvin. The climax
of the unhappy story was the Revocation of the Edict of
Nantes which was signed by Louis on October 18th, 1685.
By it Protestant worship was proscribed and all pastors
were ordered to leave the kingdom within a fortnight under
pain of sentence to the galleys. Other Calvinists who
attempted to leave the country were liable to the same
punishment.

Amid such disasters the extinction of the remaining
Huguenot colleges was inevitable. An attempt to run schools,
such as that of Melle in Xaintonge, on a *mi-parti* system, by
which a number of Catholic and Protestant regents taught
in the same establishment and to which pupils of both
religions were admitted, was foredoomed to failure. In 1681
the Huguenot college of Sedan which, owing to the conquests
of Louis XIV, was now situated on French territory, was
suppressed and the buildings were handed over to the
Society of Jesus on payment to the king of 20,000 livres.
In the same year the school at Châtillon, which had disappeared in the middle of the seventeenth century but had

---

[1] The Huguenots made a protest against this iniquitous decision.
See their *Humble Address* to Louis XIV, Quick, pp. cxxvi–vii.

since been revived, was finally shut down and given up to
a teaching community of women—the "Filles de l'Adoration
du Saint-Sacrement." In 1684 the college of Die, which for
long had been slowly throttled by the Jesuit college in the
same town, came to an end. Saumur, a school which had
been suffering from Oratorian competition, closed down at
last in 1685; and the same year marks the disappearance of
the Huguenot college at Puylaurens—an institution of whose
history we know little else.

The Revocation of the Edict of Nantes thus gave the *coup
de grâce* to the Protestant colleges. By it the king expressly
forbade "all private schools for the instruction of the
Children of those of the said so-called Reformed Religion
and generally all other things whatsoever that may bear the
sign of privilege or favour to that said Religion[1]." The only
survivor of the thirty-five secondary schools which the
enthusiasm and public spirit of French Protestantism had
brought into being was the college of Montbéliard. This
outlived the general destruction caused by the Revocation
of the Edict of Nantes because, in spite of the territorial
conquests achieved by the "Grand Monarque," the town still
lay just outside his dominions.

Such, then, was the fate of the Huguenot schools. They had
proved themselves—to adopt Quick's quaint phraseology—
"very fruitful nurseries of many excellent scholars and
furnished the Churches with some thousands of able, godly,
and painful Ministers[2]." Like the schools of Port-Royal they
were the product of a party which, in the eyes of those in
power, menaced the political unity of the kingdom and the
absolutism of its sovereign. At the Revocation of the Edict
of Nantes the Huguenot colleges perished no less victims
to Jesuit opposition and royal ambition than the Port-Royal
schools when, twenty-five years previously, they had been
dispersed for the last time. The French Protestant schools
do not furnish us with any striking innovations upon
contemporary school practice, nor with any conspicuous
improvements in teaching methods. One reason for this may
be that we know comparatively little of the inner life of the

[1] § VII; see Quick, p. cxlix.   [2] Quick, p. cxvi.

average Huguenot college and far less about the working of
the "little schools." But, for all this, Protestant education
in France is not without its significance for the modern
reader. The Huguenots knew all the horrors of war in their
very midst, of relentless persecution and grinding poverty.
Yet even when their difficulties and distresses were greatest
they never lost their belief in the value of education or
ceased to exert themselves to provide for the needs of their
schools. If their efforts to raise funds were not always
successful, it was because with many of the faithful literally
no money was available for anything beyond the bare means
of subsistence; those who had inherited wealth or become
rich through trade or industry set an example of liberality.
At no time did it ever occur to the Huguenots that education
is a luxury and one of the first upon which economies should
be practised. To us, then, the history of their schools
reiterates the eternal truth that the children of the race
are its most valuable asset and its chief hope; and that no
sacrifice that can be made so as best to fit them for their
future work—the regeneration of the world—is too great
or too costly.

CHAPTER IV

THE EDUCATION OF PRINCES—BOSSUET
AND "LE GRAND DAUPHIN"

IT is comparatively easy to label and classify the conspicuous intellectual and spiritual movements of history,
but it is often less satisfactory to attempt to analyse the
infinitely complex motions of the human mind and to
localise its operations in place or time with the precision
beloved of a school text-book. Of no movement is this more
true than of the Renaissance. Starting, doubtless, from Italy
and spreading gradually northwards and westwards, it made
itself felt in every branch of thought and expressed itself
in every department of human activity. It is with but one
aspect of that widespread and complicated phenomenon that
we are concerned in the present chapter—with the influence
which the Renaissance had upon the theory and practice of
education as applied to those who were one day to exercise
kingly power or to fill high offices of state, and upon whose
character and conduct, therefore, the well being of nations
would depend.

With the reservations already made, we can say with
approximate correctness that the fifteenth century formed
the epoch of the Renaissance in Italy, although the movement was not confined to that country. Towards the end
of the Quatrocento Charles VIII of France laid claim to the
kingdom of Naples. In 1494 his armies crossed the Alps.
Charles moved in triumph from Pavia to Florence, from
Florence to Rome, from Rome to Naples. His successor,
Louis XII, continued the Italian campaigns and from 1499
to 1512 there was a French court at Milan. Thus the French
came into close touch with Italian civilisation, and the
revival which had begun in Italy spread into France as a

result of the military activities of Charles VIII and Louis XII. In art, in commerce, and in manners the vivifying influence of the Renaissance was felt and, although in France the movement developed its own special national characteristics, it was to Italy that the original impulse was due. This was nowhere more obvious than in the stress which was laid in France, during and after the Renaissance, upon the importance of the right education of "princes." Although the problem had been debated all through the Middle Ages it had become prominent in Italy largely as an outcome of the revival of learning; but it is at a later period and in France that the question arouses most interest and is most thoroughly discussed, because there, owing to contemporary political conditions, the education of the ruling class—and more particularly of the absolute ruler himself—becomes a subject of paramount importance. Before, therefore, we embark upon an endeavour to describe in some detail a particular attempt to solve this question, it will be well to try to trace, if only in the barest outline, the reasons why the education of "princes" came into prominence in Italy and why its importance subsequently developed in France.

The humanists of Italy had looked for encouragement and financial assistance to the courts and—to a less extent—to the free communities of their native land. Augustus and Mæcenas were paralleled among the princes and nobles of many a small Italian state. The universities on the whole held aloof from the movement, or at best tolerated humanist scholars as semi-official teachers of an inferior grade. In the Middle Ages it was the Church, acting at first through the monasteries and afterwards through the universities, which had controlled education. But with the Renaissance the clergy lost their monopoly in this respect. Learned and influential laymen now began to share in the diffusion of knowledge and the importance of the universities tended to decline. When the Revival of Learning spread across the Alps in the early years of the sixteenth century this same phenomenon soon became apparent in France. The University of Paris, entrenched behind a rampart of vested

interests, looked with suspicion and fear upon the advance
of the hosts of humanism[1]. As the century advanced the
suspicion and fear were increased rather than allayed by a
tendency on the part of many French humanists to regard
with appreciative interest that outcome of the Renaissance
in north-western Europe—the Reformation. All through the
century, in spite of the interruptions caused by the Wars
of Religion, the University of Paris, owing to its great and
widespread reputation, still continued to attract the greatest
scholars of the age; yet it remains true to say that many of
these devoted their lives to opposing fiercely the system for
which the University stood, and to promoting the ideals
which it most bitterly opposed. It will be sufficient to
instance the names of Erasmus, Vives, Ramus, and Corderius.

The French humanists, therefore, like those of Italy,
looked elsewhere for support and they found it in the
sovereign—or, less frequently, in the enlightened civic
corporation such as that of Bordeaux which founded the
Collège de Guyenne in that city. But at Paris the king alone
was strong enough to override the opposition of the University; and in François I the French humanists found the
help and encouragement which their Italian predecessors
had received from such princes as Ludovico Sforza, the
Duke of Milan who had opposed Louis XII. The young king,
who succeeded to the throne in 1515, was a sincere admirer
of Italian culture and showed himself ambitious to pose as
a patron of the new learning which came thence. Budæus
or Budé, the chief French scholar of the day, was dignified
with the title of Royal Librarian; while in 1530 were laid
the foundations of the Royal College or *Collegium Trilingue*
—the Collège de France—an institution in the heart of
Paris and yet entirely independent of the University[2]. It

---

[1] Pasquier notes the barbarism which reigned in the University
at the accession of François I. Not only was Hebrew not taught,
but Greek was almost unknown. Cf. "Car mesmes lors qu'il estoit
question de l'expliquer, ceste parole couroit en la bouche de plusieurs
ignorans: *Græcum est*; *non legitur*." (*Recherches*, p. 831.)

[2] See *supra*, p. 22.

provided for the teaching of Greek, Hebrew, Latin, and mathematics on definitely humanist lines; and in spite of the strenuous opposition of the University[1], the Royal College entered upon a career of prosperity which has lasted almost unbroken down to the present day. It was clear therefore to the French humanist of the first half of the sixteenth century that he would be well-advised to look to the enlightened sovereign rather than to the Church or the University for the realisation of his ideals.

There was another influence at work which gave added importance to the position of the sovereign in the humanist scheme. The political life of the Italian city-states in the Middle Ages was characterised by party factions and civil strife; and these internecine wars were a matter of considerable concern to many of the political thinkers of the day. Not unnaturally, the establishment of the authority of a strong sovereign had often appeared to be the most obvious solution of the problem. Dante in his *De Monarchia*, which dates from the early years of the fourteenth century, had advocated the supremacy of the Emperor with a wealth of argument and analogy which seems at times fantastic to the modern reader. His thesis was a favourite one in the Middle Ages; but it has been described as an "epitaph, not a prophecy," for the Empire was already falling into decay. But in the full tide of the Renaissance we find similar theories set forward. There was—in Italy, at any rate—a reaction against Christian ethics with their stress on the value of poverty and humility and self-effacement. Classical thought had held in highest estimation intellectual ability and the civic virtues, and had tended in some measure to give a less prominent place to private personal piety. In the early days of the Christian religion it had been a common, but not unnatural, mistake for its heathen contemporaries to regard it as an anti-social institution. Something of this

---

[1] Cf. Marot's poem addressed to the king:
          ... L'ignorante Sorbonne
    Bien ignorante elle est d'estre ennemie
    De la Trilingue et noble Académie
    Qu'as érigée.   (*Œuvres*, II, 382.)

attitude reappeared under the influence of the Italian Renaissance. The great and glorious individual—the Aristotelian μεγαλοπρεπής—is now the type of virtue. Contemporary Italy, like ancient Greece, contained many city-states which were ruled by τύραννοι. Hence there was a tendency to look for the good of the State in the rule of the "hero," as Carlyle would call him. Even Machiavelli, with his theoretical respect for republican government, feels that it is not suited for Italy and so he, like Dante, sees the salvation of his country in the dominance of a strong ruler.

All these theories were borne out by the actual state of affairs in western Europe. The collapse of feudalism was leading to the growth of strong centralised national monarchies in which the whole or most of the power of the State was concentrated in one single individual will. At the same time it was inevitable that the Renaissance, which affected every department of human thought and manifested itself in many different ways, should powerfully stimulate political speculation. The nature of sovereignty began to be called in question and the conditions of good government to be re-examined and debated in a manner which recalled the political philosophy of ancient Greece. Modern democratic ideals were now formulated, but—roughly speaking—they gained most ground in those countries which were inclining towards the individualism of the reformed religion. Catholicism, with its hierarchy and its highly-organised ecclesiastical system, tended to support monarchical institutions; and this fact helps to explain the opposition of the French crown to the Huguenots. It was, in fact, in Catholic France that the theory of the enlightened despot was realised most fully[1]. With the triumph of the ancient religion after the civil wars which marked the last few decades of the sixteenth century, and with the defeat of political Protestantism in Richelieu's campaign against La Rochelle, the unification of the country under the rule of one strong man was felt to be the most satisfactory solution for the problems of the time.

---

[1] It is, of course, true that the theory of absolutism expanded at the same time in Spain and England also. See, for example, Lavisse and Rambaud, iv, 139.

Centralised and absolute government seemed to be the only safeguard of the State and in the person of so skilled a diplomat and so iron-willed a minister as Richelieu the needful τύραννος was found. The king, Louis XIII, was but his "illustrious slave." The work was continued by Mazarin, who at his death left France a united nation and the greatest power in Europe. When, therefore, Louis XIV entered into the fruits of the labours of Richelieu and Mazarin, he became in his own person the symbol of a unified France, almost absolute in his power—for there remained hardly any constitutional check upon his actions. His exclamation: "L'état, c'est moi," whether it be apocryphal or not, sums up with sufficient precision the actual state of affairs during the greater part of his reign. Political theory in France took its tone from the existing conditions of government. The doctrine of the Divine Right of Kings reaches its zenith at this period. The Gallican Church, with its dislike of ultra-montanism and its strong sense of nationality, becomes a staunch upholder of the monarchy. Bossuet, voicing the sentiments of the day, continually uses the most extravagant language about the king and his position. It must have seemed therefore to the average Frenchman of the epoch of Louis XIV that upon despotism—benevolent and enlightened perhaps, but despotism nevertheless—depended the strength and greatness and well being of his country. The educational implications of the situation at once became apparent; if the monarch is accountable to God alone in the exercise of his functions, it is essential for the welfare of his subjects that he should continually realise this moral obligation; and to ensure that he does learn to realise it, he must be educated with that end in view. Given, then, that the enlightened despot is the safeguard of the State, there remains the problem of enlightening him; and it is this fact that accounts for the large amount of serious thought that was devoted during the seventeenth century in France to what was called the "education of princes."

Of course the problem was no new one. So long as States depended for their welfare upon individual rulers the question of the proper education of the monarch was bound to be of interest. But the implications of the problem are much wider. The arguments set forward for the right education of "princes" from the days of Thomas Aquinas[1] down to the eighteenth century were at bottom much the same as those which led to a demand for universal education in a democratic age. It is ultimately a question of "educating our masters," so that they may realise their responsibilities and consult the common good. The problem is still with us and the solution of it concerns everyone who is interested in education.

How, then, was the ruling class educated? During the Middle Ages the noble had undergone the chivalric education, in which as page and squire he learnt courtly accomplishments and martial exercises. Side by side with this there had existed a purely literary education which was given to those who were destined to become ecclesiastics. But after the Renaissance the two types of education were no longer so sharply distinguished; often indeed they were fused so far as the children of noble families were concerned. Although the chivalric ideals were not lost and the emphasis on courtly manners and physical accomplishments still persisted, yet many of the nobles aspired also to a literary education such as that which humanism had to offer. The universities as a whole continued their mediaeval curriculum. In the faculty of arts the *trivium* held the field for many years to come and therefore the type of education which it implied was not suitable to those who were to be fitted for the duties of high position at court. The result was the development of what are known as "academies"; and the educational theory which underlies their practice is usually termed the "doctrine of courtesy." The most important exposition of it is found in Castiglione's[2] *Il Cortegiano* (*i.e.* the Courtier) which appeared in 1528 and was translated into English in 1561. The "courtier" is defined as the servant of a reigning prince, serving him in council or in war; but, as one of the characters in the book

---

[1] *De Regimine Principum.*
[2] His dates are 1478 to 1529; he spent a large part of his life at Mantua and Rome.

points out, the perfect courtier is himself the perfect prince. He is what the "orator" was to Cicero or Quintilian—the *beau idéal* of the man of education and affairs; but in addition to this, he is the "very parfayt knight" of the Middle Ages, refined by the grace which humanistic culture alone could bestow.

The *Courtier* of Castiglione and other Italian works of a similar type produced a remarkable effect upon educational thought not only in France, but also in England and Germany. In the latter half of the sixteenth and the early part of the seventeenth centuries "academies" for the education of children of noble birth sprang up in many parts of France, and they either supplanted or supplemented the purely literary type of education which was offered by the universities. Examples of the two types are given elsewhere in this book[1] and a detailed description of their curriculum and aims need not be repeated. But it should be noticed that to the original Italian "doctrine of courtesy" the "academies" made an addition. The boys belonging to the governing class must still be educated in true "gentle-manliness" and in social graces as well as in the arts of warfare; but contemporary progress in those branches of learning with which humanism was not directly concerned, made it necessary to equip the future statesman with a knowledge of "modern" subjects, the value of which was determined chiefly by their practical utility. Thus the curriculum of the "academies" was widened so as to include a study of the vernacular and modern languages, of natural science and mathematics; while much stress was laid on modern history and geography. In France these institutions were encouraged by Richelieu under whose patronage the Academy of Tours was founded. The Oratorian college of Juilly, although the offspring of a teaching order which had set out to devote itself to the work of the seminary, became under royal patronage what was practically an "academy."

Yet the "academy" was not the only means of education adopted for children of noble birth. With the decay of

[1] See *infra*, pp. 194–196.

chivalric education there arose a tendency to employ private
tutors in families of the governing class, and this custom
persisted parallel with the growth of "academies." It was
more common in north-western Europe than in Italy. The
reason, as Woodward points out, had originally been that
"in England and Germany the upper class was essentially
a country class; in Italy the men of wealth and status craved
for the society and comfort of a city....It was not until the
following century (sc. the seventeenth) that schools were
called into existence in northern Europe to provide that
combination of courtly training and liberal teaching which
had been exemplified at Mantua[1]." Though in France the
"academies" played a more important part than in England,
where they were often projected but less often realised[2], the
employment of tutors in noble and wealthy families became
a common practice in both countries. In England the
system is recommended by Locke who is concerned with the
education of the "gentleman"; in France, by a host of
writers, some of whom had themselves had charge of boys
of high degree. Even Rousseau in the middle of the eighteenth century still has to employ a tutor in order to
supervise the training of the "natural man." But as a
matter of practical life it is only for children of rich and
high-born parents that the services of a tutor can be
requisitioned; and since, as has been shown, the education
of the "prince" became a matter of such tremendous import
in France of the seventeenth century, much attention was
devoted to the duties of a royal tutor by some of the most
eminent thinkers of the period. In the present chapter we
propose to discuss in greater detail a particular example of
this phenomenon—the education which was given by the
illustrious Bossuet to the son of Louis XIV, who—it was
hoped—would one day succeed the "Grand Monarque." The
fact that the Dauphin died before his father and never filled
the high position for which he seemed to be destined, does
not diminish the significance of Bossuet's educational
methods. They were designed primarily as a means of

---

[1] *Education from the Renaissance*, p. 276.
[2] Milton's *Tractate* is really a project for an "academy."

training the future despot for the infinite responsibilities of governing the greatest power in Europe; and they are therefore of interest as being a solution offered by one of the ablest men of the day for what was perhaps the most important political problem with which contemporary society was faced.

Louis, eldest son of Louis XIV and usually known by the title of Monseigneur, was born at Fontainebleau on November 1st, 1661[1]. The king had just entered upon his personal rule with so much energy and intelligence that men saw in the new-born prince an earnest that the golden age, already inaugurated, was destined to continue to future generations. Special envoys announced the happy event in all the courts of Europe; poets and orators vied one with the other in predicting the future glories of the royal infant. In accordance with custom, the Pope presented a magnificent *layette*—known as "les langes bénits"—embroidered with silk and gold and worthy of the heir of the eldest son of the Church. As was usual also, a staff of servants was assigned to the infant—a wet-nurse, Mme Moreau, who held in addition the office of chief *femme de chambre*[2], seven other *femmes de chambre*, a "rocker" (*remueuse*), and even a number of valets. But the ultimate responsibility for the well being and early training of the future sovereign devolved upon the *gouvernante*. Her intimacy with the royal family and the special marks of honour which she enjoyed made her office one of the highest dignity. When she was admitted to her functions she took a solemn oath, kneeling before the king and placing her hands between his. Once appointed she could not be removed from her post against her will; she enjoyed a salary of 48,000 livres in addition to numerous gifts and perquisites; and her full stipend was continued as a pension even after the royal infant was old enough to dispense with the care of a governess. To fill so exalted and responsible

---

[1] It was on the occasion of the birth of this dauphin that Pascal made his famous remark that "there was nothing in which he would more gladly have taken part, if that had been his business, than the education of a prince." (Nicole, *Essais de Morale*, II, 214.)

[2] She enjoyed a salary of 40,000 livres a year.

an office Louis XIV selected one of the most accomplished ladies of the court. Julie d'Angennes de Montausier was the daughter of that Mme de Rambouillet whose *salon* had been the centre of all that was best in the social and literary life of France during the second quarter of the seventeenth century. It was in her honour that the *Guirlande de Julie* had been composed—a collection of verses to which almost all the most famous of contemporary poets had contributed. In the atmosphere of culture and refinement of the Hôtel de Rambouillet Julie had been brought up, and it must be confessed that as a result she had become something of a *précieuse*. She had married the Duc de Montausier and had reached the mature age of fifty-four when she was called upon to undertake the task of guiding the early education of the heir-apparent. She had not altogether lost her youthful beauty and fascination, and her appointment was hailed with approbation by the entire court. At the same time, Mme de la Chesnaye who had been *sous-gouvernante* during the infancy of Louis XIV was reappointed to this post in order to assist Mme de Montausier in her charge of his son.

Few details are available as to the methods which the Grand Dauphin's *gouvernante* adopted in the discharge of her duties. Fléchier in his *Oraison Funèbre de Mme la Duchesse de Montausier* contents himself with vague and somewhat perfunctory expressions of praise[1]. Be that as it may, her term of office was a short one. In 1664, when the Grand Dauphin was barely three years old, she resigned her position in order to become maid-of-honour to the Queen. It is not very difficult to guess at her reasons for taking such a step. The *gouvernante* was never allowed to leave her charge by day or night; and for a sprightly lady, still fond of refined society and keenly interested in intellectual pursuits, to be closely tied down to the care of someone else's infant must have proved irksome at times. Her successor was more suited for the duties of the post. Mme de la Mothe, widow of a famous *maréchal*, had brought up three children of her own and seems to have been a kind-hearted and motherly

---

[1] See *Recueil de Diverses Oraisons funèbres* (Brussels, 1682), pp. 25–29.

person. Her grandmother had already been *gouvernante* to Louis XIV and this was obviously the main reason why Mme de la Mothe was given the charge of the Grand Dauphin. The appointment caused some surprise at court and there were not wanting those who questioned her fitness for the office. But she possessed qualifications which her eminent predecessor lacked; and although again we have no detailed information as to the exact methods which she used, her maternal care and experience are shown by the fact that the Grand Dauphin, who had been a weakly infant, left her hands strong and healthy.

It was customary for a young prince to remain under the charge of a governess until his seventh year. When he had reached that age he was entrusted to the care of a *gouverneur* who was usually a courtier or soldier of great distinction. Like the governess, he was given complete charge of his pupil and was compelled to be in attendance upon him continually. The governor was allotted sumptuous apartments at court and received a yearly salary of 48,000 livres, to which a further allowance of 30,000 livres was added for household expenses. He was assisted by a *sous-gouverneur* whose position was of much less dignity and smaller emolument but tended often to be almost a sinecure. But the duties of the governor were somewhat complicated by the existence of a *précepteur* who, although definitely subordinate to the governor and receiving a salary of only 12,000 livres[1], was none the less responsible for the education of the prince. The respective spheres of the two tutors were defined in the oaths which they had to take when entering upon their duties. The governor promised "to employ all (his) care in forming the mind, the courage, and the morals of the prince, and in giving him an education worthy of his royal birth; to form his heart by reference to the practice of moral virtues and his mind by reference to what is of use in the conduct of life, in the knowledge of the world, and in success in affairs." The preceptor's oath ran as follows: "I swear to

[1] It was not always paid regularly. Cf. in a letter from Bossuet to Huet (Nov. 22nd, 1675) "...à l'oreille, je n'ai pas touché un sol." (*Correspondance*, I, 351.)

employ all my power to bring him up in the love and fear of God, to train his morals, and develop his mind by the knowledge of letters and sciences such as are suitable to an illustrious prince." It is obvious that the two duties coincided to some extent. To the governor belonged the duty of making his charge an accomplished courtier and a man of affairs, and of giving him a knowledge of men which would be of first-rate importance to the future sovereign. The preceptor's task was to impart a more purely academic education, to instruct the young prince in the various branches of polite learning and in the principles of true religion. But both alike were ultimately concerned with the moral development of their pupil and to this end they were to co-operate.

In 1668 the reign of Mme de la Mothe came to an end and the Grand Dauphin was handed over to the Duc de Montausier, husband of his first *gouvernante*. The governor seemed in many ways suited for the responsible office to which he was called. In the *Oraison Funèbre du Dauphin*, delivered many years after Montausier's death, Massillon sums up his character as follows: "He was a man of lofty and austere virtue, of an unparalleled honesty, of a sincerity which stood the test of the court, a philosopher without ostentation, a Christian without weakness, a courtier without prejudice—in short, he was one of those men who seem to be, as it were, a survivor of the moralists of old and who do not belong to the present age[1]." Montausier had been a Protestant up to the age of thirty-four and he retained, even after his conversion, some of the characteristics which one associates with the adherents of the reformed religion. His sterling worth of character was universally recognised, but his manner was cold and brusque; his regard for truth led him to speak plainly and to be little concerned as to whether he might wound the sensibilities of his hearer; in short, he was more respected than loved[2]. Such was the man to whom was committed the supreme charge of the prince who seemed destined one day to occupy the throne of France.

---

[1] *Massillon* in Migne, *Orateurs Sacrés*, XLIII, 235.
[2] He is said to have been the original of Molière's *Misanthrope*.

To aid Montausier in his task a *sous-gouverneur* was appointed; but his post was a sinecure, for the governor was not a man to delegate his duties to other people. Yet the office of preceptor, as we have seen, was of greater importance. To fill it a certain M. de Périgny had been selected; he was little known at court, although he had already acted as reader to the king and had assisted him in drawing up his *Mémoires*. The education of an isolated pupil by a tutor, however competent, has its disadvantages, and to combat these it had become customary at court to appoint certain *enfants d'honneur* to share the lessons of the royal pupil and by their society, example, and competition to compensate him to some extent for what he lost by not going to school. Four young nobles were therefore selected to work with the Grand Dauphin under the direction of Périgny. A plan of instruction for these illustrious pupils has been preserved to us[1]. It is a very ambitious course and includes such subjects as philosophy, jurisprudence, and politics. But, as we shall see, this plan was never put into effect. After teaching the Grand Dauphin to read, Périgny based much of his instruction upon fables, using those of La Fontaine in particular for this purpose. When it became necessary to begin the study of Latin, the preceptor had the good sense to copy the Port-Royalists and others of the best contemporary educationists, by preparing a short and clear text-book written in French. He sought to awaken his pupil's interest by associating Latin words, wherever possible, with their French derivatives. In fact, although he started life as a lawyer and had had no previous experience as a teacher, Périgny seems to have worked on quite successful lines. In the teaching of history he was assisted by Jean Doujat who had already been professor of this subject at the Collège de France. But Périgny's term of office was a short one. He died on September 1st, 1670, and his place was taken by one of the most eminent Frenchmen of that or any age—Jacques-Bénigne Bossuet.

In 1670 Bossuet was already at the height of his reputation.

[1] See *Desseins de M. le Président Périgny pour l'instruction de M. le Dauphin* in *Œuvres Complètes de Fléchier* (Nîmes, 1782), V, 433.

JACQUES-BÉNIGNE BOSSUET
(1627–1704)

At a period when sacred oratory reached its zenith he had proved himself one of the greatest of French preachers. As a theologian, as a "director of consciences," as a controversialist, he was unrivalled; and when in 1669 he was consecrated to the see of Condom there was in the French Church no more distinguished a prelate than he. It might seem that to appoint a man of such genius to undertake the education of a child of ten was to waste talents of so high an order. But this was not the opinion of Bossuet's contemporaries nor of Bossuet himself. As has already been indicated, the education of the future sovereign was looked upon as a matter of first-rate national importance. Bossuet himself said: "The instruction of Mgr le Dauphin is altogether a public affair"; and in undertaking it he felt that his opportunities would ultimately prove wider in scope than those even which are afforded to a bishop. He therefore willingly set aside the duties which had hitherto occupied him and seriously devoted himself to the petty details of his new task. He mapped out a careful course of instruction and re-read the classical authors which he would have to study with his pupil.

In treating of those who were concerned with the Grand Dauphin's education we may seem to have lost sight of the central figure himself; and it will therefore be interesting to attempt to discover what sort of child he was upon whom so much thought and care were being expended. The young Louis was of an amiable and harmless nature, but he seems to have been a nervous child and incapable of sustained effort. Montausier, as we have seen,—for all his undoubted worth—was a harsh and unsympathetic man and his treatment of the Grand Dauphin succeeded only in crushing the child's timid spirit and in accentuating his lymphatic proclivities. The journal of Dubois, who had been *valet de chambre* to Louis XIV and was afterwards attached to the person of the young prince, is full of references to the frequent canings by which the grim governor sought to lead his pupil into the paths of virtue. Montausier's severity became a by-word at court; the Duc du Maine, who bore the governor no very good will, on seeing him one day flourishing a light cane as he walked, cried: "Ah, Monsieur, toujours le bâton haut!"[1] But the Dauphin was not to be won by harsh methods and the only result of severity was to arouse in him an invincible spirit of contrariance. Mme de Caylus speaks of the methods of Montausier as being "more calculated to discourage a child like Monseigneur, who was of a gentle, lazy, and stubborn disposition, rather than to inspire him with the sentiments which he ought to have[2]." Thus serious damage had already been done before Bossuet was called to take over the Grand Dauphin's education. Montausier, of course, still held chief place as governor and Bossuet was definitely subordinate to him; but the bishop did not feel that the position was unworthy of his merits; in a letter written shortly before he entered upon his duties he says: "My consolation is that in order to succeed I shall only have to carry out the great and noble ideas of M. le Duc de Montausier[3]." Perhaps subsequent experience led him to alter his estimate of those ideas.

Towards the end of the year 1670 Bossuet took up his residence at the court. Lessons were given in what is now the *Salle d'antiques* on the ground-floor of the Louvre. Work began at 9.0 in the morning and continued until Mass at 11.30. Then came dinner and after it a short recreation or visits to the king and queen. At 1.30 lessons recommenced and were followed by a walk or by hunting or fishing parties in which the *enfants d'honneur* also took part. This was succeeded by supper and a third period of study, after which there was another interval for recreation before bedtime. Even on Sundays the Dauphin was not allowed to be idle. Louis XIV had given instructions that no day should pass without some employment, for "there is no life more properly a buisie life than that of kings[4]."

The education of the eldest son of the greatest European king by a tutor of such eminence as Bossuet was a matter of

[1] See Mme de Sévigné, *Lettres* (Aug. 7th, 1676), V, 12.
[2] *Souvenirs et Correspondance*, p. 71.
[3] Sept. 17th, 1670, *Correspondance*, I, 204.
[4] *Ep. ad Inn. XI*, trans. by J. T. Philipps, p. 125.

so great interest that when the time came for the *précepteur*
to lay down his office the Pope, Innocent XI, asked him for
an account of the methods which he had employed. It will
therefore be our duty to examine the letter which Bossuet
wrote in reply; the account which follows is based mainly on
this document. As we should have expected, religion is the
foundation of the whole structure. Twice a day religious
instruction was given. The Grand Dauphin learnt his catechism by heart and not only were the "general precepts of
Christianity" explained to him, but it was also pointed out
that "there are duties proper and peculiar to princes which
they can't (*sic*) omit without great guilt[1]." When the history
of the Old or New Testament was being taught, stress was
laid on examples of good kings who were rewarded, and of
those who did evil in the sight of the Lord and were appropriately punished. Above all, the Dauphin was taught to
reverence our Lord; if ever he were inattentive when the
Gospels were being studied, the book was at once laid aside
"as not to be read but with a sacred respect[2]."

In the teaching of Latin Bossuet followed the example of
the most progressive educationists of the day. "We
endeavoured," he says, "to teach him the Latin and French
tongues both together, first of all their propriety and then
their elegance. We relieved the tediousness of this part of
learning by convincing him of the usefulness of it[3]." To aid
his pupil in this task Bossuet composed a grammar written
in French prose[4]. There is also extant a manuscript Latin-
French dictionary with notes in Bossuet's own hand-writing
and the Grand Dauphin's arms embossed upon the cover.
The royal pupil, if we may believe his tutor, was soon able
to translate the best Latin authors; and it was thought
better to read through the whole of a work rather than to
study excerpts. Among prose writers Sallust, Caesar and
Cicero are mentioned; among poets, Virgil and Terence.
There was no attempt made to expurgate the works of the

---

[1] *Op. cit.* p. 126.   [2] *Op. cit.* p. 128.   [3] *Op. cit. p.* 169.
[4] There is said to be a MS. copy of this in the Bibliothèque
Nationale, although I have not been able to trace it. Cf. also Le
Dieu, *Mémoires*, I, 140, 141.

last-named author, as was done by the Jesuits and other
educators of the period; but—to quote Bossuet's letter—
"we passed our censure upon the licentious passages we met
with in this author; expressing still a much greater surprise
that many of our own writers have shown less modesty in
their pieces. This practice we condemn'd as infamous and
destructive of good manners[1]." Nor was classical study
confined to the reading of authors. On June 29th, 1671,
barely six months after entering upon his duties, Bossuet
writes that the Dauphin "began four or five days ago to
write compositions by himself....He is delighted with this
fine new amusement[2]." But the most valuable outcome of
this part of the education of the Grand Dauphin was the
preparation of a new collection of classical authors *ad usum
Delphini*—the famous "Delphine" edition. The idea of
issuing such a series is due, we are told, in the first instance
to Montausier, but the project was enthusiastically taken up
by Bossuet and the king was persuaded to finance the
undertaking. The editor-in-chief was Pierre Daniel Huet[3],
afterwards Bishop of Avranches, who had been appointed
sous-précepteur. The best scholars of the day collaborated in
the work which, begun in 1672, went on long after the education of the Grand Dauphin had been completed. In all,
some sixty-four volumes were issued, unequal in merit but
none the less a monument to French scholarship. Over
200,000 livres—if we may believe Huet[4]—were expended on

---

[1] *Ep. ad Inn. XI*, p. 172.

[2] *Correspondance*, I, 223. In Le Dieu's *Mémoires et Journal sur
Bossuet*, I, 141, there is quoted a poem which is said to be the work
of the Dauphin. It is modelled on Phaedrus and entitled *In Locu-
tuleios*. It conveys a moral against excessive talkativeness—"Os
regat animus; linguae mens præluceat."

[3] See especially *Memoirs of P. D. Huet*, trans. by J. Aikin, I,
165 ff. Huet seems to have had little to do. Bossuet, in his letter to
the Pope, says that he had himself "alone directed the education of
the prince and always alone given him his lessons." Huet's duty was
to take Bossuet's place when the latter was ill. The preceptor's
correspondence contains several letters to Huet asking him to take
the Dauphin's lessons; *e.g.* I, 257, 340, 394; II, 28, 78, 108-9. There
seems to have been always a very cordial feeling between Bossuet
and Huet.

[4] *Memoirs*, p. 169.

the work; and although the Dauphin himself doubtless profited little by it, yet the collection was welcomed by the whole of learned Europe and it contributed to the education of many generations of classical scholars[1]. A new and revised edition of the series was published under the editorship of Valpy in London between the years 1819 and 1830.

The Delphine Classics are confined to Latin authors. Although Bossuet's favourite classical author was the "divine" Homer, there is no evidence that any place was given to Greek in the education of the Grand Dauphin. As we have seen, the elder of the classical languages was not normally studied in the academies. For the professional instruction of the prince it was necessary to include subjects which did not usually form part of the secondary school curriculum of the day; and for this reason Greek was, quite justifiably, rejected. Moreover, both Louis XIV and Montausier were in favour of excluding this subject, and Bossuet, whatever his private views may have been, naturally deferred to their wishes.

In common with most of those who had theories upon the education of princes, Bossuet believed that a study of history had a special value for those who might one day be called upon to govern. In his letter to the Pope he refers to this subject as "cette sage conseillère des Princes" and says that it demands "a more than ordinary application, being the great mistress of prudence in public and private life[2]." "Even if history were useless for other men it would still be necessary to make Princes read it. There is no better way of showing them what are the results of passion and self-interest, what opportunities may occur, which counsels are good and which are evil[3]." The Dauphin was introduced to the subject by a study of the history of his own country. Bossuet selected passages from historical memoirs, such as those of Comines and Bellay, or from the letters of Jacques Bongars relating to the diplomatic affairs of the reigns of

---

[1] As Huet himself said: "It is a question not merely of the education of the king's son, but of the education of everybody."

[2] *Ep. ad Inn. XI*, p. 173.

[3] *Discours sur l'Histoire Universelle*, p. 1.

Henri III and Henri IV. These were then read and explained
to the pupil. Afterwards the Grand Dauphin wrote down in
French what he remembered of the lesson and translated
his work into Latin. Every Saturday also "he read over at
once all that he had writ out in the whole week." Nor was
history merely a question of memory. Moral lessons were
continually drawn; the mistakes which former French kings
had made and the consequent disasters and failures were
noted; and the Dauphin was constantly asked to decide
what he would have done under the circumstances which
were being investigated. "Thus from experience we formed
our rules of action." The history lesson meant that the
pupil was led to talk and to discuss, and we may conclude
that it was perhaps the most valuable part of the training
which Bossuet imparted. The great heroes to whom the
preceptor pointed his pupil were St Louis and the "Grand
Monarque" himself. "Thus we set the great example of the
father before the son, so capable of following him." Bossuet
made the utmost of the traditions of *noblesse oblige* which
the Dauphin inherited. "Destined as you are, Monseigneur,"
he says, "to rule one day over so great a kingdom, you
must render it happy[1]." Master and pupil together visited
the tombs of former French kings and in so solemn a setting
Bossuet drew the lessons of the true significance of earthly
greatness and the account of the stewardship that must one
day be rendered.

That the Dauphin was really interested in the study of
history is suggested by the fact that a *Histoire abrégée de
France* was published under his name. In Bausset's *Life of
Bossuet* it is definitely stated that this book was what it
claimed to be—the work of the royal pupil. "Le style, la
force, les réflexions n'ont rien qui surpasse l'intelligence et
les moyens d'un jeune homme inspiré et dirigé par un esprit
sage et éclairé[2]." One may be tempted seriously to doubt
this statement or at any rate to attribute any merits of
the book to the inspiration and direction of the preceptor.
It had been the fashion to publish short treatises which

[1] *Discours sur l'Histoire Universelle, avant-propos.*
[2] *Vie de Bossuet*, I, 323.

purported to be the work of royal pupils. Louis XIV at the age of thirteen appeared as the author of a *Helvetian War*, translated from the first book of Caesar's *Commentaries*. His brother published a translation of Florus. Louis XIII had also posed as a juvenile author. But in all these cases it is obvious that the real work was done by the tutor who was responsible for the education of the royal prodigy. There seems no good reason to suppose that it was otherwise with the Dauphin's French History. He may have been responsible for the groundwork of the treatise or for working up Bossuet's notes, but drastic editing by the preceptor was probably necessary before the book was fit to appear in print. One is reminded of the elaborate pencil-sketches which children used to bring home with them at the end of term and which had been "improved" by the drawing master.

Bossuet's teaching of history has a special interest for us because it leads us to consider his *Discours sur l'Histoire Universelle à Monseigneur le Dauphin*. The book did not appear until the Dauphin was twenty years of age and had been married for more than a year; but there is little doubt that it is an expansion of a course of lessons which had actually been given to the royal pupil. The first part, called *Époques*, is a summary of universal history from the Creation down to the time of Charlemagne. It was intended for the personal use of the Dauphin; as Bossuet says in his *Avant-propos*, the pupil had already studied separate histories and this summary was to be "un abrégé où l'on voye comme d'un coup d'œil tout l'ordre des temps[1]." The abridgment, although of necessity concise, is written in a not uninteresting manner. The rest of the book is based upon oral lessons which Bossuet had given to the Dauphin; it enters into greater detail and suitable reflections are appended or moral lessons drawn. The development of religion is traced from the earliest times and the history of the great empires of antiquity is sketched.

In order to render the study of history more vivid a large collection of pictures, chronological charts, and maps was made for the benefit of the Grand Dauphin. The aid of

[1] p. 4.

geography was also invoked; it was treated "as a sport and as a pleasant voyage to us[1]," and particular emphasis was given to the geography of France. Moreover, the most illustrious scholars of the day contributed to furthering the Dauphin's progress in history by preparing special biographies for his use. Péréfixe, for example, wrote a life of Henri IV, Fléchier a biography of Theodosius the Great, while Géraud de Cordemoy, who held the position of "reader" in the Dauphin's household[2], sketched the career of Charlemagne.

The study of history led on to that of philosophy which gave the royal pupil "the grounds and reasons of those maxims that are certain and of use in life....Recommending to him an equitable temper towards all sides, judging it to be for the honour of one born to govern, to protect all in their enquiries, rather than to enter as a party into any of their disputes[3]." It was for the benefit of his pupil that Bossuet composed his well-known treatise *De la Connaissance de Dieu et de Soi-même*, which was not actually published until 1722. The book is still of much interest for anyone who cares to examine it. It starts in a most modern fashion with an account of the structure and functions of the human body and leads on to a discussion of human psychology; in the third part of the volume these subjects are applied to the science of ethics. Together with editions of this book there is often found bound up a pamphlet on logic and Bossuet's *Traité du libre arbitre*. They complete our knowledge of his philosophical teachings. His main principles are taken from Plato and Aristotle[4]—"not the empty sciences of wrangling and disputing, but the art of forming the judgment." The subject is regarded not as an end in itself, but as the "ground of Rhetorick which cloaths, moves, and animates those naked arguments which Logick had collected and put together as so many bones and sinews."

[1] *Ep. ad Inn. XI*, p. 172.
[2] See Huet, *Mémoires*, I, 174.
[3] *Ep. ad Inn. XI*, p. 176.
[4] Cf. "We did not quite overlook Aristotle's *Ethicks*, and to them we joyn'd the wonderful and sublime discoveries of Socrates." *Id.* p. 178.

But Bossuet realised that a prince's responsibilities are of a special order and that in such a case the teaching of philosophy, like that of history, must be applied to this particular end. The Grand Dauphin, therefore, was made to study the machinery of government and the duties of the supreme ruler. He had to familiarise himself with the nature of contracts, testaments, inheritances, civil jurisdiction, judicial procedure, and so forth. From time to time also he was required to be present at some state function. On one such occasion, after a solemn address had been made to Louis XIV by the Bishop of Arles, the king turned to his son and said: "What efforts it would cost you to learn to speak as well as M. le Coadjuteur[1]." But still more necessary was it for the Grand Dauphin to learn to realise the principles upon which a just and humane rule is based. For this purpose the Scriptures were taken as the appropriate text-book, inasmuch as they show "not only the duties of subjects to their princes, but also how the publick worship of God ought to be directed and the ministers of religion supported[2]." These principles are explained at length in Bossuet's *Politique tirée des propres paroles de l'Écriture Sainte à Monseigneur le Dauphin*. The keynote of the book is struck on the first page. "God is the King of kings; to Him it belongs to instruct them and to govern them as His servants. Hear then, Monseigneur, the lessons which He gives them in His Holy Scriptures, and learn from Him the rules and examples upon which they ought to model their conduct." The work is arranged in *Articles* or headings, as for example Laws, Love of Country, Royal Authority, Obedience due to a Prince, War, Taxes, Temptations to which Kings are liable. The theories of divine right appear in their most extreme form. Each subject is discussed at length and illustrated by abundant quotations from Holy Writ. The book concludes with a long quotation from St Augustine's *De Civitate Dei*[3] to show in what the true happiness of kings consists—"We count kings happy if they

---

[1] Mme de Sévigné, *Lettres* (Aug. 19th, 1675), IV, 65.
[2] *Ep. ad Inn. XI*, p. 181.
[3] Bk. v, ch. 24.

rule justly, if in the midst of the flattery and servility of a
court they are not lifted up, but remember that they are but
men; if they fear God, love, and worship Him...and if for
their sins they do not neglect to offer the sacrifice of humility
and prayer."

Bossuet did not overlook the sciences in his education of
the Dauphin. The bishop himself displayed a lively interest
in the structure of the human body as is evidenced by the
first part of his treatise *De la Connaissance de Dieu et de
Soi-même*. The greatest anatomist of the day, Du Verney,
was called in to give demonstrations before the young prince
and his *enfants d'honneur*. Other scientists performed and
explained experiments in chemistry and physics; and
Bossuet and his pupil also visited the Observatory to learn
something of the marvels of astronomy. These experiences
afforded the Dauphin a "very agreeable and useful enter-
tainment[1]"; and they must also have proved invaluable
in widening the outlook of the young prince. The Port-
Royalist Nicole, in his recommendations for the education
of a prince, can find nothing better to say of the sciences
than: "A prince ought to know what is said about these
topics, for such information costs but little. But if we do
not tell him at the same time that this is but useless curiosity,
we are acting wrongly. For it is better to be ignorant of
these subjects than to be ignorant that they are useless[2]."
Bossuet, who—if we may believe Huet[3]—was an admirer of
Descartes, took a more liberal view than was customary
among those who had been brought up in the narrow
classical groove, and the Dauphin profited greatly by this
fact. He seems, indeed, to have been a boy whose tastes—if
he had any marked ones—did not lie in the direction of
literary studies. He made good progress in mathematics
which he learnt from Francis Blondel, the architect of the
Porte Saint-Denis—an "excellent master," Bossuet calls
him. The Dauphin also showed great aptitude for drawing
and took much interest in machines of all kinds and in the

[1] *Ep. ad Inn. XI*, p. 179.
[2] *Essais de Morale*, II, 237, 238.
[3] See *Mémoires*, I, 274.

science of fortification. In order to foster his military inclinations, a famous craftsman named Jessey was commissioned by the king to construct in silver an army of toy-soldiers.

The usual outdoor amusements of the young prince were hunting and walking; throughout his life, in spite of his idle and listless disposition, he remained passionately fond of the activities of the chase. He also received lessons in fencing and dancing. Mention has already been made of the *enfants d'honneur* who shared the Dauphin's lessons and recreations. They included some of the noblest youths at court. Among them for a time were numbered the two sons of the Princesse de Conti—Louis-Armand and François-Louis de Bourbon[1]. They have a special interest for the educational historian because their *précepteur* had been the Port-Royalist Lancelot, who has left us a record of the methods which he employed in the fulfilment of his task[2]. It was for the benefit of Lancelot also that Nicole composed his *Traité de l'Éducation d'un Prince* to which reference has already been made. Lancelot had on more than one occasion visited the court with his pupils. In the *Mémoires* of the *valet de chambre* Dubois, we read that on July 2nd, 1671, "their highnesses the Princes de Conti, aged about 10 or 12[3], came to study with Monseigneur, who gave an account in Latin and in French of David's sin with Bathsheba, the death of Uriah, how Absalom killed his brother, the reason for the violation of his sister Tamar, the revolt of Absalom and his death. After the lesson they heard Mass and dined with Monseigneur. In the afternoon they spent a long time on the terrace[4]." The subjects of study seem unusual ones for children of ten years of age; but Bossuet would doubtless be careful to draw the appropriate morals. In his letter to the Pope he says that his pupil "has seen the deceitful charms of pleasure and of women and the blind impetuosity of youth tormented

---

[1] François-Louis was originally called Prince de la Roche sur Yon, but he became Prince de Conti upon the death of his brother in 1685.

[2] See *Supplément au Nécrologe* (1735), pp. 161–7.

[3] Their actual ages were 10 and 7. The Dauphin at this time was 10 years old.   [4] *Op. cit.* 297.

by love[1]." If this was true it was perhaps by suitable
reflections on David's remorse and Amnon's violent death
that the result was produced. None the less the average
schoolmaster will be tempted to question the wisdom of the
method; and the subsequent history of the Dauphin and the
Prince de Conti who survived would suggest that Bossuet
was not so successful as he imagined. The Prince de Conti's
career as an *enfant d'honneur* was cut short by an unfortunate
incident. In the course of a quarrel between the two boys,
he struck his royal schoolfellow on the nose with such
violence that it was broken and the Dauphin bore the
disfigurement for the rest of his life[2]. The king himself took
a keen interest in the educational activities of Bossuet and
did his best to second his efforts. Often he would have a
private conversation with his son; and in the midst of his
business and even when absent from the court on a campaign he did not cease, by letters to Montausier and to
Bossuet, to show his solicitude for the good education of
the Dauphin. Even if Louis XIV has been accused of being
a "super-snob" and was obviously not always a pattern of
strict morality, it is pleasant at any rate to see him in the
rôle of a devoted and conscientious father.

From what has been said it may be gathered that in the
whole course of history there have been few children upon
whose education so much care was expended as upon that of
the Grand Dauphin. One of the most virtuous men at the
French court was his tutor, the most eminent ecclesiastic
of the day was his preceptor, the greatest contemporary
authorities in every branch of knowledge were ready to give
him the benefit of their instruction, and every opportunity
was afforded him of profiting by any experience which
might prove of service to one who was born to rule.
Bossuet's methods received unstinted praise not only in
France but also in other countries. Boileau, in a letter to
Bossuet dated Sept. 7th, 1675, speaks of "the marvellous
success which is due to your conduct in so glorious an
employment...and which draws upon you all the praises

---

[1] *Ep. ad Inn. XI*, p. 21.
[2] See Saint-Simon, *Mémoires*, IX, 150.

which are given you throughout France, for the happy
education of the Dauphin in which is comprised or summarised, as it were, the public well-being[1]." Yet it would
seem that Bossuet's efforts were by no means so successful
as might be gathered from remarks such as these. There is
evidence that he soon began to realise the magnitude of his
task. In June 1671, six months after the beginning of his
work as tutor, he was elected a member of the Academy.
In a speech which he made on this occasion he says: "The
king loves learned men and the sciences. It is to them, if
I may say so, that he has willed that the most precious
deposit of State should be entrusted. He wills that they
should cultivate the keenest intellect and the most beautiful
disposition in the world. This Dauphin, this amiable prince,
is surmounting happily the initial difficulties of his studies;
and if he is not discouraged by the thorns, what will be his
zeal when he is able to enjoy the flowers and the fruits?[2]"
Bossuet was still new to his task and he spoke as a courtier.
It soon became obvious that the Dauphin *was* discouraged
by the thorns. As we have seen, he was by nature sullen,
lazy, and inattentive, and his natural weaknesses had been
increased rather than counteracted by the treatment which
he had received from Montausier. There were times when it
seemed that Bossuet's methods might bear fruit. "M. le
Dauphin," he says in a letter to the Marquis de Feuquières,
"advances day by day in wisdom even more than in knowledge, even though what he does know is far in advance of his
age[3]." But no permanent improvement resulted. "I see in
him," says Bossuet in another letter, "what seem to be the
beginnings of fine qualities—a simplicity, a straightforward-
ness, a sense of right...but the world, the world, the world—
its pleasures, its bad advice, and its bad examples![4]" Yet
the Grand Dauphin, at any rate as a boy, had no vicious
propensities. He responded willingly to the requirements of

[1] See Santeul, *Operum omnium editio tertia*, I, 225. It is just
possible that the letter has been wrongly attributed to Boileau.
[2] *Œuvres*, XLIII, 31, 32.
[3] *Op. cit.* XXXVII (Feb. 22nd, 1674).
[4] *Correspondance*, I, 257.

the Church and, if we may believe a somewhat malicious remark of Mme de Sévigné[1], he preserved up to the time of his marriage a *naïve* innocence which could not have been common among those who frequented the French court at this epoch.

The fact would seem to be that the Dauphin took but little interest in the too exclusively literary curriculum which was provided for him and that any natural inclination which he may have had towards study had been stifled by Montausier. At last it became necessary to appeal to the pupil's royal father. In 1674 a long and interesting *mémoire*[2], addressed to the king, was drawn up by the *gouverneur* in which complaint was made of the Dauphin's listlessness and inattentiveness. "When Monseigneur likes, he attends, he understands, and he remembers with a marvellous ease. But he does not always like—and that is what troubles us[3]." Pellison, who after the death of Périgny carried on the task of editing the memoirs of Louis XIV, speaks of "application and concentration" as being what the Grand Dauphin chiefly lacks in his studies[4]. It was hardly likely that Bossuet himself would wish to confess that his carefully planned methods had proved vain; yet he must have realised his failure and, after seven and a half years of apparently unsuccessful effort, the truth at last escapes him in a letter to the Maréchal de Bellefonds[5]. "There is much which must be endured," he says, "with so dull an intellect; one has no outward consolation and, like St Paul, one walks hoping against hope[6]." Yet the king never wavered in his belief that Bossuet was the best tutor who could be procured for the education of his son. From time to time he expressed himself well satisfied with the progress which the Grand Dauphin was making[7], and he did his utmost to make his

[1] See *Lettres* (Jan. 24th, 1680), VI, 210.
[2] It is given in *La Vie de M. le Duc de Montausier*, II, 81–105.
[3] *Op. cit.* p. 96.
[4] *Œuvres de Louis XIV*, I, 144.
[5] *Correspondance*, July 6th, 1677, II, 35.
[6] Cf. Romans iv, 18.
[7] See, for example, letter of May 1st, 1676, in *Œuvres de Louis XIV*, V, 549.

son appreciative of the services which Bossuet was rendering him. "There is no one," he says, "to whom we owe more than to those who have at once the honour and the labour of developing our mind and our character[1]." Bossuet's task came to an end in 1680 when his pupil married a princess of Bavaria; he was promoted to be almoner to the Dauphine and in 1681 was translated to the see of Meaux. There is little doubt that he gave up his charge with a sense of relief; yet there remained no ill-feeling between the sullen, inapt pupil and his brilliant tutor. Though there was never that deep affection which always existed between Fénelon and his old pupil, the Duc de Bourgogne, yet the Dauphin cherished a feeling of friendliness[2] towards Bossuet, while the latter responded with "beaucoup d'affection et de confiance[3]."

Saint-Simon draws a most unattractive picture of the Grand Dauphin; and allowing for a certain amount of exaggeration—for the author is often unjust to those whom he dislikes—we must acknowledge that the portrait is not altogether untrue to life. "Monseigneur," he says, "had neither vices nor virtues; he possessed neither intelligence nor learning, and was radically incapable of acquiring them. He was very lazy and devoid of imagination; he lacked taste and discernment; he was by nature bored, and communicated this feeling to everyone else; he was born to be—as it were—a ball, tossed about by other people, for he was wrapped up in his own obesity and gloom. Although he had no active impulses towards evil, he would have made a pernicious king[4]." Such a judgment puts it beyond question that Bossuet's education of the Grand Dauphin was not a success, and it will be worth our while to endeavour to discover what were the real reasons for this. The prime cause of the tragedy, as has been indicated, was undoubtedly Montausier's harshness. Bossuet himself adopted gentler methods and he did his best to unbend from his dignified position and stoop to the level

[1] Œuvres de Louis XIV, I, 199.
[2] The Abbé Bossuet even speaks of the "particular affection and tender friendship" which the prince always had for his former tutor.
[3] See Le Dieu, *Journal*, Dec. 9th, 1703.
[4] *Mémoires*, IX, 152.

of his pupil. But he had neither the experience nor the insight which was needed for the direction of a not very attractive small boy. A celibate bishop would not normally make the best preparatory schoolmaster; and it was a natural lack of sympathy with the Grand Dauphin's dislikes and difficulties which was the principal obstacle to Bossuet's educational attempts. Reference has also been made already to the Dauphin's lack of aptitude for literary studies. He was too lazy to master the apparently unreasonable formalities of Latin grammar and considered it beneath his dignity to trouble himself about such things. Bossuet, in a short Latin treatise, tries to show his pupil the right way of looking at this subject. "Do not think," he says, "that you are severely blamed in your studies simply for having violated the rules of grammar in your compositions. Doubtless it is disgraceful for a prince, who ought to keep good order in everything, to fall into such mistakes;...but what we blame is the lack of attention which causes the mistakes. It is this which now leads you to deal wrongly with words; but if we allow this bad habit to persist and grow stronger, you will deal wrongly, not with words only but with things. Now you complain of the rules of grammar; soon you will find fault with the laws of reason[1]." But Bossuet's remonstrances had little effect and, as the Dauphin grew older, his distaste for Latin increased. One day a lady of the court was recounting the tale of her troubles. "Do you ever have to write proses?" interrupted the young prince. "No, Monseigneur." "Then you don't know what it is to be unfortunate." One can hardly suppress a feeling of sympathy for the Dauphin who, for all his dulness and indolence, seems to have had glimmerings of a sense of humour.

Yet, as we have seen, the Dauphin was not entirely devoid of interests. He seems to have shown some aptitude for mathematics and for geometry, in particular. He had a real fondness for drawing and even learnt to etch. It was his custom to present his particular friends at court with copies of engravings which he himself had made. But the education

[1] *Serenissimo Delphino*: in Bossuet, *Œuvres* (1818), xxxiv, 48, 49. This pamphlet is sometimes entitled *De Incogitantia*.

given by Bossuet to his pupil was based upon subjects for
which the Dauphin had neither liking nor natural skill. The
staple of his curriculum was Latin and history, leading up to
a study of philosophy with special reference to the duties of
a prince. Other subjects were definitely subordinate and
were included only as "divertissements." It was difficult—
perhaps impossible—for Bossuet, under the circumstances,
to adopt any other plan; yet his experience is not without
its lessons. The case of the Dauphin has its modern counter-
parts. Many of us have still to realise that there are children
who are constitutionally incapable of profiting by the curriculum which the ordinary school provides for them, and
who yet cannot justly be classed as "mentally deficient."
Every schoolmaster of any experience has, at some time or
other, been called upon to struggle with a class of "middle-
school thicks." These unfortunate individuals, chiefly in
virtue of their age, have drifted slowly up the school and at
last reached a stage where further promotion is, for very
shame, impossible. Like the Grand Dauphin, they alternate
between outbursts of excessive activity in the open air and
long periods of intellectual torpor. Their Latin cries to
Heaven for vengeance[1]; their French is little better; they
seem to be incapable of writing or even spelling their own
language. Occasionally they show some slight aptitude for
mathematics and usually they come into their own in the
science laboratory or in the woodwork shop. It is hardly
necessary to point out that to make such boys follow the
normal school curriculum is not to do our best for them.
They are of a special and (fortunately) abnormal type and
they call for special and abnormal treatment. If we adopt
Montausier's method and endeavour to goad a boy of this
kind to his work by continual punishments, we shall probably succeed only in giving him a profound and permanent
distaste for any kind of intellectual work. Like the Dauphin,
he will take "so great a disgust for books that he will form
the resolve never to open one when he is his own master, and

---

[1] *E.g.* (actual examples): "most people" = *populissimi*; "my
father" = *longius meus*.

6

he will keep his word[1]." It may be doubted whether such a consequence is wholly the boy's own fault. If the net result of his class-room experiences is that he has attained an invincible distaste for things intellectual much is doubtless due to the school itself. These facts are far more widely realised to-day than they were in the time of Bossuet; but it remains true that one of the most urgent needs in modern education is that something should be done promptly and in every school for those abnormal children who do not fit into the ordinary grooves. For such cases a programme of work entirely different from that of the rest of the school should be drawn up, and special forms should exist parallel to those which follow the normal curriculum. In such classes Latin would be dropped entirely; French—the only foreign language—would be taught to a large extent orally; English, although frequent practice in essay-writing is inevitable, would include a more than usual amount of *vivâ voce* reproduction and acting. But the chief stress in such forms would be laid on practical work in science and mathematics, on practical geography both indoors and outdoors, on hand-work of many kinds, on drawing and singing, on physical drill and gardening. Of course, it sometimes happens that the "middle-school thick" makes good in after life even though he has been forced through the ordinary curriculum. The writer has in mind the case of one boy who displayed little aptitude or energy at school and who afterwards built up a highly successful business in electrical models and toys; and of another of the same type who became a very skilful taxidermist. But one is tempted to feel that any success in facing the problems of adult life which such people may achieve is gained, not because of the training which the school has given them, but in spite of it.

It would seem then that, although no child ever had more care and thought expended upon his education, the Grand Dauphin was wrongly treated. It has been customary among modern French writers who have dealt with this subject to attempt to prove either that the Grand Dauphin was not so bad as he has been painted and that Bossuet's methods

---

[1] Cf. M[me] de Caylus, *Souvenirs et Correspondance*, p. 72.

were in fault, or that education, even in the capable
hands of a Bossuet, sometimes lamentably fails[1]. The lesson
which, to the present writer, seems more naturally to spring
from the story of Bossuet and the Dauphin is that wrong
methods in education are just as provocative of positive
harm as wrong treatment in medicine. To punish certain
children because they continually and habitually make bad
mistakes in their Latin prose, or their geometry, is as un-
skilful as to prescribe a diet of nuts and wholemeal bread
for a patient who is recovering from typhoid fever. The
diagnosis in the former case is doubtless far more difficult
than in the latter; but when once, after fair and searching
trial, it has been definitely made, the patient should be set
aside for the special treatment that has already been suggested. Had such methods been adopted with the Dauphin
the tale might well have been different. As it was, he was
wrongly dealt with from the very beginning and his defects,
instead of being remedied, were steadily increased.

Yet we must not altogether blame Bossuet, for he had
special difficulties to face. As a matter of fact the education
of a prince, although invariably entrusted to men of
eminence, very frequently did not succeed. The survivor of
the two Princes de Conti, who had shared the Dauphin's
lessons, hardly did credit to Lancelot and the Abbé Fleury
who had been his preceptors. Even if he became conspicuous
for the brilliance of his intellect, he became equally conspicuous for the depravity of his morals. "He had been,"
says Saint-Simon, "extremely well educated, as is usual in
the case of those of his rank; he was very learned. The
irregularities of his life merely eclipsed his intelligence
without extinguishing it[2]." Sainte-Beuve acutely.sums up
the situation in an epigram: "Pauvre Lancelot!" he exclaims,
"il voulait même d'un prince faire un saint; et voilà qu'il
sortit de là un Alcibiade[3]." Louis XIV himself seems to
have owed but little to his preceptors Péréfixe and la Mothe
le Vayer. The former, for instance, had instilled into his

---

[1] M. Floquet, for example, inclines to the former view; M. Henri
Druon to the latter.

[2] *Mémoires*, VII, 58.   [3] *Port-Royal*, III, 563.

pupil that war should be shunned and that *impudicos amores* are shameful; the latter had instructed him in "economics," or the science of family life, in which mutual love and trust between husband and wife are laid down as the guiding principle.

We must realise that every tutor who undertook the education of a boy of the royal house, or one closely allied to it, laboured under several disadvantages, the effects of which could rarely be annulled even under the most favourable circumstances. In the first place, the division of control between the governor and the preceptor inevitably led to difficulties. Montausier and Bossuet, apparently, were always upon friendly terms, but it must sometimes have proved irksome to the most illustrious prelate in France to have to defer to the authority of the ex-protestant Duke. Then again, the environment under which the young prince was brought up savoured too much of the hot-house. The concentration of the French nobility in the court at Versailles had the inevitable result that henceforth the kings of France knew but little of their dominions. The whole country was now centred and epitomised in Paris; and, unless it were to go upon a military promenade, the sovereign and his court rarely made a journey of more than the three or four leagues which separated Versailles from the Louvre. Thus it came about that, although Bossuet did not neglect to give the Grand Dauphin lessons in the geography of France, it was studied not at first-hand but from the maps which hung in his schoolroom. Throughout the ten years during which Bossuet and his pupil were associated, they apparently left the neighbourhood of Paris upon one occasion only. It was in 1674, at the time of the second conquest of the Franche-Comté, when Louis XIV was absent from the capital with his armies in the field. Montausier and Bossuet, together with their royal pupil and his *enfants d'honneur*, took up their abode for six weeks in the preceptor's native city of Dijon, not far from the scene of operations. The Dauphin was not only allowed to visit the delightful environs of the town[1], but he even journeyed as far as Dôle

[1] At Plombières-les-Dijon an obelisk was set up in honour of the

which was still in a state of siege and there gained his first practical experiences of the art of war. But normally the exigencies of court-life confined the Dauphin to Paris or its neighbourhood, and we may heartily agree with Chateaubriand when he says: "Louis XIV, who otherwise justifies his proud title, did his race a great injury by isolating the princes of France behind the barriers of an oriental education[1]."

But the greatest difficulties of all were due to the differences in rank between the preceptor and his pupil. One of the first principles of the educative process is that the teacher shall be in a position of authority and that the pupil shall look up to him with respect. Even the most modern theories of co-operative class-discipline have not vitally affected this relationship. But it was practically impossible for it to be established between a prince and his tutor, when the royal house was enclosed in inviolate sanctity by a wall of elaborate ceremonial and when every member of it shone with a glory reflected from *Le Roi Soleil* himself. The tutor was always inferior to his pupil, and no attributes of learning or piety could atone for what he lacked in rank. Even Lancelot, amid the Jansenist austerity of the Conti household, where earthly distinctions had less value than they possessed in other noble families, feels his position acutely and is humiliated by the scant respect which is accorded to him[2]. The prince was constantly exposed to the danger of flattery; even the preceptor himself, as we have seen in Bossuet's own case, was not always free from blame in this

---

frequent visits which the Grand Dauphin paid to this village during his stay in Burgundy. On it was carved a portrait of the prince, executed by Du Bois, a famous Dijonnais sculptor. The obelisk no longer remains; but the writer remembers seeing, about fourteen years ago, in the *Musée* at Dijon a *bas-relief* portrait of the Grand Dauphin as a boy. Subsequent reference to the 1883 catalogue of the *Musée* discloses the fact that it is ascribed to Du Bois. It therefore seems quite possible that this sculpture was actually taken from the obelisk at Plombières.

[1] Letter to Duchesse de Berry, in *Revue rétrospective* (Dec. 1884— July, 1885), p. 92.

[2] Cf. *Supplément au Nécrologe*, p. 162.

respect. But continual adulation corroded the moral nature
of those subjected to it and counteracted any efforts which
might be made to develop character along the right lines.
Add to this the absence of engrossing work, the laxity of
life at court, the easy avenues to vice which wealth can
provide—and it is not hard to realise the enormous difficulties which confronted such men as Bossuet and Lancelot.
The right education of the prince was a harder task even
than was realised by those who wrote upon it or experi-
mented with it; and we cannot feel that it was the true
solution of the ills of society. But it does not become us to
make light of the efforts of such men as Bossuet, for we
ourselves are still experimenting and we can profit by their
mistakes.

CHAPTER V

THE ORATORIAN SCHOOLS

IN the field of secondary education the seventeenth
century in France was a period of great activity. Another
chapter of this book deals with the work which was carried
on by the Faculty of Arts in the University of Paris. But
the rigidity of the curriculum and the laxity of discipline in
the University were among the reasons which explain the
decline of its schools and the conspicuous success of rival
institutions which came into prominence about this time.
As with the University itself, these schools were all ultimately under the control of the Church which is at this
period almost the sole administrator of education[1].

The non-university secondary schools may be divided into
two types—the seminaries and the colleges of the Teaching
Congregations. Of these the second are immeasurably the
more important; but the work of the seminaries, though
restricted in aim, is for all that worthy of passing consideration. In accordance with the requirements of the Council of
Trent these institutions were founded by bishops or arch-
bishops in their various dioceses for the education of those
who aspired to holy orders. It has been the policy of the
Roman Church, where possible, to supervise the education
of candidates for the priesthood from a comparatively early
age. The Anglican Church usually adopts a different plan;
she prefers to allow those who wish to be ordained to receive
a wide general education in company with others, who are
aiming at different professions and vocations, before they

---

[1] Cf. "Le droit d'enseigner est essential à l'Église...les écoles
chrétiens ont esté pour l'ordinaire sous la conduite et direction des
evesques." Joly, *Statuts*, pp. 225 and 227. The only teachers (apart
from masters in Huguenot schools) who escaped ecclesiastical control
were tutors in private families; and one of the *statuts* (No. 62) therefore
besought parents not to employ such persons.

enter at the age of twenty-two or later upon a specialised course in preparation for a bishop's examination or under the distinctive *régime* of a theological college. One may be inclined to criticise the Roman system of training as being too exclusively professional; but no adherent of the English Church, be he never so ardent, can pretend that the possession of a university degree supplemented by a smattering of divinity, is a really satisfactory preparation for holy orders. Yet each system has its merits, as can be judged from its results. The English "clergyman" is perhaps more a man of the world and therefore more able to appreciate the layman's point of view than the Roman priest; whereas the latter bears more definitely the impress of the professional ecclesiastic and exercises more definitely the authority and influence of his high calling. But in France of the seventeenth century the character and attainments of the priesthood had sunk to a low ebb. Continually we read of the ignorance—and worse—of the clergy, and of the scandalous mal-administration of ecclesiastical affairs. In 1595 the assembly of the clergy of France laid before Henri IV a report[1] complaining that three-fourths of the parochial churches were without incumbents, a large proportion of archiepiscopal and episcopal sees without occupants, many abbeys without superiors, while the sin of simony was so rife that a mere child[2] could be appointed to an archbishopric; and the king in his reply pointed out that the grave misconduct of many of the clergy themselves was largely responsible for the abuse and corruption that abounded. The Wars of Religion, also, and the progress of the Reformation had weakened the hold which the clergy had upon their flocks and the crying need of the Church was for a regeneration of her ministry.

Fortunately there were not wanting those who realised the need and were eager to do their utmost to supply it. Chief among them was St Vincent de Paul who in 1626 founded his community of missionary clergy known as

---

[1] See *Procès-verbaux des Assemblées du Clergé de France*, I, 276.

[2] Charles of Lorraine, the fellow-student of Ramus (see *supra*, p. 20), was only eight years old when he became Archbishop of Rheims.

"Prêtres de la Mission." Appropriately enough they were housed in the ancient Collège des Bons Enfants of the University of Paris and here large numbers of candidates were prepared for ordination. Mention may also be made of the Sulpitians, founded by the Abbé Olier, the Eudistes, and the seminary of St Nicholas de Chardonnet. All these institutions were *grands séminaires* which were open to young men of about eighteen who had already received a general education elsewhere; thus they corresponded more nearly to the theological college as we understand it. This type of seminary gradually prevailed during the latter half of the seventeenth century, but in the earlier part it was more usual to model the seminary on the plan laid down by the Council of Trent. In this case the pupils were admitted at the age of twelve to fourteen, and it was hoped that an early acquaintance with and a long training in habits of devotion and discipline would bear fruit in later life.

According to regulations which were finally drawn up by the Church of France in 1610, candidates for admission to a seminary must be at least twelve years of age, of legitimate birth, and must show some aptitude for intellectual pursuits. Those who were in need of help received a free education, but fee-paying pupils, who were the sons of wealthy parents, could be admitted if they showed a desire to serve God and the Church. The school day was strictly regulated. The pupils rose as a rule at 4.0 a.m. and attendance at daily Mass was compulsory. All alike wore the tonsure and a clerical costume "ut in disciplina ecclesiastica commodius instituantur." The pupils might not leave the precincts of the seminary without express permission; they were not allowed to speak to their comrades except at recreation times, and even then it was forbidden that two pupils should keep together apart from their fellows. The school rules were chiefly negative: no talking in church or during lessons or preparation-time; no letters to be sent out or received except under censorship by the Superior; no games which entail too great expenditure of energy and involve over-heating of the participants; no conversation outside recreation hours save in the Latin tongue—the use of French was punished by the use of the cane, except in the case of the younger boys. The character of the curriculum may be inferred from the duties of the teaching staff. There was a master who taught the younger boys "grammar"—*i.e.* the dry bones of elementary classics; while for the elder pupils there were teachers of Latin, Greek, theology, scholastic theology, philosophy, and the explanation of confession, penance, and the other sacraments. In addition to these regents there were a procurator, a principal, and several *maîtres de salles* (*magistri cubiculorum praefecti*), one of whom acted as the grammar master and whose general duties were much the same as those of the modern *répétiteur*.

The physical well being of the pupils was not overlooked. It was provided that seminaries should be built in healthy places and should be properly equipped; under this latter head the provision of a good library is specified. Each pupil was to have a separate bed and to be furnished with clothes and other necessary equipment, all of which he had to keep in good order. Although the seminary was essentially a boarding-school, it is just possible that *externes* were in some cases admitted. There is a regulation which forbids the *internes* of seminaries to have any dealings with *externes*; but this probably implies only that pupils from these theological schools occasionally took special courses at the colleges of a neighbouring university or elsewhere, and in such cases any intercourse with outsiders would be strictly prohibited.

The seminary schools with their highly specialised course and their ecclesiastical atmosphere naturally did not play a part of first-rate importance in the secondary education of the period. But there were institutions which, although they started as seminaries, soon lost their restricted outlook and either became or added to themselves secondary schools in the wider sense of the term. Of the schools of the Teaching Congregations those of the Port-Royalists[1] and Oratorians were in origin seminarist and were primarily designed as an attempt to combat the ignorance and vice which prevailed among the French clergy in the early part of the seventeenth

---

[1] See Barnard, *The Little Schools of Port-Royal*, p. 61.

century. But the Port-Royal schools soon lost this character; while the Oratory, though not neglecting the training of ordinands, quickly became assimilated to the other Teaching Congregations which, like the Jesuits and the Benedictines, gave—and still give—an education which while definitely religious in character is by no means confined to those who aspire to the priesthood.

In the present chapter it is proposed to treat in some detail of the work of the Oratorians who, for some reason, seem to have suffered an altogether unmerited neglect. They carried on their educational work in France from the early part of the seventeenth century down to the Revolution; their school at Juilly can worthily challenge comparison with the Jesuit colleges of Clermont or La Flèche; while their methods of teaching and the breadth of their curriculum entitle them to a high place among the pioneers of modern education.

The society known as the Oratory of France owed its foundation to Pierre de Bérulle. He came of an ancient family of Champagne and was born near Troyes in 1575. He was an eldest son and heir to a considerable estate; but he showed his disinterestedness by renouncing his chances of worldly advancement and embracing an ecclesiastical career. He was educated at Paris, at the colleges of Boncourt, Bourgogne, and Clermont, and gave early signs of great intellectual promise. Ordained to the priesthood in 1599[1], he quickly gained a reputation as a confessor, a controversialist, and a converter of heretics. His merits soon earned recognition. He was appointed one of Henri IV's almoners and the king also offered him no less than three bishoprics, as well as the archiepiscopal see of Lyons; but De Bérulle preferred to remain a simple priest. It was largely owing to his instrumentality that the Carmelite Order, which had been founded by St Theresa in Spain, was introduced into France.

But it is from the foundation of the Oratory that the name of De Bérulle derives its chief lustre. The unsatisfactory

[1] In a letter to his family De Bérulle said that his ordination "terminait tous ses souhaits."

condition of the French clergy at this period was realised
by no one more seriously than by him. In a letter to
St Vincent de Paul he says "le clergé y était sans discipline,
le peuple sans crainte, les prêtres sans dévotion et sans
charité." In 1601, while reading in his daily office the words:
"Annuntiate inter gentes studia eius," De Bérulle realised
that it was to be his mission to remedy this scandal in the
bosom of the Church[1]. Owing to his labours in connection
with the establishment of the Carmelites in France he was
unable to put his plans into action until 1611. His aim was
to found a congregation of priests which should be a free
society and not monastic. There were to be no vows[2] other
than those of the priesthood itself, and the system of the
society was summed up in the phrase "Entre qui peut, sort
qui veut." The Oratory was thus in origin designed as a
union of seminaries for the perfection of the priesthood.
They were to be open both to those who aspired to orders
and to those who had already been ordained, and their
members were free to enter or leave as they wished.

De Bérulle's scheme was not altogether an original one
for it was closely modelled on the Italian Oratory which
St Philip Neri (1515–1595) had already founded at Rome.
This also was a free society, consisting of priests and secular
clerks who had united to further their own spiritual life and
to benefit their neighbours, but who were not bound by any
special vows. The Marquis de Sillery, afterwards Chancellor
of France, was a great friend of De Bérulle's and had been
ambassador at Rome; and it was probably through this
channel that the future founder of the French Oratory first
heard of its Italian prototype. The two societies are exactly
alike in that they consist of priests or candidates for the
priesthood and that no special vows are required of their
members. But whereas the Italian Oratory aimed merely at

[1] He had also been urged to undertake work of this kind by Mme
Acarie, who was associated with him in introducing the Carmelites
into France.

[2] "La politique de l'Oratoire sera de n'en point avoir" (Lamy,
Entretiens, p. 188); "Le lien véritable de la Congrégation est la
charité" (De Condren, *Œuvres*, p. 383).

M.^r le Cardinal de Berule.

Paris chez Crepy rüe S.^t   Jacques au Lion d'Or &c.

Pierre Card.^{al} de Berule né le 14.e feur.^r
1575. a Jnstitüé la Congregation de l'O:
ratoire a la persuation de S. François de
Salles et du B. H. Cæsar de Bus en 1611. Co:
nfirme par Paul V. 1613. est mort le 2.e Octobre
1629. disant Messe lors quil prononçoit Ces
paroles hanc igitur Oblationem.

PIERRE DE BÉRULLE

(1575–1629)

the regeneration of the priesthood locally, De Bérulle had in view a national institution which should benefit the Church throughout France; his object was to found a number of institutions all united under the government of one superior-general acting from Paris.

The society started work in 1611. It consisted of a congregation of six priests, living together in simplicity and religion, and occupying a house on the site of the present Val de Grâce. Royal letters patent were granted in 1612 and a bull[1] of May 10th, 1613, gave papal sanction to the institution. The object of the society may be summed up in the following passage from this document: " ...principale ac praecipuum institutum sit perfectioni status sacerdotalis totaliter incumbere......insuper et aliorum ad sacros ordines aspirantium instructioni, non circa scientiam sed circa usum scientiae ritus et mores proprie ecclesiasticos se addicere volentes[2]." Great stress was laid on the power and the practice of prayer (*oratio*) and it was this which gave its special title to the Congregation—*Oratorium Jesu Christi Domini nostri*.

The Oratory grew with wonderful rapidity. Within a few years it had institutions all over France as well as at Louvain, Madrid, Savoy and Rome. In Paris the society was favoured with court patronage; the Oratorian chapel in the rue St Honoré[3], which was consecrated in 1630, was elevated to the rank of a "chapel royal" and many persons of quality "assisted" at its services or listened to the preaching and singing[4] of the Oratorian fathers. The success of the society

---

[1] *Sacrosanctæ Romanæ Ecclesiæ*: see *Magnum Bullarium Romanum*, III, 371 ff.

[2] § 3, *op. cit.* p. 372. Bossuet splendidly sums up the spirit of the Congregation in his funeral oration for François Bourgoing, third superior-general of the Oratory.

[3] It lies just behind the Louvre and is now used as a Protestant *temple*.

[4] The Oratorians paid special attention to music and were known as "les pères au beau chant." It is interesting to remember that Palestrina had been an adherent of St Philip Neri and had composed hymns, etc. for his Congregation. It is said that the word *oratorio* owes its derivation to the name of this society.

redounded on its founder. During the early years of Louis XIII and the regency of Marie de Médicis the internal condition of France was greatly disturbed and De Bérulle was one of the intermediaries who arranged the Treaty of Angoulême (1619) by which a formal reconciliation was effected between the king and the queen-mother. In 1624 De Bérulle was again sent on a political mission to Rome in connection with the proposed marriage between Henrietta of France and the Protestant prince Charles. The Pope— as might be expected—was disinclined to favour such an alliance, but eventually De Bérulle succeeded in over-ruling his objections and the necessary dispensation was granted. When therefore the French princess left her native country she was accompanied to England by De Bérulle in the capacity of almoner. He returned a year later and in 1627—much against his will, so it is said—he was made a cardinal. Other honours were showered upon him; but in October, 1629, while celebrating Mass in the chapel of the rue St Honoré, he was suddenly taken ill and expired shortly afterwards. He had lived to see the foundation of no less than fifty institutions of various kinds, all connected with the Oratory and scattered over the whole of France.

It will be seen that, although the Oratorian Congregation regarded the training of candidates for the priesthood as an important part of its functions, it did not originally concern itself with secondary education in the usual meaning of that term. De Bérulle in his original scheme definitely excluded the direction of colleges from the work of the Oratory. In his first project he says: "Thus one of the functions of this Congregation will be the training not of youths (as with the Jesuits) but of priests only." Even as late as the *Règlements de la Congrégation de l'Oratoire*[1] drawn up in 1631 by Charles de Condren, the second superior-general of the society, there is no mention of *collèges*; the rules there given are confined to the conduct of priests and aspirants to holy orders. It is possible that De Bérulle had expressly excluded secular education from the work of the Oratory for fear of arousing jealousy and incurring opposition on the part of the Society

[1] See De Condren, *Œuvres complètes*, pp. 379 ff.

of Jesus. He had a warm admiration for the Jesuits; they had been his teachers in his youth and at one time he had contemplated entering their society; among them also he numbered many of his best friends. But a breach between the two societies soon became apparent and it widened as time went on. They differed, in fact, fundamentally both in constitution and in outlook. The Jesuits were regulars; the Oratorians a society of secular priests bound by no special vows. The Jesuits, being directly subordinate to the Holy See, were ultramontane in tendency; the Oratory was a national and Gallican congregation under the ultimate control of the bishop in each diocese. De Condren, who succeeded De Bérulle as superior-general of the Oratory, was less favourably inclined than his predecessor towards the Jesuits; and the Oratorians' admiration for Descartes and suspected leanings towards Jansenism also helped to increase the antagonism. In spite, therefore, of De Bérulle's wishes— even contrary to them—the Oratory may well have opened schools in order to keep pace with the Society of Jesus, which had resumed its educational work in France early in the seventeenth century, and had rapidly achieved a remarkable success. The influence of the Oratorians was bound to be eclipsed by that of the Jesuits so long as they neglected that means of "peaceful penetration" which the Society has always used with such remarkable effect. But, apart from these considerations, the work of the priesthood inevitably includes teaching and this was particularly the case at a period when the work of education was very largely in the hands of the Church. Although De Bérulle had definitely expressed a desire to exclude ordinary school-teaching from the scope of his congregation, the bull granted by Paul V said merely that the education of the priesthood was to be the *chief* work of the Oratorians (*principale ac praecipuum*); and thus a loophole was left for secular education. Even before the death of De Bérulle himself the Oratory had already undertaken work of this kind and under the superior-generalship of De Condren it developed in a remarkable manner.

The first suggestion of the change seems to have come

from outside the Congregation. As we have seen, the Oratory soon became fashionable at court. Even Richelieu, whose disfavour De Bérulle incurred shortly before his death[1], gave the society some tepid encouragement[2]. But it was the Cardinal de Joyeuse who, quite early in its career, had first introduced the work of secular education into the Oratory. He had already given the society a seminary in Paris for twenty-five or thirty ecclesiastics, but in 1614, while he was Archbishop of Rouen, he handed over to it the *collège* of Dieppe and endowed it at his own expense. Other endowments were added by private individuals and by the municipal authorities; and eight priests of the Oratory, with one Paul Métézau as superior, were sent down to begin operations. The school had a successful career; its pupils, who received gratuitous instruction, numbered between five and six hundred by 1642, and although the buildings were destroyed during the bombardment of Dieppe by the English and Dutch fleets in 1694, they were afterwards rebuilt and the work of education continued.

In an appendix[3] will be found a detailed list of the Oratorian colleges which in course of time sprang up in all parts of France. There was always a great deal of freedom in the constitution of the various schools, and their regulations were evolved gradually. In some colleges education was free; elsewhere fees were paid which varied as a rule between 200 and 400 livres *per annum*. Sometimes—as at Mans or Langres or Agde—a college is offered to the Congregation by the local bishop who makes himself responsible for the endowments of the institution; and in such cases the *écolâtre* of the diocese has rights of inspection and supervision. Elsewhere it is the municipality which invites the Oratory to staff its secondary school and provides the necessary funds for maintenance. There are many examples of this—the colleges of Riom, Pézenas, Montbrison, Beaune and Saumur

---

[1] For the reasons see Jervis, I, 314–316, and Perraud, ch. IV.

[2] Berthault (see *infra*, p. 164) dedicated his *Florus Gallicus* (1644) to Richelieu and refers to the minister's "propensa in Presbyterorum Oratorii D. Jesu Societatem voluntas."

[3] See Appendix H.

are cases in point. Sometimes the "education grants" were not promptly paid and difficulties arose in consequence; sometimes the sums allotted were insufficient and the deficit had to be met by endowments from private individuals. But on the whole these municipal schools flourished and did a most valuable work, particularly in the smaller French country towns. They help to show that throughout the seventeenth century and well into the eighteenth also there was a strong feeling on the part of the city and municipal authorities in favour of entrusting education to the care of professional ecclesiastics. The town handed over its *collège* to a teaching congregation; the Society of Jesus was most often favoured, but, as we have seen, there were many municipalities which preferred the Oratorians or some other body. The popularity of the Jesuits waned somewhat during the early eighteenth century, and when in 1762 the Society was expelled from France for the second time, seven of its principal colleges were handed over to the Oratory. But even where a town-school was staffed by Oratorian *professeurs* the municipality usually retained certain rights of inspection or control. Thus these Oratorian schools must have played a large part in the life of the towns where they were situated, and in the course of a career which in many cases lasted well over a century, must have had a deep and lasting influence upon it. As has been said, many of these schools gave a free education; and even where a fee was charged to boarders, *externes* were often educated gratuitously. Although a large part of the endowments might come from the town or out of the pockets of private benefactors, additional expenses which might prove necessary were met out of the funds of the Congregation itself. Thus in all parts of France there arose schools giving a full secondary course of an unusually wide and varied character, which involved no cost to the central government and little or none to the parents of the pupils.

In other cases the Oratory took over the management of a college of some provincial university. The first example of this was the Collège d'Anjou in the University of Angers, which in 1619—partly owing to the good offices of Marie de

Médicis[1]—was handed over to the Oratorians. A similar college in 1625 was attached to the University of Nantes. In 1631 the Collège de Guyenne[2] in the University of Bordeaux was offered to the Congregation; owing to opposition on the part of the Jesuits the charge was not accepted until 1639, and throughout the history of this institution there was friction between the Oratory and the Society of Jesus. When the Oratorians undertook to staff a college of this kind the principal and regents usually became members of the Faculty of Arts of the local university. There were often difficulties due to rivalry or jealousy. At Angers, for example, the University at first refused to matriculate pupils who came from the Oratorian college. Sometimes there was trouble with the *pédagogues*, with whom the pupils known as *pensionnaires* lived, and many of whom were licensed to teach reading, writing and the elements of Latin— *i.e.* were *maîtres d'école*. There was a continual tendency for these teachers to carry the instruction which they gave beyond the limits to which their licence confined them. The history not only of the University of Paris but also of the provincial universities is full of examples of this[3]. Thus at Nantes two *maîtres d'école* introduced into their school all the classes up to the Rhetoric; this made the institution *ipso facto* a *collège* and not merely a *petite école*. Not content with this enormity, one of the *maîtres d'école* had even advertised a theatrical representation to be played by his pupils with the assistance of three young ladies. So great a scandal, joined to the encroachments of the so-called *petite école* upon the sphere of the Oratorian college prompted the Congregation to make a protest. It was successful. The offenders were forbidden to organise plays for their pupils and were directed to confine their energies to preparing pupils for the Vth class of the secondary school and to assisting their *pensionnaires* who attended the college, with the preparation of home-work. Similar friction occurred at Nantes between the authorities of the Oratorian college and the local *pédagogues*.

---

[1] De Bérulle was a *persona grata* with her; see p. 152.

[2] Montaigne had been educated here.

[3] Cf. *supra*, p. 47.

To put an end to encroachments, the latter were strictly prohibited from teaching any subjects which formed part of the curriculum of the Oratorian college, or even from assisting their *pensionnaires* in such subjects set as home-work[1], unless express permission were given.

It can be seen from what has been said that the Oratorian schools were of various types, that they depended for their success largely upon local conditions, and that their system allowed a considerable amount of freedom. At the same time, the internal arrangements of all these schools were similar and were based upon a document which was gradually evolved as the result of experience[2]. The *Ratio Studiorum a magistris et professoribus Congregationis Oratorii Domini Jesu observanda* appeared in two parts. The first, published in 1634, is inspired by De Condren, although not actually written by him; it deals with the general internal administration of the Oratorian colleges. The second part, drawn up by Jean Morin, one of the most eminent of Oratorian educationists, appeared in 1645[3]; it concerns itself with syllabuses, teaching methods, and other matters of professional interest to the staff of the schools. But there was one Oratorian college in particular which always led the way and was regarded by the rest as the example to be followed as far as local conditions allowed[4]. This was the famous Collège de Juilly.

In 1637 the Congregation took over an ancient abbey, dating from 1184, at Juilly, some twenty miles from Paris in the direction of Soissons[5]. It was designed as a seminary

[1] The French verb for this whole phrase is *répéter*, but there is no exact English equivalent in one word.

[2] In the same way the Jesuit *Ratio Studiorum* did not appear till 1599, although the Society had been in existence since 1534.

[3] The two parts were published in one volume by Vitré, Paris, 1645. So far as is known, no copy of the book is now extant, but from various other sources much of its substance can be gathered.

[4] In the *Ratio Studiorum O.D.J.* Morin definitely stated that the teaching methods which had been in vogue at Juilly for some years past should be adopted in other Oratorian colleges. See Adry, p. 10.

[5] It lies two miles south of the station of Dammartin on the C. de F. du Nord.

for "ecclésiastiques et aspirants à l'état de prêtrise et autres qui, par dévotion, viendraient y demeurer quelque temps pour faire retraite." Thus its original aim was in accordance with De Bérulle's intentions. But Louis XIII, who had already shown an interest in the work of the Oratory in Paris, was desirous of entrusting to the Congregation the education of some boys of noble birth. De Condren was approached on the subject, and in 1638 Juilly became a "royal academy" under the patronage of the king. As a sign of this honour the college was granted as its coat of arms the royal lilies joined with the insignia of the Congregation. The institution may be regarded as the fine flower of the Oratorian educational system and the account of this which follows is based to some extent upon the actual practice of this particular school at Juilly.

The staple of instruction in the Oratorian colleges—as indeed in all other institutions giving a secondary education at this period—was the Latin language. This is explicitly laid down in several memoranda issued by the triennial General Assembly of the Society and is also specifically mentioned in many of the agreements drawn up between the Oratory and the towns which confided to it the administration of their colleges. But this did not entail a study of Latin as taught by the University or the Society of Jesus. Both of these continued to regard Latin as a living language and to make the power of speaking and writing it the chief aim of instruction. At Juilly the pupil was introduced to Latin grammar not through a primer written in this language—as was the almost universal custom of the day—but through a *Nouvelle Méthode* drawn up in 1640 by De Condren, in which all explanations were given in French. This was a notable innovation. The rules were tabulated and the understanding of them was facilitated by the use of different colours[1]. In the case of substantives, adjectives and pronouns, masculine forms were given in red, feminine in green, neuter in yellow; while forms which are common to all three genders were shown in black. With verbs red was used for

[1] For an example see Barnard, *The Port-Royalists on Education*, p. 257.

tenses formed from the present stem, green for those derived from the perfect, while forms containing the participle (*e.g.* compound tenses in the passive) appeared in yellow. It may be doubted whether such devices are of any great assistance to the learner[1]. "If there were only two or three things to remember," says the Port-Royalist Nicole, "perhaps this method might be of service; but since there is an enormous number the mind is overwhelmed[2]." The book is none the less a landmark in the history of Latin teaching. The Port-Royal *Nouvelle Méthode Latine* of Lancelot is one of the earliest Latin grammars for school use published in France in which the foreign language is approached through the vernacular. But Lancelot's *Méthode* appeared in 1644, whereas by 1640 De Condren's grammar was already in use at Juilly. Are we then to conclude that the Port-Royal *Méthode* is an imitation of, or was suggested by, a device already employed by the Oratorians? This seems unlikely. De Condren had his grammar printed privately for the special use of the college at Juilly and there is no evidence that the volume was used outside the schools of the Congregation until a much later date. It was not published in book form until 1675. Apart from the use of the French language (which is doubtless an important resemblance), the two books have little in common. Lancelot turns the doggerel Latin verses of Despauter into French rhymes, hoping that the learning of grammar rules may thereby be facilitated; De Condren aims at the same end by the use of his "quatre différentes couleurs." It would seem fair to conclude that there was no conscious plagiarism on the part of Port-Royal. Both Congregations were deeply influenced by Cartesianism. De Bérulle had been a friend of Descartes[3] and as the Oratory stood for no particular system of philosophy or theology it was easy for the society to adopt his doctrines. Descartes had written in French and his system involved a freedom of thought and

---

[1] In his preface De Condren says that he realises that the success of his method lies not only in the *cartes* themselves, but also in the manner of teaching them.

[2] *Essais de Morale*, II, 292.

[3] See Haldane, *Descartes, his Life and Times*, pp. 108–10 and 125.

judgment which appeared dangerous alike to a rigid theology
and to absolutist theories of government. Hence the up-
holders of Cartesianism tended to arouse the opposition both
of the Society of Jesus and of Louis XIV. In this way the
Oratory shared to some extent in the persecutions which
were levelled at Port-Royal—although in the case of the
latter there were, of course, many other factors which
complicated the situation. The Oratory succeeded in purging
itself to some extent of this "heretical" tendency; but it
always included a large number of influential men—as for
example Lamy, of whom more will be said later—who
welcomed the teachings of Descartes and introduced them
into the schools of the Congregation. The truth is that both
Port-Royal and the Oratory were co-operating—probably
unconsciously—in an educational reform which was due
ultimately to the influence of Descartes; and for this reason
coincidences in teaching methods are to be expected. This
fact does not in the least detract from the merits of either
De Condren's grammar or the *Méthode* of Lancelot.

We may return from this digression to complete our
account of the teaching of Latin in the Oratorian schools.
Great stress was laid on translation and the explanation of
authors and comparatively little on the writing of Latin
prose. Every week, on Thursday morning, an examination
called *composition* was held and on its results places were
awarded. The marks gained in these tests were recorded and
counted towards the final order at the end of the school-year.
It is interesting, in passing, to remember that a similar
custom exists in the modern French *lycée* and that the term
composition is still used. In the early stages of writing proses
the master first of all worked out the translation from
French into Latin *vivâ voce*, and the pupils afterwards made
their written copies. This method deserves to be widely
adopted and would commend itself to any practical teacher.
Verse composition seems to have played but a small part in
the curriculum. "On perd ordinairement beaucoup de tems
à faire des Vers dans les collèges," says Lamy[1], the most
famous of all the Oratorian teachers. The pupils were made

[1] *Entretiens*, p. 170.

to build up their own vocabularies by collecting words from the authors which they read. Continually the emphasis is on reading—"l'usage est le meilleur maître en matière de langues[1]"—and the method of retranslation, which Roger Ascham recommended, was employed by the Oratorians. The authors most frequently studied were Terence, Phædrus, Cæsar, Sallust, Cicero, Livy, Virgil, Ovid, and Horace. In the Rhetoric form Quintilian and Cicero's *De Oratore* and *Orator* were prescribed. At the same time an intensive study of the set books was preferred to a wider and shallower acquaintance with Latin authors. Morin quotes with approval the dictum: "multum legendum sed non multa."

It has already been indicated that the use of Latin as a medium of instruction was not obligatory throughout the Oratorian school. In the colleges of the University or the Society of Jesus all instruction was given in Latin and this language formed the only medium of communication between the masters and their pupils. The Port-Royalists were bold enough to throw off the yoke of the Middle Ages and to make a whole-hearted use of their own language in their schools; but the Oratorians did not venture to adopt so complete an innovation and they therefore took a middle course. Lamy in his *Entretiens sur les Sciences*[2], in the manner of a modern apologist for the direct method, refers to the advantages of acquiring a foreign language by natural means, as when children learn to speak. He thinks that it would be helpful if there were institutions where Latin was the only language spoken[3]; but he realises the difficulty of the proposal, and its great drawback is that it would involve cutting off the pupil's connection with those who speak only the mother-tongue. None the less it is valuable to *use* a language "au lieu d'étudier une langue dans un cabinet." As a compromise instruction was given by the Oratorians in French up to and including the fourth class, in which the pupils would be of about the age of twelve; after this, except in the history lessons, Latin was the medium

[1] *Op. cit.* p. 153.   [2] 4ième *Entretien.*
[3] One is reminded of the household in which Montaigne was brought up.

employed in teaching. In three respects therefore—to sum up—the teaching of Latin in the colleges of the Oratory far surpassed the methods in use in contemporary schools, with the possible exception of those of Port-Royal. The emphasis is on the reading and explanation of authors, not on the writing of proses; Latin is used not so much as an end in itself, but as an aid to the fullest use and appreciation of the vernacular and as the basis of a literary education; the employment of Latin as a teaching medium, if not entirely abolished, is at any rate restricted.

The study of Greek in the schools of the Oratory, though not neglected, was not given that prominence which it had in the University, among the Jesuits, or at Port-Royal. At Juilly Greek authors were read and explained, but there appears to have been no composition in Greek. In the *Constitutions* of the College of Loudun, founded in 1628, the Oratorians undertake to teach "la grammaire et langue grecque." At Pézenas—a town which had entrusted its school to the Congregation in 1619—the municipal authorities in 1632 stated that "depuis longtemps" Greek had been taught and with success. When the Collège de Guyenne at Bordeaux was taken over in 1639 "la leçon de grec" is definitely mentioned in the document relating to the transaction. In spite of instances of this kind which might be multiplied, there are indications that Greek tended to take a subsidiary place in the time-table. François Bourgoing, the third superior-general of the order, complains in 1647 of the "ignorance of the Greek language" shown in the society's schools. In 1705 the inspector of the colleges at Saumur, Nantes, and Le Mans warns the regents in his report not to "neglect Greek which the superior-general wishes to be studied." An order from the general assembly of the Congregation held in 1690 directs that masters in charge of forms IV and V shall furnish to the inspector proofs of their knowledge both of Latin and of Greek. In the earlier days of the Oratory's existence instruction in Greek, where it was given, was in the hands of the ordinary regent, or form-master, as we might call him; but later on special courses were formed and entrusted to a *professeur* who devoted himself particularly to this subject. A course of this kind was established at Juilly in 1757. Lamy in his *Entretiens* classes Greek and Hebrew together as two languages which must be learnt for the proper understanding of the Scriptures and historical writers; and in his *Lettre du R.P....touchant les Humanitez* (which was addressed, be it noticed, to a young ecclesiastic who was in charge of the teaching of *belles lettres* in an Oratorian school) he gives advice on the choice of Greek grammars. But except for a number of sporadic and haphazard references, we find nothing very definite as to what actually was *done* in most of the colleges of the Congregation; and the writer therefore inclines to the view that in at least a few of them Greek may not have been taught at all; while elsewhere it did not as a rule go beyond an elementary stage or was confined to the readings of the New Testament or a simple text of Lucian. The influence of such Greek scholars as Mitre Mérindol[1], Pierre Thomassin, and Bernard Lamy doubtless made itself felt as time went on; and at any rate the curriculum of the Oratorian school always included so much of importance that was neglected by contemporary educationists that we can afford to pardon their apparent neglect of the elder of the classical languages.

The value which it set upon the study of history is one of the Oratory's chief titles to fame. At Juilly as early as 1634 there was a special teacher of this subject. In the two lowest forms sacred history was studied; the middle school learnt Greek and Roman history; while the elder boys took a three years' course covering the whole history of France. The lessons usually took the form of lectures or dictated notes which the boys afterwards worked up and thus the history lesson became also an exercise in French composition. There is a good deal of material extant which helps us to gain a clear idea of Oratorian history teaching. At Vendôme the professor of history, Lecointe, gave dictated notes which were freely used in other Oratorian colleges and became the model for this kind of exercise throughout the Congregation.

[1] He was superior of the Oratorian college at Toulon and wrote several works on Greek grammar. He died about 1670.

Some of these notes are preserved in the Bibliothèque
Nationale[1]; one of them deals with the state of Europe in
1649 and describes the progress of the Thirty Years' War.
It forms a succinct and vivid *résumé* of contemporary
events which must have proved of extraordinary interest to
boys at a time when the dry bones of Latin and Greek were
the staple instruction of the average school of the day. We
can well believe that the pupils of the Oratorian colleges
took up the study of history with enthusiasm and that there
arose in the ranks of the Oratory a succession of teachers to
carry on this work. Chief of them was Pierre Berthault who
entered the Congregation in 1622. Eight years later appeared
his *Florus Franciscus, sive Rerum a Francis bello gestarum
epitome in iv libros distincta*. This tiny volume, which would
easily fit into a waistcoat pocket, contains a summary of
French history from the days of Pharamund down to 1630.
It is written in Latin and, as its subtitle implies, is largely
an account of wars. In 1644 Berthault published his *Florus
Gallicus* which is a more detailed work than its predecessor.
It begins with the history of Gaul from the year 1986 A.M.
and comes down to 1630 A.D. It includes a chronological
table of French kings and a list of dioceses and universities.
The *Florus Franciscus* and *Florus Gallicus* were for long
in use at Juilly and at other Oratorian colleges. From a
modern standpoint it is easy to belittle the value of such
books, but that they did help to stimulate an intelligent
interest in history is abundantly evident. There is extant a
note-book made by a pupil at Juilly who had followed a
course of history in 1715 under Père Sauvage, who not only
taught this subject but was also superior of the college. It
is perhaps permissible to quote the character of Louis XI
as given in this note-book, although the original must
inevitably lose much of its force in a translation:

He was extremely clever and full of tricks and artifices; but
his evil disposition, his low cunning, his distrust, and his
deceitfulness will always debar him from a place among our
most illustrious kings. He was too partial to tortuous paths;

[1] F. Fr. 17571.

he overemphasised the value of dissimulation. Owing to his underhand methods he landed himself in difficult situations; he might have won over the great by kindness without rendering them obsequious through fear. He has been described as the greatest politician of his time because, always preferring expedience to honour, he thought nothing of breaking his oaths and violating the most solemn treaties. He was always ready to violate peace—though this sometimes cost him dear—always ready to lay down the arms which he had just taken up—a strange line of action for a prince who was so terribly afraid of civil rebellions. He often carried on negotiations without any desire to come to an agreement; he signed treaties at the very moment when he was plotting to break them. He risked nothing in warlike operations; he disliked battles; he thought little of foreign conquests....By nature he was neither kindhearted nor liberal. He never hesitated to carry on an intrigue, to corrupt and suborn the most devoted servants of sovereigns who were his enemies. It was easy to incur his displeasure, but it was difficult to maintain his goodwill. Innumerable were the heads cut off during his reign; innumerable the nobles and magistrates who were imprisoned, shut up in iron cages or, as galley-slaves, loaded with heavy chains called ironically "king's daughters." There was, again, in his character a ferocity which one usually associates only with barbarians. Bad brother, bad son, bad father, unfaithful husband, bad friend, bad neighbour, bad ally, bad king—yet pious, or pretending to be so—he made his confession once every week, often went on a pilgrimage, and gave gifts to the Church, for he feared the devil, and death still more.

The national character of the Oratory is nowhere more clearly marked than in the honour which it paid to the teaching of French history. At times it is a little difficult to avoid a feeling that there is something exotic about the Jesuit schools. In spite of their splendid efficiency they seem ever to look beyond the aims of education and to subject the individual to a rigid system. The true home of the Society of Jesus—and it would be proud to acknowledge the fact—is not in the country where it happens to be domiciled, but at Rome. The Oratorians, while abating nothing in their loyalty to the Holy See, were essentially Gallican and national, and they breathe a spirit of freedom, of keen enquiry, and of noble patriotism which stamps them as essentially French.

The teaching of history naturally involved that of geography. The class-rooms at Juilly were hung round with maps which the pupils could examine at their leisure. There was also a special library of historical books which the older boys were allowed to consult. But it was not only in history teaching that the Oratorians were far ahead of their times. The study of mathematics was held by them in the highest esteem. Within two years of its foundation, the Collège de Dieppe possessed a chair in this subject and there are innumerable references to the teaching of it in the records of other Oratorian schools. Manuscript note-books are still preserved which were written by former professors of mathematics at Juilly[1]. Nor did these teachers confine themselves to the lower branches of the subject. Trigonometry, conic sections, the calculus, mechanics, all came within their purview, though it is of course unlikely that all these subjects were taught in every Oratorian school. It was to be expected that a society which contained so many enthusiastic followers of Descartes should pay special attention to the teaching of mathematics. Lamy found time to write several text-books on the subject. His *Élémens des Mathématiques* affords an interesting treatment of the science. The book is not divided into separate compartments labelled "Arithmetic" or "Algebra" or "Geometry." Instead Lamy takes *grandeur* as his unit and he treats it in different ways, now arithmetically, now algebraically, now geometrically; he even includes an account of logarithms[2]. In short, he does for number what the Port-Royalists attempted to do for language in their *Grammaire générale*. He believes strongly in the value of mathematics as a factor

---

[1] At Juilly the boys used more particularly a book written by Jacques Fournenc especially for this school. In it, says Adry (p. 15), "ce Père en substituant l'autorité de la raison à celle d'Aristote, préparait la voie aux ouvrages plus parfaits qui ont été donnés depuis."

[2] Invented by Napier in 1614.

in education[1], because this subject teaches *truth*; and he says:
"Les mathématiques tenans donc entre les Sciences humaines
un des premiers rangs, l'on ne peut pas, sous prétexte de
piété, en défendre l'étude à la Jeunesse[2]." The contrast
between the attitude of the Cartesian and of the opponent
of Descartes is implicit in the whole passage. A society
which contained men of the type of Lamy, Malebranche,
Poisson, author of a *Traité de la mécanique de Descartes*, and
Jacques de St Denis who composed a *Traité physique du
Monde*, could not but favour any endeavour to discover
exact truth and thus encourage the study of any branch of
mathematics or physical science.

A description of the school arrangements at Juilly will
give an idea of the internal administration of a typical
Oratorian college. There were six[3] forms, known as *chambres*,
to which boys were drafted according to their age and
ability. The *chambre des minimes* corresponded to the
sixième of the University or of the modern *lycée*; then
followed the *chambres des cinquièmes, des quatrièmes*, and *des
troisièmes*. The *deuxième* or *Humanité* was usually called
chambre des moyens; it consisted of boys of the average age
of fourteen to fifteen and had the reputation of being the
rowdiest form in the school. The rhetoric form or *chambre
des grands* took itself more seriously and was allowed special
privileges. Its members were not forced to walk in line, two
by two, in the "crocodile" fashion affected by girls' schools
at a later date, and they were permitted within limits to make
their own rules—a democratic concession which is characteristic of the general constitutions of the Congregation. Above
the ordinary school course, which lasted six years, there was
the usual two years' course in philosophy.

[1] Lamy also makes a *practical* application of mathematics in his
Traité de Perspective and his *Traitez de Mécanique, etc.* The latter
includes a design by B.A.L.Y.M. (? *BernArd LamY Mathématicien*)
for a perpetual motion machine.

[2] *Élémens de Mathématiques*, p. iii of Preface.

[3] In some of the Oratorian colleges there was a preparatory form
below the regular school course. It was known as the *chambre des
abécédaires* and would correspond to the *Salle* and *Pater* (VII and
VIII) forms of the *petites écoles*.

The school-year began on St Luke's day—the 18th of October. The highest forms were allowed from two to three months' holiday in the summer, but for the lower school work went on until September 13th. The pupils rose at 5.0 and prepared their lessons until 7.30, when a meal was served. After this there was a short break followed by Mass at 8.0, masters and boys alike assisting at the Holy Sacrifice. At 8.30 the boys went to their class-rooms and the lesson, as was the invariable custom, began with a prayer. Each form had its own monitor or decurion whose duty it was to collect the work and within limits to hear the repetition of his fellows. This method, which was initiated from the Jesuits, relieves the teacher of a large amount of mechanical and uninteresting work; but it is easily open to abuse and would perhaps need to be applied with caution in an average English school. Morning lessons ended at 11.0 with the recitation of prescribed prayers or a reading from the *Lives of the Saints*. Then came dinner, followed by a period of recreation. After an hour of private preparation afternoon school began at 1.30 and lasted until 4.30 when a light meal was served. There followed another break and more preparation until supper at 6.0. In the evening there was a third period of private work during which history in particular was studied or the boys were allowed to write home to their parents. At 7.30 evening prayers were said in the school chapel, after which the pupils retired to bed.

Each class had its own form-master who was in charge of the greater part of its work. On entering upon his teaching career the Oratorian regent began with a set of boys in the sixth form—the lowest—and accompanied them as far as the third; at this stage he usually remained for two years and he also spent two years with the *moyens* or second form. This was followed by two or three years in the *rhétorique* and one or two with the *philosophie*. Thus every Oratorian schoolmaster normally spent ten or twelve years in ordinary class-room work, after which he was given special administrative or ecclesiastical duties. For the first five years of his teaching experience he was dealing with the same set of boys and he took most, if not all, of their work. One may perhaps be permitted to criticise this system. The young school-master, fresh from the university, is often more fitted to take the upper forms where a knowledge of his special subject is of greater value than experience in teaching. But as he learns the technique of his craft he becomes more fitted to handle classes where teaching-skill is of the first importance; and it would not be wholly unreasonable if the crown of the schoolmaster's teaching career were his promotion to take the lowest form of all. Yet, in spite of what has been said, the Oratorian system was not without its advantages. The influence of a good teacher with a vigorous personality, if applied in concentrated form for a space of five years, is a powerful means of moulding the character of his pupils. Moreover the ecclesiastical status of the Oratorian schoolmaster gave him a special kind of authority which a lay teacher in a so-called Protestant country can rarely possess. On Saturday evenings at Juilly each form-master catechised his boys and gave them religious instruction—a procedure which is either formal and worse than useless, or else a character-moulding influence of the highest value. In short—though there were doubtless many exceptions—the relationship between master and pupil in the Oratorian school was of a most intimate kind. It was far more akin to that which exists between the form-master or house-master and his boys in a modern English school than to the purely professional acquaintance which the *professeur* in the French *lycée* has with the boys whom he teaches with consummate skill, but with whose moral well being and out-of-school interests he is as a rule less concerned.

Yet it remains true that continuous association even with the most skilful and inspiring of teachers runs a risk of becoming monotonous. The Oratory sought to avoid this by varying the lessons as much as possible. "Professores," says the *Regulæ*, "per dimidias horas quoad fieri poterit, in classibus exercitia partiantur." The half-hour lesson, at any rate in the secondary school, is rarely of much real value. The periods of preparation also in Oratorian colleges never exceeded an hour and were sometimes shorter. The atmo-sphere of change and unrest which these regulations must

7

have introduced into the school organisation is a noticeable weakness in the Oratorian system.

At Juilly, drawing, music, fencing, horse-riding and dancing were all taught; but it must be remembered that Juilly was a "royal academy" for the education chiefly of young nobles. In the municipal colleges which the smaller country towns entrusted to the Oratorian fathers, we may well suspect that such polite accomplishments as these were unknown. Of games, as known to the modern English schoolboy, we hear little in the records of the Oratorian schools. Walks under supervision were permitted on Sundays and holidays, while simple ball-games, tops, battledore, etc. were not unknown. In wet weather the boys were encouraged to play at chess, draughts, backgammon and various instructive card-games similar to those which were employed in the Port-Royal schools[1]. In later days at the outbreak of the Revolution the elder pupils in the Oratorian schools—in common with those in all other colleges—were forced to undergo a form of military training which suggests the modern O.T.C. The cadets, armed with dummy muskets, went through their drill to the sound of the drum and were even to be seen route-marching in the surrounding country, headed by their school flag and accompanied by their regents.

In the *Regulæ a prefecto et professoribus observandæ* the acting of plays in Oratorian schools is strongly discouraged. Such representations were not uncommon at the time; the Jesuits had made them fashionable and one remembers that Racine's *Athalie* and *Esther* were composed for the young ladies of Mme de Maintenon's school at Saint-Cyr. If therefore the municipal authorities of some school staffed by Oratorians were to clamour for a play presented by the pupils, the project was to be discouraged and in its stead "exercices littéraires, qui ont les mêmes advantages sans avoir les mêmes dangers," might tactfully be suggested. Should the town authorities remain obdurate, "une tragédie sans ballets" might under protest be permitted.

The Oratory was more happy in imitating the Jesuits in

[1] See Barnard, *Little Schools of Port-Royal*, p. 158.

the formation at Juilly of an *académie*. It was a school
society open to members of the three highest forms and its
officers were chosen from and by the boys themselves.
Meetings were held every week and compositions, both prose
and verse, in French or Latin, were read aloud. At the end
of the year prizes were awarded to those members of the
académie who had most distinguished themselves.

Towards the end of August each class underwent a
rigorous examination and promotions were decided. There
was also a public speech-day at which prizes were awarded.
At Juilly the summer examinations were presided over by
the superior-general of the Society, who spent a week at the
College for this purpose. Three times a year the parents of
each Oratorian pupil received a report upon the progress of
their sons in manners, morals, piety, and school-work. The
document had to be signed and returned to the school
authorities. This practice was by no means usual at the time
and one may recognise in such an endeavour to win the
interest and co-operation of the parent, yet another point
of kinship between the Oratorian system and that of the
modern secondary school.

Something remains to be said of the administration and
staffing of the Oratorian colleges. At the head of each school
was a *superior*. "Superior," to quote the *Regulæ*, "toti
collegio et studiis universis præest." He is the final
authority in all matters connected with the college; but he
must temper gentleness with authority, remembering that
his power comes from Him who is at once "Roi et Agneau."
De Bérulle in his instructions to superiors[1] says: "Watch
over your charge. Feel a great respect and a great tenderness for the souls of your subordinates. Rarely command.
Seldom find fault, but continually set the example. Often
exhort; be a father rather than a superior; show more
patience than zeal." Such then was the spirit of the Oratorian school—"douce sans mollesse, ferme sans dureté."
Discipline was mild; the use of corporal punishment, though
not forbidden, was strictly regulated. To cite once more the
Regulæ: "Professores verborum contumeliis scholasticos ne

[1] Mémoire de direction pour les supérieurs; ch. XXII.

lædant; nunquam pedibus, manu, aut libris cædant; sed legitimis pœnarum generibus utantur." These legitimate kinds of punishment are elsewhere specified as impositions, detentions, and caning; but more extreme measures were not adopted until the sanction of the superior had been obtained.

The superior, or *proviseur* as he would be called nowadays, was aided by the *Père Assistant* or *Père Économe*[1], and the *Père Préfet* or *Grand Préfet*. Of these two officials the former acted as bursar. In his charge was an iron box containing the cash and valuables of the college. The *Père Préfet* (*studiorum moderator*) not only supervised the curriculum in the capacity of *préfet des études*, but was also responsible for the discipline of the school (*censeur*). His part it was to be the "Argus du collège." "Ipsius est invigilare assidue studiorum directioni et providere ut leges tam publicæ quam privatæ tum a professoribus tum a studiosis observentur." He drew up the time-table, placed the new boys, decided removes, inspected forms, had charge of the library and was ultimately responsible for the *académie*.

The actual teaching was in the hands of the regents or *professeurs*. The normal course of preparation for this work was a three years' novitiate at one of the training-colleges belonging to the Congregation. There were three of these institutions—at Lyons, at Aix-en-Provence, and at Paris (Notre-Dame des Vertus). Candidates were required to be not less than seventeen years old and must have passed at least through the rhetoric form of a *collège*. There was an entrance examination in Latin and French and also a searching passing-out test; but if the candidate's moral and intellectual attainments were satisfactory he became a member of the Congregation and started on his ten or twelve years of teaching in a college. So long as he was not in orders he ranked as a *confrère*.

The Oratorian teacher had a much less free hand than have most modern schoolmasters. His lessons had to be prepared according to a plan laid down in the regulations.

---

[1] Sometimes the offices of *Père Assistant* and *Père Économe* were separate.

His work was continually being inspected. Not only was
the *Père Préfet* frequently present at the lessons which he
gave, but an official *visiteur*, sent out by the superior-
general of the Congregation, also made periodic descents.
His visitations not only involved inspection of teaching but
also personal interviews with the members of the staff. His
official reports were sent in to headquarters, and in addition
the superior of each college twice a year furnished statements
as to the conduct, efficiency, and piety of each of his regents.
Those who survived this searching test of competence and
character were singled out for special commendation. The
English schoolmaster who, at any rate in the older type of
school, is practically supreme in his own class-room (if his
discipline is good) and tends to resent interference from
outside, would agree that in the Oratorian colleges the
system of inspection was greatly overdone. Yet it remains a
characteristic of French educational administration and it
makes for a high level of general efficiency. Regents who
could not stand the test were drafted out from teaching work
into some other post inside the Congregation for which they
were more fitted. Again, the fact that the Oratorian regent
normally spent only ten or twelve years in actual class work
must have ensured a vigour and freshness of teaching that
is lacking where a school staff includes many men who have
for a long period been teaching the same subjects to the
same forms and on the same methods. If a system of school
inspection can weed out, before it is too late, those who have
not and never will have any aptitude for teaching, and can
help the rest of us to avoid getting into grooves, it will
justify itself abundantly.

In spite of the Oratorians' thoroughness in teaching, we
can trace a tendency—especially in the early days of the
Congregation—to disparage mere knowledge; and sometimes
it is difficult to forget that even in the case of the Oratory
we are still dealing with a seventeenth century religious
congregation. De Bérulle says: "La plus nécessaire (*sc.*
vertu) à ceux qui enseignent est l'humilité contre la pré-
somption, la soumission, et la modestie de l'esprit contre la
science." We may spoil the Egyptians, but we should use

secular knowledge as a bait to win our pupils for God. In this spirit the Oratorian regents applied themselves in their vacations not so much to preparation of school-work for the coming term as to a course of retreat and prayer. Intellectual instruction is recognised by the Oratory as good, but the first aim of the regents is ever to win the affection and respect of their pupils and so to make moral education easy. Lamy, in a passage where he is pointing out the necessity of "patience et douceur" in teaching, says that sowing truth in the soul is like cultivating plants in a garden. If pupils prove contrariant it is often the fault of their master; but "when a teacher is gentle, when he loves children, he finds them gentle, he is loved by them, especially if he knows well how to inspire them with the fear of God; for he holds them by this bond and makes them do whatsoever he wishes." Not even at Port-Royal could the ideal relationship between master and pupil and its results upon the training of character be more effectively expressed.

The career of the Oratorian schools, although on the whole very successful, was not without its troubles. Some of these arose from the support which many members of the Congregation gave to Descartes. It has already been said that De Bérulle was a personal friend of the philosopher; but the Cartesian teachings involved a challenge to absolutism in politics and religion alike. Hence the works of Descartes were put on the Index—*donec còrrigantur*—and were condemned by Louis XIV and the University of Paris. Any society which favoured the new philosophy rendered itself suspect in the eyes of the political and ecclesiastical authorities. The troubles came to a head in the superior-generalship of Bourgoing (1641–62), a well-meaning but severe administrator. He endeavoured to limit the philosophy programme for the schools of the Congregation so as to exclude the possibility of teaching Cartesianism. This action provoked considerable opposition. André Martin[1] at Angers and Poisson[2] at Vendôme were the most prominent

[1] Author of *Philosophia Christiana*, under the pseudonym of Ambrosius Victor.

[2] See *supra*, p. 167.

of those who were made to suffer for what they considered to be the truth. But the movement could not be stopped. Malebranche, who had been a member of the Oratory since 1660, published in 1674 his *De la Recherche de la Vérité*. He has been described as "Descartes Christianised," and it was in fact Descartes' treatise *De Homine* which first attracted him towards the study of philosophy. The sixteenth general assembly of the Oratory, held in 1678, declared that any doctrines could be taught in the schools of the Congregation save those expressly condemned by the Church. This pronouncement was obviously levelled chiefly at Jansenism (of which more hereafter), but it evidently covered also the case of Cartesianism, and the king was graciously pleased to approve of the attitude taken by the official assembly of the Congregation. But this body could not control the beliefs of the more advanced members of their Society. Bernard Lamy, who taught philosophy at Angers[1], refused to deny the truth that was in him and was therefore removed from his post; none the less we find him writing four years later in his *Entretiens sur les Sciences*: "I cannot make out what has induced some of our writers to endeavour to render him (Descartes) suspect; it means grudging France and our own times the glory of having produced the greatest of all the philosophers." Many other Oratorians endured persecution for the same cause; "the fathers of the Oratory," says Mme de Sévigné in 1678, "are forbidden to teach the philosophy of Descartes and therefore blood is forbidden to circulate[2]." In the midst of these disturbances another assembly was held and the king compelled the inspectors (*visiteurs*) of the Congregation to sweai that they would allow no teaching of Cartesianism in the districts for which they were responsible. But the ferment of the new doctrine was too powerful to be confined by unyielding rules and regulations. In time the noise of the quarrel died down and the Oratorian schools took a leading place among those educational institutions which encouraged a spirit of free enquiry.

---

[1] Louis XIV referred to him as "votre petit homme d'Angers."
[2] *Lettres* (Oct. 12th, 1678), v, 493.

But there were more serious controversies in which the Oratory became involved. The Jansenist heresy, which is associated particularly with Port-Royal, had its adherents also among the Oratorian fathers. It was Bourgoing who, as superior-general, had this problem also to face. He showed himself even more uncompromising with Jansenism than he had been with Cartesianism. In 1657 he drew up a letter of submission to the Pope and induced 400 out of the 425 priests of the Congregation to sign it. His successors Senault (1663–72), De Sainte-Marthe (1672–96), and De la Tour (1696–1733) had a difficult course to steer. On every hand were dangers—papal bulls fulminating against heresy, discontented Jansenist enthusiasts in the very bosom of the Oratory, a court jealous for its authority, bishops divided among themselves. The secession of Quesnel and Du Guet from the Oratory in 1685 somewhat eased the situation, and they became the leaders of the Jansenist movement after the downfall of Port-Royal. But the quarrels dragged on well into the eighteenth century and at times the Congregation seemed to have lost much of its original spirit. The suspicion of Jansenism reacted on many of the Oratorian colleges and some of them even were wholly or partially closed down. The Society as a whole, however, remained faithful to orthodoxy and its last act, before the storms of the Revolution overwhelmed it, was to send a letter[1] of loyalty to the Pope.

Speaking broadly, the seventeenth century was a period of growth and progress for the Oratory, but the eighteenth century was a time of change and decline. The number of pupils educated by the society dropped from 1100 in 1700 to 389 in 1753. The school of Voltaire and the philosophical encyclopaedists were alike anti-clerical, and the spread of free thinking and the decay of reverence were fatal to religion. The Society of Jesus soon fell a victim, although its enemies within the Church joined with the most advanced spirits of the times to bring about this. Its expulsion from France in 1762 left a gap in the educational system of the

---

[1] It was dated May 10th, 1792.

country that was hard to fill[1]. The Oratory was made responsible for seven[2] of the colleges vacated by the Jesuits, but the question of staffing them presented difficulties. The situation was met by employing as many *confrères* as possible and introducing lay teachers as "associates," for not more than two or three Oratorian priests could be assigned to each school. This was clean counter to the original design of the Congregation as set forward by De Bérulle, and as a result much of the characteristic spirit of the society was lacking. Again, extended work meant increased cost; and thus lack of sufficient revenue was added to the troubles and difficulties which the Congregation already had to bear.

In the midst of these perplexities a new charge was laid upon the Oratory, and one which tended still more to change its original character. A project, emanating probably from Louis XV himself, was set on foot to provide "military schools" for the sons of officers in poor circumstances. The majority of the pupils were to be destined for the army. The first school of this type was set up at La Flèche in 1764, and twelve years later the scheme was extended. Ten colleges, in various parts of France, were opened and all alike were entrusted to religious congregations. Of these ten schools the Oratory received three—those at Vendôme, Effiat, and Tournon. The first two had already been Oratorian colleges of the usual type, but Tournon had been a Jesuit college before the expulsion of the Society from France. The curriculum in these military schools was of an extremely progressive type and had much in common with that of the "academies" of an earlier period. Latin was studied, but it was by no means the chief subject of the curriculum, while Greek did not appear at all. Special prominence was given to history, geography, mathematics (up to a very high standard), modern languages (especially German and English), drawing, music, dancing, and fencing. To some extent the courses were elective and it was possible, though

---

[1] See *infra*, pp. 231–232.
[2] See List of Oratorian Colleges in Appendix H.

not customary, for each pupil to have a separate time-table. There is perhaps little to be gained from a more detailed description of these schools. The religious aspect of education was not neglected; the pupils attended Mass every day and went to confession once a month. But the old strictly ecclesiastical character of the Congregation was obviously declining and the Oratory of the latter half of the eighteenth century was something very different from the society in the days of De Bérulle or De Condren. Doubtless the changes brought their advantages. The Oratory by its very constitutions was open to progress and new ideas. The convulsions which it underwent owing to Cartesianism and Jansenism are enough to prove this. When therefore the Revolution broke out in 1789 the Congregation as a whole welcomed the movement. In January, 1791, 101 Oratorian priests entered the ranks of the "new clergy"; and when the Assembly voted the abolition of ecclesiastical orders the Oratory was exempted owing to its educational aims and achievements. But the respite was not for long. A law of August 10th, 1792, decreed the suppression of all secular congregations and this time the Oratory did not escape. The college at Juilly was closed after the August prize distribution[1] and the buildings were shortly afterwards converted into a hospital for wounded soldiers. The houses of the Congregation were shut, the members dispersed, and their possessions confiscated. At the time of its suppression the Oratory presided over seventy-one institutions of various kinds, including thirty colleges and six seminaries. Of the 751 members who composed the Congregation 236 were priests, 394 *confrères*, and 121 *frères servants*[2]. The "assistants" would not of course be included in this number. An attempt was made in the nineteenth century to revive the teaching work of the Congregation; but it has little in common with that of the institution the history of which we have

----

[1] The writer has before him a copy of *Télémaque* given as a prize in 1792 to a pupil "in schola militari regia Effiatensi sacerdotum Oratorii Domini Iesu."

[2] Notice the proportions. In 1657 there had been 425 priests of the Oratory.

outlined, and we may do well to leave our account of it here.

The educational influence of the Oratory was not confined to its colleges. Reference has already been made to several school text-books which were written by members of the Congregation and which won a wide popularity. The histories of Berthault were for long used at Juilly, while the mathematical treatises of Lamy went through many editions. But Lamy was far more than a mathematician; in his versatility and wide outlook he is indeed the Oratorian schoolmaster *par excellence*. He taught *belles lettres* and philosophy successively at Vendôme, Juilly, Saumur, and Angers; but, as we have seen, he was deprived of position owing to his Cartesian tendencies. In his retirement he composed his most important work, the *Entretiens sur les Sciences*, a book which even to-day has a deep interest for the schoolmaster[1]. He looks at education definitely from the standpoint of religion; "sciences" (and by this he means knowledge in general) are useless unless they redound to the glory of God and the service of one's neighbour. To study aright we must learn to distinguish the true from the false, the certain from the probable; and for this purpose "il n'y a point d'étude plus propre que la Géométrie et les autres parties de Mathématiques[2]." He also recommends the study of logic and of this subject he gives an "idée." When this fundamental attitude towards knowledge has been acquired the pupil may proceed to a study of language, of history, and of geography. True to the traditions of his Society, Lamy is an enthusiast for history. "One should know the history of one's country[3]," he says, "...A knowledge of history is necessary to avoid being a stranger in the world[4]...History is a great mirror in which one sees oneself at full length. A man does nothing which another man may not or cannot

---

[1] Rousseau had a high opinion of it; he says "I read and re-read it a hundred times and decided to make it my guide" (*Confessions*, p. 205). He also learnt his geometry from Lamy's *Élémens des Mathématiques*. He found Pétau's chronology less interesting (*op. cit.* p. 213).

[2] *Entretiens*, p. 39.   [3] *Op. cit.* p. 103.

[4] *Op. cit.* p. 111.

do[1]." History, when rightly studied, shows us our dependence upon God, and for this reason the teacher must always be careful to give the right turn to the subject and so render it morally instructive. The book goes on to deal with the study of the classics and of philosophy. The writer's recent experiences evidently have not discouraged him, for he praises whole-heartedly the system of Descartes; "it is Descartes who opens this road, it is to his Method that we must attach ourselves[2]." The volume also contains "l'Image d'une sainte Communauté"—a description of the Oratory—and a list of books on all the subjects which the author recommends for study. The treatise as a whole is of great value not only because it sheds a side-light on Oratorian school-methods, but also because it seems to concentrate the essential spirit of the Congregation.

We cannot stay to consider in detail the other text-books which emanated from the Oratory. Lamy's *l'Art de Parler* is a handbook of the usual type for use in the rhetoric form. The author seems to regard poetry as a doubtful blessing[3] and condemns the theatre unreservedly. "L'on ne peut assister aux spectacles sans péril." Where a love-motif is introduced, the spectator must either imitate it or hate it—"necesse est aut imiteris aut oderis[4]." Thomassin's *Méthode d'étudier et d'enseigner les lettres humaines* is a huge and discursive work in six volumes. The main object of the book is to establish an accord between secular studies and the Scriptures. The problem had already exercised several of the early Fathers, and ever since the Renaissance crossed the Alps the necessity for reconciling humanism with Christianity hȧd once more been realised, and the task of doing so had sometimes proved a difficult one. Thomassin, however, is rarely at a loss. Athene's protection of Odysseus is paralleled by the story of the Angel Raphael and Tobit; the history of Noah is an antitype of the fables about Bacchus; Hercules is suggested by Joshua, Iphigeneia by the daughter of

---

[1] *Op. cit.* p. 112.   [2] *Op. cit.* p. 298.
[3] He takes up the same attitude in his *Entretiens*. Of the poets Virgil is said to be "le plus raisonnable de tous" (4ième *Entretien*).
[4] Seneca, *Ep.* 7.

Jephthah; Plato is proved to have had glimmerings of the doctrine of the Trinity. These attempts to render the classical writers *Christi præcones* are not without their interest, but for those whose chief concern is with the work of the Oratorian schools they have less value. Of greater importance is the *Lettre sur les Humanités*[1] of Du Guet, who after a career as an Oratorian *professeur* left the Society with Quesnel in order to throw in his lot with Jansenism; and the *Traité des Études* of Charles-François Houbigant who taught at Juilly and other colleges. The latter volume is of special assistance to us in attempting to estimate the methods which the Oratory adopted in teaching the classics, history, and French literature; but since the account already given of these subjects is in some measure based on the works of Houbigant and Du Guet, no useful purpose would be served by giving a more detailed description of them here.

From what has been said in the present chapter, it is evident that the contribution which the Oratorians made to French education was of first-rate importance, and it is somewhat surprising that this has hitherto been so little realised. For the best part of two centuries their schools flourished and many parts of France benefited by their activity. They did not confine themselves to pupils drawn from any particular social class; if the sons of "persons of quality" were to be found at Juilly or in the military schools, children of *bourgeois* parents enjoyed a gratuitous or cheap secondary education in many of the municipal colleges which were staffed by the Congregation. In point of numbers and influence the Oratory is, of course, eclipsed by the Society of Jesus; but as regards the character of the education given by the two institutions the Oratory easily wins the suffrages of the modern critic. The emphasis which its members laid on the teaching of history, mathematics and science, their spirit of free enquiry, their freedom from political aims, the mildness and sanity of their discipline—all these character-istics give the Oratorians a claim to be considered the most "modern" of French educators of their time. Theirs was the

[1] See Du Guet, *Lettres*, VII, 48.

spirit which made possible the Revolution; one of their
number was a deputy at the States-General of 1789 which
initiated representative government in the place of monarchical absolutism. Even when in 1792 the Assembly
abolished secular congregations, the Oratory—although
involved in the general downfall—was commended for its
progressive attitude and was declared to have deserved well
of the State. We may well agree with Compayré[1] when he
says that if we had lived in the seventeenth century it is to
the Oratorians that we should have entrusted our children.
With the Jesuits, for all their brilliance and thoroughness,
the individual tended to be sacrificed to the system and the
education which they gave ran the risk of being tainted by
the political and ecclesiastical aims of the Society. At Port-
Royal the teaching of the classics and the mother-tongue
surpassed anything that the Oratory could offer; but here
again the Jansenist theology complicated the aims of the
"little schools." Education came to be regarded as a
desperate attempt to save souls, and the schools of Port-
Royal never wholly lost their sombre other-worldliness.
Suggestive and inspiring as they are to the student of
educational history, they remained always something of an
experiment; they lasted for only about fourteen years and
were staffed by a body of men such as no other school,
perhaps—before or since—has ever possessed. Again, in the
colleges of the University, as we shall see in the next
chapter, the curriculum in the seventeenth century was still
mediaeval, and although reforms were from time to time
effected, the University was conservative in tradition; so far
from leading the march of progress, it usually followed the
example set by other teaching bodies when it at last realised
that it would suffer by not doing so. Moreover the fact that
students of more mature years as well as boys of secondary
school age were alike members of the University introduced
certain difficulties; and it was partly for this reason that
the tone was not always good, the discipline lax, and the
punishments severe. Against each of these three types of
contemporary secondary education—that given by the

---

[1] *Histoire des doctrines de l'éducation*, I, 236.

Jesuits, the Port-Royalists, or the University—the Oratorian system shows up with a lustre all its own. Its absence of artificiality, its practical thoroughness, its gentleness, its cheerfulness, its progressiveness, its high moral tone—all these characteristics lead us to feel that it was the best education of its kind that was given in France, or indeed in any European country, during the seventeenth and eighteenth centuries.

CHAPTER VI

THE UNIVERSITY OF PARIS (2)—ROLLIN

IN many respects Ramus was as one born out of due time. He indicated necessary reforms in the curriculum and administration of the University, but in his day little heed was paid to his recommendations. The University of his time was already on the downward grade and he was unable to arrest its decadence. The Wars of Religion so disorganised the social life of the period that the colleges were frequently shut down and the students disbanded. Henri III, in a document dating from 1584, complains that the college buildings were let out as lodgings instead of being occupied by scholars. Another cause of the decline of the University was the competition of Jesuit schools[1]. The Society of Jesus had established itself in Paris under royal protection in 1561. Two years later they opened the famous Collège de Clermont in which a full secondary education, as well as courses in theology, were open to all without payment of fee. Naturally the University could not expect to compete successfully with such a system, and in spite of the vigorous and persistent opposition of the older institution, the Jesuit College grew rapidly while its rivals languished. By the end of the sixteenth century the University of Paris had almost ceased to exist. Although forty-three colleges still remained, not one of them was carrying on the work for which it had been originally intended. The lecture-rooms had been converted into stables where the soldiery lodged their horses or in which farm animals were kept. Some of the buildings had been burnt down or damaged during the civil disturbances, and such parts as remained were occupied by persons who had no connection with the University, but who lived on

[1] The Protestant Hubert Languet writing from Paris on Aug. 26th, 1571, says: "Iesuitae obscurant reliquorum professorum nomen et paulatim adducunt in contemptum Sorbonistas." *Epp. ad Camerarium fratrem*, p. 107.

college premises together with their wives and children[1]. The accession of Henri IV in 1594 put an end to the Wars of Religion and so removed the principal cause for this unhappy state of things. The Béarnais was favourably inclined towards learning; addressing the professors of the Royal College, he once said: "I would rather have my expenses cut down and my meals reduced in order to pay my Readers[2]." Realising, therefore, that the University was in evil case, he turned his attention to its needs. He had a double task to perform; not only was it necessary to revive and re-start the whole institution, but at the same time some kind of reform was imperative. Amid all the wonderful progress of the Renaissance the University as a whole had stood still, hypnotised by the scholastic methods of the Middle Ages, though they had long since lost their original value and significance. Now a new era had dawned, heralded by Petrus Ramus. It is true that the reforms actually achieved by Henri IV fell far short of what was needed and of what had been advocated by Ramus and re-echoed by the most progressive thinkers of the period; yet the University did at last take on a new lease of life; it recovered something of its old-time dignity and in face of the competition of the Society of Jesus and afterwards of other teaching congregations its colleges continued their work with their former traditions infused by a new spirit.

But to accomplish this reform the direct intervention of the king was necessary. A royal commission was appointed and placed under the presidency of Renauld de Beaune, Archbishop of Bourges and Grand-Almoner of France. In passing, it is interesting to note that although the ecclesiastical powers are nominally represented in the person of the archbishop, yet the real control is with the Crown[3]. This

[1] There is an interesting and amusing contemporary account of these disorders in the *Satire Ménippée* (see *Harangue de Monsieur Le Recteur Roze*).

[2] See Poirson, *Histoire du règne de Henri IV*, II, 425.

[3] Cf. "La puissance séculière rentrait dans ses droits; et les rois avoient enfin compris que c'étoit à eux qu'il appartenoit de donner les loix à une compagnie établie dans leur capitale et destinée à l'instruction de leurs sujets." Crevier, VII, 54.

affords another indication of the fact that the University, although ecclesiastical in origin, had in the process of time passed under the power of the State. The doctrine of the supreme authority of the Crown over the University was definitely set forward by the Advocate-General Servin at this juncture when the proposals of reform were formally presented to the Faculties. It is a principle which has prevailed in France, but it is only within recent times that it has become operative in this country; and even yet, in the case at any rate of the older Universities, in spite of University Commissions, it is by no means fully realised.

After visiting the colleges, where they were horrified to discover the abuses already described, the Commissioners conferred with the Rector of the University, the proctors of the Nations, the deans of the higher Faculties, and the principals of the colleges. It was agreed that most of the regulations drawn up by Cardinal d'Estouteville a hundred-and-fifty years previously, should again be put into force, although various modifications and additions would be necessary. The revised code was approved by the king and laid before a general assembly of the University authorities on September 18th, 1600. Dissentients were not lacking. The Faculty of Theology, in especial, bitterly resented the transference of University control from ecclesiastical to civil authorities. The ultramontane and disloyal tendencies of some of the theologians were countered by a regulation that all members of the University, before taking a degree, should swear fealty to the king and the magistrates and should promise not to write against the liberties of the Gallican Church, the government, and the authority of the Crown. Other protests were made by the regents who feared lest their already exiguous remuneration might be still further diminished if the price of pupils' *pension* were cut down and if what the Commissioners described as "festins, accompagnez souvent de dissolutions et de débauches," were entirely suppressed. None the less, the cause of reform won the day and the revised regulations were adopted.

There remained the task of putting them into practice. This duty was entrusted to a committee in which the leading spirit was Edmond Richer. He was principal of the Collège le Moine and afterwards showed himself a doughty champion of the liberties of the Gallican church and an uncompromising opponent of the ultramontanism of the Jesuits. Richer and his colleagues had no easy task to perform. Some of the regents were ignorant or of evil character; there were even college principals who could be described as "peu reglez[1]." It was found necessary to punish the most recalcitrant with imprisonment, but an attempt was made to win over the rest by patience. At the end of six months little success seemed to have resulted from the efforts of Richer and his coadjutors. They therefore instituted a system of inspection of colleges and, with the help of their principals, some semblance of decent order was introduced. The chief difficulty that remained was to fix the amount of *pension* paid by *convicteurs* and *caméristes*[2]. The regents in particular resented the abolition of the *lendi* or *Minerval*, as it was sometimes called. Some of them went so far as to stir up their pupils and furnish them and the college servants with arms; so strong was the evil tradition of former years. Members of the Committee of Reform were insulted and even maltreated in the streets of the University quarter. The disturbances were so great that many parents who could afford to do so took their children away from the colleges of the University and employed tutors to educate them at home. Félibien dates from this period this custom, which became increasingly common among the wealthy classes in the seventeenth and eighteenth centuries. The Jesuits also reaped a benefit from the troubles of the University. In spite of their temporary eclipse consequent upon Châtel's attack upon the life of Henri IV and Mariana's writings on the subject of regicide, they were soon ensconced in Paris again and their success henceforward was unbroken. But in spite of these setbacks Richer and his colleagues did not relinquish their efforts and in the end their perseverance was rewarded. By the end of 1601, we are told, the face of the University was changed, the *lendi* was abolished, regents whose learning or morals left something to be desired had

---

[1] Félibien, ii, 1256.   [2] See *supra*, p. 6.

been supplanted by others who were better qualified for the position, and proper order and discipline had been established throughout the University.

We proceed now to consider the articles which constitute the reformed regulations as set forth by Henri IV, and under which the University was governed down to the time of the Revolution[1]. Naturally one cannot do more than indicate a few salient features and, as has been said, many of the statutes merely reiterate regulations which had been in force (if not always observed) for many years past. Educational administrators do not always recognise—even in these enlightened days—that the character of the teacher rather than the scope of the curriculum or the commodiousness of the school-buildings, is ultimately the determining factor in securing good education. One is glad therefore to find that the first thing recognised by the Commissioners was that unless the colleges were suitably staffed no progress would be possible. Article 1 lays it down that the regents must be "men whose conduct and learning are alike praiseworthy...so that while teaching children literature they may at the same time inculcate good morals." Masters and pupils alike must attend Mass daily; no Protestant may be received as a boarder and even *externes* are warned against making the reformed religion a topic of conversation. Vain swearing and reference to the name of the devil are proscribed. Masters and pupils are to take their meals together, and stress is laid on the necessity of seemly table-manners. Non-members of the University are not to be allowed to have lodgings on college premises. To ensure discipline, each college is to have a porter who will prevent pupils from leaving its precincts without permission. Principals are enjoined to maintain the full number of scholars on the foundation and to read to them the statutes of the college twice a year. No person may hold at the same time two scholarships or other benefices in two separate colleges. The *lendi*, as has already been indicated, was utterly abolished; "præceptores discipulis candelarum,

---

[1] They are given in Bréchillet-Jourdain, *Histoire, pièces justificatives.*

scamnorum, telarum, indicti, ut vocant, prætextu nihil exigent[1]." The fees payable to regents were limited to half an *écu d'or* a month in the upper forms and a slightly smaller amount in the VIth, Vth, and IVth classes. Masters who demanded, or even accepted, fees in excess of this amount were liable to lose their office. The cost of *pension* was of course additional to this fee for tuition, but it also was strictly regulated every year by a committee whose jurisdiction extended over all the colleges alike[2].

The curriculum as prescribed by the reformed statutes does not show any considerable advance upon that of the time of Ramus, although it is in the Faculty of Arts that the greatest progress is seen. By Article x of the statutes it was clearly laid down that no pupils under the age of nine were to be admitted to a college of the University. At this age they left the *petites écoles* where they had already learnt reading, writing, Latin grammar, the elements of arithmetic, the catechism, and church singing. When they entered the University they had, before anything else, to accustom themselves to the use of Latin for conversational purposes, because it was the medium of instruction. There are evidences that this custom had grown slack, but the regulation is now strictly reinforced—"nemo scholasticorum in collegio lingua vernacula loquatur, sed Latinus sermo eis sit usitatus et familiaris[3]." At the same time a real reform was made in that the teaching of Greek became something of a reality; here at any rate the labours of Ramus had borne some fruit. The stress was laid largely on the writing of Greek proses; but as the seventeenth century progressed the study of this language in the University declined and, in spite of the 1600 reform, Greek in the Faculty of Arts never bulked so largely as it did in the Jesuit colleges or at the "little schools" of Port-Royal.

The list of authors to be studied was prescribed in some detail and "libros neotericos[4]"—"misérables livres modernes"—were forbidden. The following texts are specified: for the lower forms, Cæsar, Terence, Cicero's *Letters*, Sallust, Ovid, Virgil; and in the rhetoric class, Cicero's *Orator* and

---

[1] Art. XXXII.   [2] Art. LXVII.   [3] Art. XVI.   [4] Art. XXV.

philosophical works, Quintilian, and poetical writers. Composition in both prose and verse was obligatory. As a
grammar the verses of Despauter were employed in the first
five years of the course, after which a work of the Dutch
scholar Vossius was used in the *rhétorique*. The chief Greek
authors recommended were Homer, Hesiod's *Works and
Days*, and Theocritus—a rather curious selection; while for
the rhetoricians Demosthenes and Isocrates were prescribed.
The philosophy course was but little changed, at any rate
so far as its content was concerned. In the first year
Aristotle's *Organon* and *Ethics* were studied and in the
second year the same writer's *Physics* and *Metaphysics*. At
the same time it is definitely laid down (Article XLII) that the
emphasis is to be laid on the subject-matter rather than on
mere grammatical points—"ut magis pateat rei scientia
quam vocum energia." The custom of holding Saturday
revisions (*Sabbatines*) was retained and the principals of
colleges were instructed to examine note-books periodically.
Promotions from one form to another were to be determined
by annual examinations and it was also specified that
exercises for the *maître-ès-arts* degree should be held publicly
and should not be taken before the statutory time. The
school-day for the ordinary forms consisted of six hours in
class and five hours of private study; but the pupils who
were following the philosophy course did an extra hour of
class-work from 6.0 to 7.0 in the morning. Thirty-eight
saints'-days were allowed as whole-holidays[1], although the
members of each college would be compelled to assist at
High Mass on such festivals. The school-year began on
October 1st. For the philosophers it ended on August 31st,
for the rhetoric form on September 7th, and for the rest of
the college on September 14th; so that not only were the
school hours longer than is customary nowadays, but the
length of the academic year was also greater.

If we compare the statutes of Henri IV with those which
had been in force during the previous century we may be
tempted to conclude at first sight that very little change or
progress is discernible. Yet the reform of 1600 was none

[1] See Art. XXXVII.

the less a notable event in the history of the University of Paris. To begin with, an institution of respectable antiquity and high dignity was revived from the ashes of its former self. In the last years of the sixteenth century it had become practically extinct; within the first decade of the next century it had taken on a new lease of life. By 1611 it was sufficiently vigorous to head a spirited attack against the Jesuits, in defence of the liberties of the Gallican Church[1]. A firmer yet less brutal discipline was at the same time enforced among its students, with the result that the seventeenth century can show us no parallel to the *lendi* riots which were so frequent in earlier days. Administration was strengthened and purified. During the reigns of Henri IV and Louis XIII the professorial chairs in the University were always occupied and often by men of considerable eminence. Such scandals as those against which Ramus protested in 1565 are not repeated after the 1600 reform. Again, the curriculum, although little altered in outward appearance, was henceforth to be expounded with something of a new spirit. Scholastic methods still persisted, but not with all their pristine vigour. The humanism of the Renaissance, as interpreted by Rabelais and as advocated by Ramus, had at last penetrated to the University.

Yet the reforms of 1600 were only partially successful. They revived for the moment the moribund University, but its decadence soon recommenced. "O misfortune," cries Étienne Pasquier, writing soon after the reform and remembering the University of the first half of the sixteenth century before it was devastated by the Wars of Religion,— "O misfortune—to my great regret this word escapes me—I certainly find a few sparks, but not that great brilliance in studies which used to shine during my youth[2]." The chief hindrances to progress have already been indicated. The Jesuits were spreading rapidly all over France; in every town of note there sprang up a Jesuit college staffed by expert teachers and administered with military precision. By 1627 there were no fewer than 3595 boys in the schools

---

[1] For details refer to Jervis, *Gallican Church*, I, 271 ff.
[2] Pasquier, *Recherches de la France*, ch. LXIII.

of the Society within the province of Paris alone. Nor were
the Jesuits the only rivals whom the University had to fear.
The Oratorian colleges, if not so numerous as those of the
Jesuits, were equally efficient. The "little schools" of Port-
Royal, although short-lived and insignificant in size, breathed
a new spirit into education and left an imperishable memory.
The Barnabites—or "Regular Clerks of the Congregation of
St Paul," to give them their proper title,—the Benedictines,
the Carmelites, the Premonstratensians, the Augustinians,
the Doctrinaires, and many other Orders began to busy
themselves with educational work, and some of them had
colleges of their own in the University quarter at Paris.
These schools, doubtless, did not all attain to the standard
set by the Jesuit or Oratorian colleges, but they tended to
compare quite favourably with the colleges of the University.
The records of a rectorial inspection made in 1642 show that
University discipline had some real improvement since the
reforms of 1600; but of the forty-three colleges under review
not more than half-a-dozen were specified as being able in
any degree to challenge comparison in this respect with the
Jesuit schools. Again, the curriculum in the Faculty of Arts
tended still to be too formal[1]; the vernacular was still
prohibited; the teaching of Latin was imparted largely by
the aid of antiquated text-books; the exercises of the
rhetoric and philosophy forms, even yet, were often barren
and unprofitable. The influence of Cartesianism was strongly
resisted by the rank and file of the University, though there
were not wanting isolated individuals like Pourchot, professor at the Collège Mazarin and seven times Rector of the
University, who welcomed it and were largely responsible
for its ultimate official reception into the philosophy course.
Another difficulty arose from the salaries paid to the regents.
Their fees, no longer amplified by the customary *lendi*

---

[1] In 1675 Louis XIV said to a deputation from the University:
"The way in which youth is instructed in the colleges of the University
leaves much to be desired; the pupils there learn at most a little
Latin, but they are ignorant of history, and geography, and most
branches of knowledge which are of use in everyday life." This
charge could never have been levelled against the schools of the
Jesuits, Oratorians, or Port-Royalists.

offerings and diminished by the rising cost of living, proved utterly inadequate, and a discontented and inadequate teaching staff was the result. So great was the difficulty of recruiting the ranks of the regents that in 1645 Dumoustier, the Rector who held office at the time, put forward a scheme by which "enfants distingués" were to be offered a gratuitous education if they promised to engage in teaching when they were qualified to do so. The honesty of enticing candidates into an inadequately paid profession by the offer of a free training will perhaps not be apparent to those who engage in other walks of life; but it is a method by which educational authorities of the present day sometimes seek to counteract the shortage of teachers. Fortunately for the "enfants distingués" Dumoustier's proposal proved abortive. Little wonder then that parents preferred to send their children to schools which were run on progressive lines and which sometimes provided a liberal education without charge.

Not unnaturally the University, in spite of the weight of its traditions, made some attempt to profit by the example set by its rivals. At first it tended to imitate Jesuit methods; afterwards the influence of the Port-Royalists, Arnauld[1] and Lancelot, began to be felt. But it was more difficult to emulate the gratuitous tuition offered by the Society of Jesus. In 1661, however, the Collège Mazarin or Collège des Quatres-Nations was founded by the will of the Cardinal. In it no fee was charged for tuition and the institution at once entered upon a career of prosperity unbroken down to the time of the Revolution. The number of its students varied between 600 and as many as 1200. But the Collège Mazarin was only one college among many, and it was not until the year 1719 that an arrangement at last was made whereby education in all the colleges of the University was given gratuitously[2].

A criticism often levelled at the University in the seventeenth century by contemporary critics was that the type

---

[1] It is said that his *Règlement dans les lettres humaines* had been followed in several colleges long before Rollin formally adopted it. See Bréchillet-Jourdain, *Histoire*, p. 214.

[2] See *infra*, pp. 201–202.

of education that it gave was too exclusively bookish and
suitable only for such as were destined for the Church. The
Jesuit schools did not disdain to teach riding, fencing,
swimming and other manly exercises, but the University
altogether neglected a number of pursuits which were
essential to the training of the future man of action. It was
the clerkly character of the ordinary type of secondary
education which led to the rise of the "academies" in Italy
and Germany—and to a less extent in England—as well as
in France[1]. In them the customary classical subjects of the
curriculum were supplemented by such "modern" branches
of learning as mathematics, modern history, geography,
modern languages, and accomplishments such as fencing,
dancing, riding and instrumental music. The curriculum of
the University at the reform of 1600 was not widened so as
to include subjects such as these; but during the seventeenth
century it became not uncommon for members of the Faculty
of Arts, especially the sons of wealthy parents, destined for
employment at court or in the army, to take extra classes,
either during or directly after their University career, at
institutions which were usually called *académies de manège*
or *académies militaires*.

Typical of such a school was that kept by a certain
Pluvinel who had been riding-master to Henri IV and had
taught horsemanship to Louis XIII. He is said to have been
the first man to set up a riding-school in Paris; previously
the sons of the *noblesse* had been forced to go to Italy for
this part of their education. By special permission of the
king, Pluvinel gave his lessons in a part of the Louvre which
was reserved for this purpose, and he was assisted by masters
who taught vaulting into the saddle, fencing, pike-thrusting,
dancing, lute-playing, drawing, mathematics, and "beaucoup
d'autres choses bienséantes à des personnes de qualité[2]."
These instructors were chosen not only for their skill but
also for their character, so that they might not merely
impart accomplishments to their pupils, but at the same
time set them a good example of life and conduct. In short,

[1] There is a good account of the "academies" in Adamson, *Short
History of Education*, chap. x.   [2] Sauval, II, 498.

there was not in Europe "maison tant accomplie ou famille mieux ordonnée[1]."

Another example of a similar kind of school was the military academy founded in 1613 by Pierre Laboureur and Samson de Lobarede; the latter, like Quentin Durward, was an archer of the Scottish Guards. They had invented a new kind of arms drill and applied to Louis XIII for permission to open a school in which it could be taught. The students were graded as lieutenants, ensigns, sergeants, corporals, *anspessades*, drummers and privates; the two captains were Laboureur and Lobarede. The whole life of the school was conducted upon military lines. Each member had his own arms and equipment and was not allowed to use those of another *académiste* under penalty of fine. A similar punishment was exacted from those who made repeated mistakes in fencing, who left the ranks without permission, or who so far forgot themselves as to indulge in profane oaths. The sums thus collected were handed over to the sergeant-major and devoted to charitable objects. Those who quarrelled were promptly put on sentry duty until they were prepared to compose their differences amicably. The school was closed on Thursdays, Saturdays, and Sundays; Fridays in Lent and the whole of Holy Week were also observed as holidays.

This institution was a military school pure and simple; it did not, like Pluvinel's academy, provide instruction in more intellectual "modern" subjects. But academies of both types rapidly became popular in France when once they had been introduced. They were not all of so irreproachable a character as those which have been described, and some of them fell into ill repute. At the same time academies were kept by most noted *écuyers* of the seventeenth century, such as Du Plessis[2], De Disancour, De Veau, Benjamin, Potrincourt, Nesmond—mere names to-day, but

[1] Alexandre de Pont-Aymery, *Institution de la Noblesse Françoise*, p. 2.

[2] John Evelyn visited the "Academy of Monsieur du Plessis"— "to see them ride and exercise the Greate Horse...here also young gentlemen are taught to fence, daunce, play on musiq, and some thing in fortification and the mathematics." (April 1st, 1644)—→ *Diary*, p. 60.

popular and important teachers in their time. In their
schools the sons of the nobility supplemented the education
which they had received from private tutors or in the
colleges of the University. Some of the teaching congregations, as has been pointed out, endeavoured to combine
the two kinds of education; but it is in the academy as
founded by Pluvinel that we see the germ of the *écoles
militaires* which Louis XV afterwards developed from some
of the colleges of the various religious societies[1].

The history of the University in the seventeenth century,
in spite of the reforms of Henri IV, is a record of mediocre
achievement. The dead weight of a tradition that had lost
most of its vitality proved a serious handicap, and the
competition of more efficient institutions was an almost
insuperable obstacle. But towards the end of the century a
new effort towards reform was made. The guiding spirit this
time was Charles Rollin. Inspired by Port-Royal, he took up
the task which Ramus had begun; and since he held an
influential position in the University, he had an opportunity
to put into practice the reforms which he advocated. It
will be worth our while therefore to study shortly the life
and work of one who deserves a conspicuous place in the
history of French education.

Charles Rollin was born at Paris in the year 1661. Like
his illustrious predecessor Ramus, he was of obscure parentage, his father being a poor cutler. While still a child Rollin
attracted the notice of a philanthropic Benedictine whom
he used to serve at Mass at the monastery of the Blancs-
Manteaux. This institution was one of the Benedictine
houses in Paris which engaged in educational work, and
Rollin's benefactor may well have been himself a teacher.
Be that as it may, he realised that his server was a "lad of
parts" and procured for him a scholarship at the Collège de
Plessis. The time was a favourable one for the studiously
inclined. The storms raised by the Jansenist controversy
seemed to have been allayed by the Peace of the Church in
1669, and Rollin, undisturbed by theological controversy,
pursued a brilliant career and in due time graduated in the

[1] See *supra*, pp. 177–178.

CHARLES ROLLIN
(1661–1741)

Faculty of Arts. He then embarked upon a three years'
theological course at the Sorbonne; but he decided not to
aspire to the priesthood and to the end of his life he was
never more than a tonsured clerk.

It was to the work of the teacher that Rollin felt himself
called. In 1683 he was appointed professor of the second
class[1] and four years later was promoted to the charge of
the rhetoric form. In 1688 he succeeded his former teacher
Hersan[2], a friend of Port-Royal, in the professorship of
Latin Eloquence at the Royal College; but the holding of
this position did not of course entail the resignation of his
teaching post at the Collège de Plessis and he continued to
discharge the latter duty until 1693. In that year he retired,
intending to devote himself to study and writing; but in the
following year he was invited to become Rector of the
University. The work entailed by such a position was not
that which he would have chosen, but he was ready to
serve his *alma mater* as best he could. "The burden which
you have desired to lay upon me," he says, "I promise to
discharge in full, so far as I can achieve it by toil, by
watchfulness, and by industry[3]."

Rollin made good use of the opportunities which his office
afforded him. In 1693, in company with his old friend
Hersan, he had visited the convent of Port-Royal. There
perhaps he had been shown the *Mémoire sur le Règlement
des Études dans les lettres humaines,* which had been drawn
up by "le grand Arnauld," probably for the use of those
who taught in the famous "Little Schools." At any rate,
there was a copy of this document with copious marginal
notes written by Rollin himself; and several of the reforms
introduced into the University during the rectorship of
Rollin are definitely recommended in the *Mémoire* itself[4].
We may instance his emphasis on the study of French, both

[1] Average age about 15 + .

[2] Cf. "Mr Hersan, ancien Professeur au Collège de Plessis, sous
qui j'ai eu le bonheur d'étudier trois années entières." *Traité des
Études,* II, 9.   [3] *Opuscules,* II, 240–1.

[4] The Preface to vol. XLI, p. iv (1775 and ff. edition), of Arnauld's
works says: "Nous ignorons la date de la composition de ce Mémoire;
mais il est vraisemblable qu'il a été dressé pour diriger ce qu'on

prose and verse, his advocacy of Greek, and his attempts
to render more regular and rigorous the examinations for
the degree of *maître-ès-arts*. His Jansenist propensities are
also shown in his disapproval of theatrical representations,
which some of the colleges had inaugurated in imitation of
the Jesuit practice, and in his earnest endeavour to reform
above all else the moral condition of the University. He
laid it down that in all the colleges a passage of Scripture
should be expounded to the students each day. Candidates
for the master's degree were to furnish testimonials as to
character. Rollin also took the opportunity afforded by an
extension of his period of rectorship (it lasted in all for two
years) to carry out a systematic inspection of the various
colleges of the University. The reports of his rectorial
visitation are still extant, and they help us to form an
estimate of the condition of the colleges at the end of the
seventeenth century. In all but a few cases the report is
distinctly unfavourable; the discipline is bad—"in eo
collegio non minimam esse disciplinæ dissolutionem" is a
typical remark; the administration is lax; in many cases the
proper number of scholarships has not been filled up. In
every instance Rollin makes detailed recommendations;
curriculum, discipline, administration, dress, and many
other topics are touched upon, and it seems obvious that
his inspection was at once necessary and beneficial.

Towards the end of 1696 Rollin's term of rectorship
expired and he hoped once more to take up the life of
study and literary activity which he had planned for himself
two years previously. He bought a house with a quiet
garden not far from the church of St Étienne-du-Mont.
Over its door he inscribed the Latin couplet:

Ante alias dilecta domus quo ruris et urbis
Incola tranquillus meque Deoque fruor.

But the opportunity of retirement and meditation was again

appelle les Écoles de Port-Royal. La copie sur laquelle nous le
donnons nous est venue du Collège de Beauvais, avec les notes de
M. Rollin, et d'un autre Professeur, qui prouve l'usage qui en a été
fait dans l'Université de Paris."

denied to him. He was prevailed upon to accept the
principalship of the Collège de Beauvais. The post was no
sinecure. The college had—so we are told—"peu d'écoliers
et pas de discipline"; but under Rollin's able administration
the tone of the place rapidly improved and the number of
its members increased so greatly that there was no longer
accommodation for all who wished to enter. It is said that
a certain father, fearing lest for this reason his son should
be refused admission, sent a bed with his boy's luggage,
together with a message that it might be set up in any hole
or corner of the buildings if only its owner could become a
member of the college. Rollin instituted several important
reforms at Beauvais. Not only did he tighten up the
relaxed discipline, but he rendered the general administration more effective by holding weekly conferences of the
staff. Remembering his own career as a student, he was
extremely liberal in aiding those who had difficulty in
following the University course owing to lack of means.
One of the most illustrious of the pupils who thus enjoyed
his bounty was the historian Crevier to whom we owe a
valuable account of the University. Rollin's admiration for
the methods of Port-Royal is shown by his introducing
into the college the study of French; and for this purpose
he recommended the *Grammaire générale* of Arnauld and
Lancelot.

Rollin's association with Jansenism was not confined to
educational matters. He was of a pious and even austere
disposition, and the gloomy doctrines of the Jansenists had
made a strong appeal to him. The Peace of the Church was
only a hollow truce, although for ten years Port-Royal
enjoyed some feeble autumn sunshine; but in 1679 the
persecution of the community and the attacks upon the
Jansenist theology with which they were associated, began
once more. An unholy alliance between the Court, who
hated anything which challenged absolutism, and the Jesuits,
who had never forgotten or forgiven the *Provincial Letters*,
waged bitter and unrelenting war against the unhappy
community. In 1709 the aged nuns of Port-Royal des
Champs were turned adrift from the abbey which their

8

Order had occupied for 500 years, and shortly afterwards
Jesuit malignity secured the demolition of the very buildings
in which they had lived. What was hoped would prove the
death-warrant of Jansenism itself was procured from Rome
in 1713. In that year Pope Clement XI fulminated the bull
Unigenitus in which one hundred and one propositions from
a Commentary on the New Testament, written by the
Jansenist champion Quesnel, were censured as "false,
captious, ill-sounding, offensive to pious ears, scandalous,
pernicious, injurious both to Church and State, seditious,
blasphemous, and suspected of heresy." Many Jansenists
had already migrated to the Low Countries, but the movement, in spite of all, still continued in France. Its adherents,
however, had much to risk, especially if they occupied
positions of eminence and influence. Rollin had openly
identified himself with the unpopular party and, like Ramus,
he was not likely to be converted by fear of persecution.
He had corresponded with the Jansenist leader Quesnel.
This correspondence came into the hands of the civil
authorities, and for a time Rollin ran a grave risk of being
incarcerated in the Bastille. It was also cast up against him
that in 1707 he had appointed two confessed Jansenists to
his staff at the Collège de Beauvais. At last, in June, 1712,
he was forced to resign from his principalship, though he
continued to lecture as Professor of Latin Eloquence at the
Collège Royal. In spite of the persecutions coming from
outside it is evident that he had endeared himself to those
who were under his care. Two letters have been preserved,
addressed by the students of the Collège de Beauvais to the
king; they put on record their sense of the efficiency and
kindness with which Rollin has administered the college and
they humbly pray that he may be continued in his position
as principal. Even after the blow had fallen and Rollin was
no longer with his pupils, their affection remained undiminished. On the occasion of his birthday in January, 1713,
we find them sending a Latin poem[1] in which they express

---

[1] It is dedicated "Ad vigilantissimum Gymnasiarchum Carolum
Rollin." This curious piece of academic Latin verse is reprinted in
Rollin's *Opuscules*, II, 437.

their continued regard for him and their unmitigated regret at his departure.

In spite of the persecution levelled at himself and at those whom he so highly esteemed, we may perhaps conjecture that Rollin found his compulsory retirement not without its compensations. He installed himself once more in the house which he had bought and betook himself to his literary labours. Of these we shall have occasion to say more hereafter. But Rollin's abilities could not be altogether overshadowed by the fact that his theological views happened to be in disfavour at court. University officials often used to call at the little house with the big garden, in order to ask advice of their former Rector. The most frequent visitor of them all was Charles Coffin, Rollin's successor at the Collège de Beauvais and, like himself, an adherent of Jansenism. Coffin perhaps kept his religious opinions somewhat in the background, but he is described by Sainte-Beuve as "un maître de la lignée de Port-Royal[1]." However, the clouds which had gathered round the Jansenist party were beginning to clear. On the death of Louis XIV in 1715 a reaction against the *Unigenitus* set in under the auspices of the Regent, Philip Duke of Orleans. To the mortification of the Jesuits, men of marked Gallican sympathies were appointed to the most influential positions in Church and State, and the Sorbonne formally annulled its acceptance of the bull and expunged the record of this from its registers. Doubtless, the question was not yet settled and the controversy continued to sway this way and that for many a year to come; but into the details of the contest it is not for us to enter. It is sufficient if we realise that Rollin's eclipse, for the reasons already outlined, was only a temporary one. In 1715 he was appointed Proctor of the French Nation in the University. In 1719 a reform advocated many years before by Ramus and re-echoed by Rollin himself, was at last effected. The *collèges de plein exercice* were now thrown open to all comers and tuition was imparted without fees; henceforth the University would be better equipped to compete with its rivals. This measure was made possible by

---

[1] *Port-Royal*, IV, 103.

the University giving up her old postal rights (*messageries*[1]);
in return for this the regents were paid out of the State
treasury and they were strictly forbidden to accept any
additional fees. Thus the University became "indépendante
du caprice des parens[2]," who might aspire to call for the
tune so long as they had to pay the piper; and at the same
time any student who was anxious and able to profit by the
course of training, which the colleges of the University
offered, would no longer be debarred from doing so through
lack of means. We can realise the joy with which Rollin,
who had known all the trials of an impecunious student,
would welcome this reform; and he was recognised as the
most suitable representative to express to the king the
gratitude of his "eldest daughter."

In the following year Rollin was once more elected Rector
of the University and he entered upon his duties on October
10th. But on December 11th he delivered an injudicious
speech in which he proclaimed his undiminished enthusiasm
for Jansenism. Although the heresy was not in so evil a
repute as it had been eight years previously, such an action
could hardly pass unnoticed. A *lettre de cachet* was sent to
the officials of the University directing them to depose their
Rector and to choose in his stead "un sujet plus modéré."
On December 16th, therefore, Rollin ceased to hold his
position. His place was taken by Coffin, his successor at the
Collège de Beauvais, whose Jansenism was doubtless as
sincere but not so much in evidence as that of Rollin.

Now at last he was free to return to his literary labours, and
the more important of his works all appeared within the
twenty-one years which elapsed between the end of his last
rectorship and his death in 1741. He refers to this period
as that of "le tranquille loisir que la divine Providence m'a
procuré[3]," and he dedicated it without reserve to the cause
of education. It is true that, as the Jansenist squabbles
continued and the Jesuit and Ultramontane factions again
triumphed, Rollin did not escape abuse. But he worked on
in his urban retreat, undismayed by the tempests which

---

[1] See *supra*, p. 4.   [2] Rollin, *Traité des Études*, I, 199.
[3] *Traité des Études*, I, 86.

raged without. During the last few years of his life his mind lost something of its former vigour and Rollin became involved in the extravagances which disfigured the later phases of Jansenism. Reputed miracles were worked at the tomb of the Jansenist deacon François de Pâris. Unedifying spectacles were witnessed when nervous invalids, worked up into a state of delirious frenzy, foamed at the mouth and declared themselves cured through the mediation of the holy deacon. But Rollin showed an intense and credulous interest in the *convulsionnaires*, and was a frequent and devout visitor to the wonder-working tomb in the cemetery of Saint-Médard [1]. The movement degenerated at last into open indecency and immorality until no respectable person could any longer countenance it; but for all this Rollin's adherence to Jansenism never wavered. Early in 1741 he was struck down by a serious illness which prevented him from carrying on his work. On September 14th he died, having reached his eightieth year. Contemporary feeling against his theological views was so strong that no eulogy or public discourse was pronounced—as was and is still customary—at his funeral. A belated attempt to do honour to his memory was made by Louis XVI who erected a statue of him in the Sorbonne. A picture of him also adorns the upper vestibule of this building.

The character of Rollin was one of singular charm. In an age when religious matters were too often only a form of party politics he was conspicuous for his innocency of life and his sincere, if somewhat credulous, piety. Every day he assisted at Mass and he never failed to read his breviary offices at the appointed times. In Lent he observed unusual austerities, and his pilgrimages to the tomb of the Deacon

---

[1] In a letter dated January 31st, 1732, Cardinal Fleury wrote thus to Rollin: "Je ne puis vous cacher qu'un homme de votre mérite et de votre capacité ne devrait pas être exposé au juste soupçon que donnent contre lui les assiduités à tout ce qui passe d'indécent et, on peut même ajouter, de ridicule à Saint-Médard." To which Rollin replied: "J'ai été quelquefois à Saint-Médard, qui est à ma porte, avec confiance dans l'intercession d'un grand serviteur de Dieu, dont j'ai connu et admiré l'humilité profonde, l'austère pénitence et la solide piété." See Sainte-Beuve, *Causeries de Lundi*, VI, 223.

Pâris have already been recorded. His pure and undefiled religion expressed itself in innumerable acts of charity. Yet he was never a wealthy man; at the time of his greatest prosperity his annual income is said to have been no more than 3000 livres, but his way of living was simple and he was content with little; he even refused to accept a pension levied on an ecclesiastical benefice. Like Ramus, he was a son of the people and he never forgot nor was he ever ashamed of his humble origin. Rather did it help him to appreciate the difficulties which beset the path of the impecunious student, and it explains his enthusiastic welcome of gratuitous education at the University. In allusion to the fact that his father had been a cutler, Rollin composed the following epigram to accompany a knife which he sent as a present to a friend:

" Ætna hæc non Pindus tibi mittit munera, morem
        Cyclopes Musis præcipuere suum.
Translatum Ætneis me Pindi in culmina ab antris
        Hic te, si nescis, culter, amice, docet."

At the same time Rollin had none of that contempt for rank and noble birth which sometimes characterises the best type of man who has worked his way up from humble conditions through sheer force of intellect or personality. He himself says: "It must be acknowledged that in nobility of birth and antiquity of family there is a certain powerful influence for gaining esteem and winning hearts. This respect which it is natural to feel for nobles is a kind of homage which we still feel it our duty to pay to the memory of their ancestors on account of the great services which they have rendered to the State, and, as it were, the continuation of the payment of a debt which we have not been able fully to discharge in respect to them and which for this reason must be continued for ever to their posterity." It is this kind of remark that helps us to realise that Rollin, eminent as he was, could not rise conspicuously above the level of his age. He was not a fiery, far-seeing innovator, like Ramus, impatient of abuses and sighing for a better world where truth and justice held sway. Rollin tended to take things as he found them and to make the best and the most of them; and thus, though he did much to reform the University of his day and is eminent among French educationists, he cannot claim a position in the history of human progress comparable to that which belongs of right to his illustrious predecessor.

What attracts us most about Rollin in his single-hearted devotion to his profession. He is not a statesman or a philosopher or an ecclesiastic or a man of letters, who happens to have an interest in education; he is above all things a teacher. He had all the virtues requisite for a man in his profession; he was enthusiastic about his work and regarded it not as a source of profit but as an endeavour towards an ideal; he was a skilful schoolmaster who could win the interest and affection of his pupils; he was a strict but not brutal disciplinarian; he was a sound scholar and yet could realise that the ultimate aim of education lies in the moral rather than in the intellectual well being of the pupils. Bréchillet-Jourdain says: "With Rollin there was extinguished one of the brightest lights which have ever shone upon public instruction[1]"; and it is perhaps worth recording also the entry in the register of the Faculty of Arts, which is the University's own epitaph upon Rollin and which does something to atone for the slights which his contemporaries offered to his memory at the time of his death: "Quamdiu vixit operam omnem suam ad id unam convertit, ut iuventutem bonis artibus, bonisque moribus informaret, tum viva voce, tum scriptis immortalibus quæ ab omnibus Europæ populis avide accepta et unanimi plausu comprobata, suis ætatibus, qualis ipse fuerit, satis declarabunt[2]."

Some account of Rollin as a teacher and university reformer has already been given; but there remains for us to examine his "scripta immortalia," which, even if they have not achieved that undying fame which was predicted for them, were at any rate immensely popular at one time and exerted a considerable influence upon the course of education in France. For the schoolmaster the most important of Rollin's writings is an interesting though some-

[1] *Histoire*, p. 376.   [2] *Op. cit.* p. 376 n.

what prolix treatise in four volumes, entitled *De la manière d'enseigner et d'étudier les belles-lettres par rapport à l'esprit et au cœur"*—or, more shortly, *Traité des Études*. It was written during the latter years of Rollin's life[1] and its special value lies in the fact that it is a kind of personal memoir; it sums up the writer's long experience and shows us a picture of the education which was given by the most progressive teachers in the University of his day. Rollin himself says: "My object in this work is not to give a new plan of studies nor to propose new regulations or a new method of teaching youth; but simply to describe the actual practice of the University of Paris, as I have seen it carried on by my masters and as I myself have tried to observe it by following in their steps. Thus, with the exception of a few points in which I shall venture to express private opinions (*e.g.* on the necessity of learning the French language systematically and of giving more time to history), I shall not in all the rest of this book do more than reproduce faithfully what has been the practice for many years past in the Colleges of the University[2]." As we might have expected, the book continually betrays the influence of Port-Royal. But whereas the methods of the Solitaires had been adapted to classes of only five or six pupils, taught by men of exceptional capacity, Rollin had applied them—with modifications, doubtless, but such as were necessitated by the altered conditions—to the forms in the Colleges. It is true that the influence of such educationists as Nicole, Lancelot, and Arnauld had already penetrated into some of these colleges—*e.g.* Plessis, Navarre, les Quatre-Nations, and above all Beauvais—because the men who happened to be their principals were sympathetic with Jansenism or its educational implications. But the rest of the University was not greatly affected; its excessively conservative tendencies had not materially altered since the days of Ramus. The value of the *Traité des Études* was that it traced a plan which was applicable to all the colleges of the University alike and which had already been applied in the most

---

[1] The first two volumes were published in 1726.
[2] *Traité des Études*, I, 79.

efficient of them. The author's own example and influence doubtless stimulated the circulation of the book when it appeared; but it stands on its own merits as one of the most important French treatises on education published during the eighteenth century. To compare it with the *Émile* is perhaps hardly fair. The latter work was written by a brilliant theorist whose influence on education was unbounded; but in spite of his short career as a private tutor Rousseau can hardly claim to be considered as a practical teacher. The *Traité des Études*, on the other hand, is above all a handbook for the use of the regent who is entering upon his profession, and Rollin also expresses a hope that his work may be of use and interest to parents[1]. Teaching methods are described in detail and are abundantly illustrated by examples which can be straightway applied in the everyday work of the class-room. Books of this type have become familiar in recent years, but they were by no means common in the France of Rollin's day, and this fact helps to explain the popularity and widespread influence of the *Traité des Études*. The reforms introduced by Rolland in 1766 were based on Rollin's suggestions, and the book continued to be reprinted, translated, and re-read until within quite recent times.

As is pointed out in another chapter, many of the characteristic French treatises on education during the seventeenth century had dealt primarily with the education of princes or nobles. Rollin strikes a new note; he dedicates his work not to some member of the royal house but "Amplissimo Rectori et almæ Universitati Parisiensi." Although he realises the special importance of the proper training of boys belonging to noble families, he has in view the education of all classes. "La jeunesse est comme la pépinière de l'État[2]," and therefore the aim of education is to make "bons chrétiens, bons fils, bons pères, et bons citoyens." Following one of the articles of the reforms of Henri IV, Rollin distinguishes a threefold aim which the teacher should always

[1] This is one of the reasons why it was written in French rather than in Latin. See *Traité des Études*, I, 85.

[2] *Traité des Études*, IV, 200.

have in view—the development of intellect, of character, and
of the religious sense. Each of these has its own value, but,
as we might have expected, Rollin makes religious education
the greatest of the three; to it the other two must contribute
if they are to be of any real value.

The *Traité des Études* is divided into several books; the
first deals with the study of languages, the second with
poetry, the third and fourth with rhetoric, the fifth with
history, the sixth with philosophy, while the last treats of
the internal administration of a *collège*[1]. These different
sections are naturally of varying value and interest for the
modern reader, but it will be convenient to retain Rollin's
own order in giving a short *résumé* of the contents of his
book.

Rollin starts by emphasising the importance of the study
of French. In most of the colleges of the University of his
day Latin conversation was still *de rigueur*. As early as 1532
Corderius had advocated the use of the vernacular as a
teaching medium and we have already seen how earnestly
Ramus had preached the same reform. The Port-Royalists,
and to a lesser extent the Oratorians, had put it into practice,
but the University as a whole remained uninfluenced by the
movement. The publication of an authorised dictionary of
the French language in 1694, the wonderful florescence of
French literature as regards prose and poetry alike, and the
adoption of French as a diplomatic and court language all
over Europe[2], had all assisted the reform; and all these
facts gave added weight to Rollin's contention that it was
a kind of shameful lack of patriotism for a Frenchman to
abandon the use of his mother-tongue in favour of a language
"the use of which can never be so widespread or necessary."
But Rollin is not content with using the vernacular merely
as a teaching medium; he regards it as a subject worthy of
study for its own sake and in his curriculum he devotes
two or three half-hour periods every week to this purpose[3].
He points out the importance of acquiring early a good
pronunciation and of avoiding dialectical peculiarities; he

[1] In the 1745 edition books VI and VII are erroneously numbered
V and VI.   [2] See *Traité des Études*, I, 296.   [3] *Op. cit.* IV, 400.

advocates the study of French grammar and recommends the Port-Royal *Grammaire générale* for this purpose; he would have his pupils study the style of great French writers such as Pascal, Nicole, Racine, and Bossuet; and by translation from Latin into French and by essay-writing in the vernacular he would teach the art of self-expression in the mother-tongue. Nowhere are Rollin's suggestions more fruitful than here.

He proceeds to consider the question of Greek. The classics were naturally the basis of education in the University of Rollin's day, as they were in all contemporary institutions which gave a secondary education. But in spite of Rollin's rather florid eulogy of the University's Hellenism and the statutes of Henri IV which deal with Greek, the study of this subject was not normally carried very far in the Faculty of Arts. Readers of Molière's *Femmes savantes* will remember the astonishment which greeted Trissotin's assertion that he knew Greek[1], and there is much evidence besides to indicate the rarity of this accomplishment at the time. Molière's play appeared in 1672; and although from 1683 onwards Rollin was teaching at the University and his enthusiasm for Greek doubtless spread beyond the walls of his own college, yet there is little to show that the University as a whole had greatly extended or improved the teaching of this subject. Rollin advocates the study of Greek not only for the sake of its literature—and it is for Homer that he has the deepest reverence—but also as a means to the right understanding of the New Testament. Like so many scholars of an earlier day when the dawn of the Renaissance broke over north-western Europe, Rollin found some difficulty in reconciling the study of the classics with the claims of religion. He is driven to extracting moral lessons from inoffensive pagan writers or he reads the truth of Christianity into the legends of classical antiquity—a favourite occupation of scholars in a bygone age. But a more profitable measure was the enactment, due to Rollin himself, that a passage of Scripture, preferably of the New Testament, should be studied every day by members of the

[1] Act iii, Sc. 3.

University; and this in itself would give some impetus to the cause of Greek.

We pass to Rollin's views on Latin—"le fond des exercices du Collège." Like Greek, it must be learnt through the medium of French. The reading of authors is introduced early, but easy prose composition is also begun in the fifth form where the average age would be about eleven. The usual texts are prescribed, but Rollin thinks it necessary to apologise for the introduction of Terence. The comedies of this author had been highly esteemed as school-books by many Renaissance scholars—especially by Erasmus—and had been advocated by many educationists since. But the Jesuits had banned his works, the Port-Royalists had extensively expurgated him, and now Rollin character- istically recommends the use of a *Terentius Christianus* compiled by a Dutch scholar named Schonæus. In the upper forms Latin conversation is introduced, but only during school-hours and even so only at stated times. It must be remembered that Latin was still the language of the Church and, to some extent, of the learned world, and that therefore the power to converse in Latin had still a practical value.

Rollin's views on the subject of poetry need not detain us, but it is interesting to note his attitude towards Latin verse composition. This accomplishment was still held in great honour in the University, because it was customary to celebrate events of academic or national importance in ponderous pentameters. In spite, therefore, of the small honour in which verse composition was held at Port-Royal and in the Oratory, and of the violent attacks which were being made on the practice by Fleury and Du Guet, Rollin still feels obliged to recommend this exercise and would begin it in the fourth form. In dealing with rhetoric he is more inspired. The subject, as has already been indicated, occupied the attention of the first form, the last of the ordinary school course; it thus formed a preliminary to the two years' study of philosophy. But the method of teaching it, which had become stereotyped in the University, consisted in dictating formal Latin rules—a practice which Ramus had condemned when it was applied to the teaching of philosophy. What Ramus therefore advocated for philosophy, Rollin put into practice for rhetoric. He recommends the study of authors; we must note for ourselves the methods which they use in order to produce the effects which they desire, so that we may apply to our own particular needs the rules which we discover.

One of the most interesting parts of the *Traité des Études* is that in which Rollin treats of the study of history. The reforms of Henri IV had not included this subject in the curriculum of the University, but the Oratorians and the Port-Royalists had already demonstrated its utility. Moreover, there was a marked and widespread interest at this time in this particular study. Bossuet, like most of those who had views on the education of princes, had advocated it, and Rollin, although he is not primarily concerned with *gens de qualité*, realises its value to the ordinary citizen. The three lowest forms, therefore, are to study Bible history; the third specialises in classical mythology and antiquities; the second takes Greek history; the rhetoric, the history of Rome down to the end of the Republic; while the philosophy form specialises in the history of the Roman Empire. "Chronology," after the manner of Archbishop Ussher, and geography are prescribed as ancillary subjects. One notices of course that the scheme makes no mention of the history of France and Rollin has repeatedly been reproached (sometimes, it would seem, by those who have not read the *Traité des Études*) with this omission. It is worth while to ascertain his own views on the subject. "I do not speak here," he says, "of the history of France because the natural order requires that ancient history should come before modern and I do not think it possible to find time during the school course to study French history. But I am very far from looking upon this subject as of no account; and I see with great regret that it is neglected by many to whom it would be extremely useful—not to say, necessary.... If we have no time to teach our pupils the history of France, we must at any rate try to inspire them with a taste for it...and make them anxious to study it when they have

time[1]." There is perhaps another underlying reason for
Rollin's attitude. History by him—as by many of his
contemporaries—was regarded largely as a means of inculcating morals; it was not so much a study of facts, of
movements, of tendencies, as a holding-up of examples which
the young should be encouraged to imitate or to avoid.
Hence with Rollin history tends to be mainly a study of
selected biographies each of which shall furnish a model of
virtue or an awful example; but in each case the moral must
be carefully pointed, as was always done in the stories in
children's magazines fifty years ago. Under a pronounced
monarchical *régime* it was obviously much easier to treat in
this way the careers of the great men of ancient times than
those of some of the conspicuous characters of French
history; for many of the latter were connected with the
still reigning house or with a system which was still flourishing.
When Rollin does have recourse to the story of his own
country in order to illustrate how history should be taught,
he chooses examples, such as the Chevalier Bayard or
Turenne, where the difficulty could not arise.

Rollin's views on the teaching of history have a special
interest because they are amplified in two works upon which
his reputation has largely rested. His *Histoire Ancienne*
which appeared between 1730 and 1738 consists of no less
than thirteen volumes. It covers the whole field of the
history of the peoples of the ancient world—Egyptians,
Carthaginians, Assyrians, Babylonians, Medes, Persians,
Macedonians and Greeks; but the book is full of excursus
and moralising reflections, and to the average modern
reader soon becomes tedious. At the age of seventy-eight
Rollin began his *Histoire Romaine* which, like Grote's
History of Greece, was written with a "purpose." Its object
was to show how the whole career of the Roman people
was but a preparation for the coming of Christ and how it
reached its climax and fulfilled its real purpose in making
possible the spread of the Christian religion. Judged from
the standpoint of the professional historian, this method
of treatment leaves something to be desired, and Rollin's

---

[1] *Traité des Études*, III, 9.

advanced age and special pleading led him again into long and wearisome digressions. However, he succeeded in finishing eight volumes of the book before his death in 1741, and the work was completed by his pupil Crevier, the historian of the University of Paris. He successfully imitated the unattractive features of the earlier volumes.

Though we may feel that Rollin's historical writings are of little value compared with the best works of modern historians or even with those of his contemporaries, yet this is not altogether a fair method of estimating their importance. We may not believe that Rollin's aim in writing history is the true one; but once having granted that aim, we must admit that he was remarkably successful. He was not impartially judicial nor even brilliantly inaccurate; but his writings gave a less critical age something which it wanted, and they therefore won praise which to us seems so little deserved. Rollin was compared to Thucydides and dubbed the "Fénelon of history." Montesquieu says of him: "Un honnête homme a, par ses ouvrages d'histoire, enchanté le public....C'est l'abeille de la France"; and thereby subtly suggests a resemblance to Xenophon.

The sixth book of the *Traité des Études* deals with the study of philosophy. It was not a subject in which the writer was very deeply versed. He himself says—somewhat ambiguously—"I have applied myself only superficially to the study of philosophy, and I have often had occasion to repent of this[1]." At the same time Rollin does realise that the subject is an invaluable part of the curriculum and he therefore recommends those for whom he writes "not to fail to give so important a branch of knowledge all the application of which they are capable[2]." In spite of the reforms advocated more than a century before by Ramus, and of the influence which Descartes had exerted on the teaching more particularly of the Oratorians and Port-Royalists, the University of Rollin's day—as has already been said—had only just begun to be affected by the reform. It was not until 1720 that Descartes's *Discours de la Méthode*, published in 1637, at last made its appearance side by side with the

---

[1] *Traité des Études*, IV, 120.   [2] *Op. cit.* IV, 121.

prescribed texts of Aristotle in the curriculum of the Faculty
of Arts[1]. Even so, formal logic still provided the basis of
the course and, as with rhetoric, its rules were dictated in
dog-Latin formulæ which had become stereotyped in the
course of time. Rollin strongly disapproved of these methods,
but he did not give to philosophy the function which would
be assigned to it in a modern scheme of education. For him
philosophy is not primarily a search for truth, a security for
freedom of thought. With Rollin its end has already been
determined; like history, it must be moralised and it is a
vain and profitless and dangerous study unless it leads the
philosopher to a surer belief in and more intimate understanding of the truths of religion which have been predetermined by revelation. Rollin therefore sets great store
by moral philosophy; he is interested in astronomy because
a realisation of the infinite in the realm of nature will aid
man to appreciate his own insignificance and the immensity
of God. So also is it with the study of plants and flowers
and animals—all redound to the praise of their Creator, and
the contemplation of His works should produce "the most
essential fruit of philosophy—namely to raise man to a
knowledge of the greatness of God, of His power, His
wisdom, and His goodness; to lead him to God Himself by
the consideration of His marvels in nature; to make him
appreciative of His benefits and able to find everywhere
reasons for giving Him praise and thanks[2]." The whole aim
of nature is to lead man to God; "la nature toute entière
est faite pour l'homme," and therefore the sciences are to
be studied not for their own sake, but for the moral and
religious lessons which they teach. It is easy to criticise
Rollin's attitude, even if one withholds no whit of admiration
for his sincere piety and his enthusiasm for religious education. A study of philosophy which is not inspired by a
free and independent spirit of enquiry, but is directed along
a prearranged path and towards an already determined
goal, may run a serious risk of becoming formal and vain.

[1] See New Statutes for the Faculty of Arts (1720), Cap. III, § xxii,
given in Bréchillet-Jourdain, *Histoire pièces justificatives*, p. 173.
[2] *Traité des Études*, IV, 194–5.

But it is only fair to bear in mind that Rollin is dealing with a two years' philosophy course for boys of seventeen or eighteen. To the writer—if he may be allowed to express a personal opinion—it would seem that a course in philosophical subjects, where independent thought was encouraged and its results, however heterodox, welcomed and discussed, would be extremely profitable to boys in the highest form of a secondary school. But there is still a large body of opinion that would regard this practice as too dangerous for youths at so critical an age. The subject known as *morale* in the curriculum of the modern *lycée* plays a part not unlike that which Rollin claims for philosophy, though it is studied by rather younger boys than those who take the philosophy course. As is pointed out elsewhere[1], its avowed aim is the inculcation of certain standards of conduct which should be adopted by the good citizen, just as the aim of philosophy for Rollin is to strengthen those influences which will produce the good Christian. In both cases the end seems to vitiate the means.

Rollin concludes his *Traité* with an interesting memorandum on the internal administration of a college. Like many writers on education from Quintilian downwards, he begins by debating the relative advantages of boarding-schools and tuition at home; and he advocates a *via media*— that of keeping boys at home and of sending them as day-boys to a college; but he makes the wise reservation that parents must ultimately decide each individual case according to its particular circumstances and must realise the infinite importance of their decision. In his remarks on school management Rollin acknowledges his debt to Fénelon and Locke, but it is obvious that he is drawing mainly on his own long experience at the Collège de Beauvais. The schoolmaster must study the individual characters of his boys; if faults are committed, he should seek to remedy them by discovering and dealing with the cause, rather than by resorting to punishment. He must jealously preserve his authority; to parody Horace—"puerum rege, qui nisi paret, imperat[2]." Yet he must command respect rather through

---

[1] See *infra*, p. 248. [2] See *Satires*, I, 2.

love than fear. Punishments as far as possible should be avoided and never given in anger; "boxes on the ear, blows, and similar punishments are absolutely forbidden"; the cane is a last resource and must be administered with due solemnity and after mature deliberation. Usually a reprimand will be sufficient and an appeal to a child's reason or sense of honour will prove more effective than a punishment. Politeness, punctuality and cleanliness must always be insisted upon. Study must be rendered as pleasant as possible and the fullest use made of the child's own instinct of curiosity. Adequate recreation and rest are essential. Rollin advocates out-of-door pastimes such as ball-games or battledore and shuttlecock; but, like James I, he feels that chess demands so much mental energy that it cannot be recommended as a relaxation for brain-workers. Finally the masters must set continually an example of good living and must learn to rely always on God in the infinitely important work which they have to do; they must pray for the help of "the Spirit of the Lord...the Spirit of wisdom and understanding, the Spirit of counsel and might, the Spirit of knowledge and of the fear of the Lord."

A chapter on the special professional duties of the principal and the regents ends the treatise. The principal stands to the college in the same relationship as the father to the family. His special care will be for the boarders; he must see that their food is plentiful and good and that the college buildings are kept clean and in good repair. He will inspect the teaching and will be responsible especially for the religious instruction of his flock. The discipline of the college is also ultimately his responsibility. Remembering perhaps his own youth, Rollin lays it down that the principal should take a particular interest in the poor scholars and not neglect them in favour of the fee-paying *pensionnaires*. Moreover, candidates for entrance to a college must be carefully selected and should any *mauvais sujet* have inadvertently been admitted, he must be expelled before his evil influence has had time to spread. The duties of the regents have already been touched upon. Rollin realises fully the great importance of obtaining the most suitable and best qualified men possible to staff the colleges. When principal at the Collège de Beauvais he had consistently followed this course, with the result that Beauvais became under his rule a kind of "normal college," where by association with the best regents in the Faculty of Arts students were trained for the teaching profession. It was largely for the benefit of these "jeunes gens studieux," who wished to become teachers, as well as for "jeunes maîtres qui n'ont point encore d'usage[1]," that the *Traité des Études* was composed.

Our ultimate estimate of the book must not be formed from a modern standpoint but, so far as is possible for us, from that of Rollin's contemporaries. We cannot help noticing that there is practically no mention of mathematics nor of modern languages, that the fine arts make no contribution to Rollin's conception of education; that philosophy and history are admitted only so far as they do what is expected of them; that education is still "bookish" and that the development of any kind of bodily skill is much neglected. In one or other of these respects Rollin had already been surpassed by the Jesuits, the Oratorians, the Port-Royalists, the "academies," and many another educational institution. But for all that Rollin marks an advance because he left a deep and lasting impression on the teaching of the Faculty of Arts of the University. His stress on the study of French for its own sake, the part which he gave to history in the college curriculum, were both of epoch-making importance. But far more than this, his personal influence in improving the college discipline, his indefatigable labours in systematising the details of administration, his contagious enthusiasm for the work of the class-room, his wonderful kindness towards his pupils and his colleagues—all entitle him to a high place in our esteem. The *Traité des Études* is the mirror of Rollin's professional career and therefore we can understand perhaps why Voltaire—while the memory of the author was still fresh in people's minds—called it "un livre à jamais utile." Time has lessened its importance, though the modern schoolmaster can still find in it much by which to profit.

---

[1] See *Traité des Études*, 1, 80.

But the influence of the *Traité des Études*, like that of
Rollin's historical writings, was very considerable in France.
Villemain, writing in 1838, said: "In educational matters
no progress has been made since Rollin[1]." Nisard, in his
Histoire de la littérature française, dating from 1861, re-
echoes the same sentiment—"In educational matters the
Traité des Études is the only book—or rather, it is *the* book[2]."
Both writers undoubtedly overestimated Rollin's importance,
but they serve to illustrate how his reputation as an edu-
cationist persisted in his own country. At this distance of
time we are perhaps better able to form a just estimate of
Rollin's contribution to educational progress. He is the
schoolmaster *par excellence*; he has some of the failings of
his tribe—a tendency to unreasoning conservatism, a somewhat exaggerated regard for detail, a propensity to become
garrulous upon matters of purely academic interest. But he
has also in a marked degree those characteristics which
distinguish every teacher who is worthy of the name—the
intense love of children; the deep sense of responsibility
for their highest well-being; and the recognition of the
teaching profession as a true vocation, to be carried on as
in the sight of God. For these things our hearts warm to
Rollin when the eloquent theorising of Rousseau leaves us
unmoved. We feel that Rollin would have been a good
colleague and a good friend. Such men, even though they
do not bear the stamp of genius, win our admiration and
our affection.

[1] *Cours de littérature française au XVIIIe siècle*, I, 226.
[2] Vol. IV, p. 122.

CHAPTER VII

A PLAN OF NATIONAL EDUCATION—
LA CHALOTAIS

IN the year 1561 the Society of Jesus established itself in Paris under royal protection and two years later opened there the Collège de Clermont which rapidly became famous and flourishing. Although the Parlement of Paris registered the royal letters-patent which sanctioned the admission of the Jesuits, there was considerable misgiving among its members at the intrusion into the city of a society of so markedly ultramontane a character. The political opposition between the Parlements—not only that of Paris but those also of the provincial towns—and the Society of Jesus became more vigorous as time went on. An antagonism of a more theological character developed during the seventeenth century between the Jesuits and those who followed the teachings of Jansen with regard to St Augustine and predestination. The Jansenists, like their adversaries, performed important services to the cause of education; they founded the short-lived but well-known "Little Schools" of Port-Royal. But the Society of Jesus, owing to its influence with the French Court, secured the discomfiture of the followers of Jansen. The Peace of the Church in 1669 brought a temporary respite in the struggle, but the strife was soon renewed. The Papal bull *Vineam Domini* once more condemned the Jansenist doctrines, and the destruction of Port-Royal was the result. Yet Jansenism continued to exist. Quesnel's *Commentary on the New Testament* provoked another outburst of criticism and theological hatred, and the Pope condemned the book in 1713 by his constitution *Unigenitus*. But even Papal fulminations could not calm the storm and the acceptants, who acquiesced in the bull, and the appellants, who protested against it, were as sharply divided as ever. The former party included the ultramontanes led by the Jesuits and supported by the Crown; while the latter were the adherents of Gallicanism who were backed by the Parlements. In 1730 a newly-consecrated Archbishop of Paris made an attempt to enforce the acceptance of the *Unigenitus* throughout his diocese. The king supported him by a royal edict, and demanded the immediate registration of this by the Parlement of Paris, without any opportunity being given for discussion. The magistrates made a spirited resistance and henceforth the breach between the Parlement and the Crown grew wider. The persecution of those who would not accept the *Unigenitus* continued; a system of "billets de confession" was introduced whereby the last Sacraments were refused to such as were not ready to sign an unconditional acceptance of the bull[1]. The Parlements of Paris, Rennes, Rouen, Aix and Toulouse distinguished themselves in their opposition to this uncharitable practice.

Meanwhile there had been growing in France a spirit of scepticism. Its causes were manifold and can be indicated here only in outline. The champions of the Reformation had cried up the right of private judgment and the liberty of personal interpretation of the Scriptures for every individual; and they had forthwith proceeded to contradict themselves by setting up rigid confessions of faith and enforcing them as binding upon conscience. Calvin, in short, had shown himself quite as narrow and intolerant as any champion of orthodox Catholicism, without having even the excuse of being logical. At the same time Protestantism split up into innumerable discordant sects, each condemning the other with almost as much enthusiasm as they showed in uniting to condemn the Church of Rome. From such a spectacle many thoughtful men turned away in perplexity and even in disgust. But when they contemplated Roman Catholicism they were confronted with difficulties no less great. Even if they were prepared to accept its dogmatic teachings, they were repelled by the unedifying sight of the one Holy, Catholic and Apostolic Church rent asunder by internecine

[1] Cf. Chapter XVI of Voltaire's *Traité sur la Tolérance* (pp. 159 ff.).

squabbles over the *Unigenitus*, by the bitter persecution
of Jansenist by Jesuit, by the savage treatment which the
Catholics of France meted out to their Protestant fellow-
countrymen, and by the unworthy lives of some of the
ecclesiastical dignitaries of the day. Thus there arose a not
unnatural tendency among those who called themselves
"philosophes," to identify Christianity with the various
ecclesiastical systems—whether Catholic or Protestant—
which professed to expound it. Wherever they looked they
saw a spirit of intolerance and against this they made a
determined attack. "They lifted up their voice," says
Condorcet[1], "against all the crimes of fanaticism and
tyranny; withstanding in religion, in political government,
in morals, in legislation, whatever bore the character of
oppression or harshness or barbarism....Their war-cry was
reason, toleration, humanity." They included in their ranks
writers and thinkers of the highest genius—Voltaire,
Rousseau, Montesquieu, Helvétius, Diderot, D'Alembert,
and many another—all bent on reforming the abuses which
abounded in the state and which to many of them seemed
to be fostered and perpetuated by the Church.

To such men the Society of Jesus—the champion of the
Unigenitus, the persecutor of Jansenism, the anti-Gallican
opponent of the Parlements—appeared to be a powerful
obstacle in the way of reform. Besides this, the Jesuits had
added yet another to the list of their enemies; they had
offended Mme de Pompadour, the mistress of Louis XV,
and this involved the ill-will of her protégé, the Duc de
Choiseul, who had recently been made minister for foreign
affairs. The tide of public opinion therefore was setting
strongly against the Society of Jesus—Parlements, Jansenists,
philosophers, and now even the Court were united in antagonism to it, when an event occurred which involved the
Society in a public scandal and delivered them into their
enemies' hands. A Jesuit named Lavallette, who was connected with a mission in Martinique, had for many years
been engaged in trade; and this had proved a very profitable

[1] *Esquisse d'un tableau historique des progrès de l'esprit humain*,
pp. 244–5.

πάρεργον, although it was an occupation expressly forbidden to missionaries. On the resumption of hostilities between England and France in 1754 several of Lavallette's ships, laden with coffee, fell into the enemy's hands and the cargoes were confiscated. The loss fell upon a firm in Marseilles to whom the vessels were consigned. An appeal for reimbursement was made to Lavallette's superiors in Paris; but while the matter was still unsettled, the Marseilles firm, being pressed by creditors, became bankrupt. The General of the Society of Jesus—Lorenzo Ricci, who had recently been appointed—disclaimed responsibility for Lavallette's liabilities; whereupon the creditors sued the defaulting missionary and were awarded a sum which he was utterly unable to pay. At this, the creditors determined to attack the Jesuits as a body, holding them responsible for the debts incurred by their agent. The court at Marseilles upheld their claims and decided that the property of the whole body was available for the discharge of the liabilities of Lavallette. The Jesuits thereupon acted with a conspicuous lack of their usual discretion; they committed the grave error of laying the matter before their most implacable enemy—the Parlement of Paris. They argued that in accordance with the constitutions of the Society there was no corporate responsibility, but that each separate college[1] was independent as regards its temporal property. The Parlement immediately demanded that these constitutions should be examined and the Jesuits were ordered to furnish a copy of them. The resulting report was unfavourable. It appeared that the Society not only claimed to be exempt from ordinary ecclesiastical jurisdiction, but that being subordinate directly to the Pope, it was in an anomalous position as regards the French Crown. Judgment was given against the Society and it was held to be fully responsible for Lavallette's debts. The decision was received with great delight. A contemporary writer tells us that the public "escorted the first president to the door, clapping their hands, and the result has been canvassed all day with the utmost satisfaction

---

[1] The mission at Martinique was dependent upon the *collège* of La Flèche in Anjou.

throughout Paris, which proves the great unpopularity into which this Society has fallen[1]."

The action of the Parlement of Paris in demanding an examination of the constitutions of the Society of Jesus was followed by several provincial parlements; among them was that of the city of Rennes in Brittany, which, as we have seen, had already signalised its opposition to the Jesuits on the question of "billets de confession." There the duty of examining and reporting upon the constitutions was entrusted to one who has a special interest for us; although he contributed to the downfall of the Society in France and therewith to the extermination of the Jesuit schools, yet he did much to show how a new and better scheme might take their place, and he was one of the first to adumbrate the modern lay and national systems of education. Louis-René de Caradeuc de la Chalotais had been born at Rennes in 1701 and, after a brilliant career as a student, had embraced the legal profession. At the age of twenty-nine he was already *avocat-général* of the Parlement of his native city. He early identified himself with the cause of progress and reform. He championed the wrongs of the down-trodden "lower classes" and induced his Parlement to address several memorials to the king on this subject. In 1761, when the question of the Jesuit constitutions came up, La Chalotais had been *procureur-général* of the Parlement of Rennes for nine years; but although he had acquired a considerable local reputation, he was unknown outside his own province. Such then was the man who on the 1st, 3rd, 4th and 5th of December, 1761, made his famous *Compte Rendu des Constitutions des Jésuites*. The bearing of the document is mainly political; but at this epoch, even more than usually, questions of politics and of education are inextricably intermingled and it will therefore be necessary for us to examine this *Compte Rendu* of La Chalotais before we can proceed to discuss his educational proposals.

He begins by laying it down that a religious Order in a State must have no rules contrary to those of the State itself; if it transgresses this rule it must be proscribed. Its aim

---

[1] Barbier, *Journal*, IV, 389.

should be to benefit the human race; an Order "which has for its object nothing but its own glory and self-interest would be essentially bad and vicious[1]." La Chalotais then proceeds to examine the history of the religious Orders in general. Their original purpose was "the conversion of sinners and the instruction of the faithful, the heathen, and heretics[2]." But in the course of time they have arrogated so much to themselves that now they dominate schools, churches, seminaries and missions, while the secular clergy have come to regard them as their "masters and instructors." Yet many of these regulars are idle folk, forgetting the purposes for which their Orders were founded. Looking back over the history of his country for the previous century and more, La Chalotais comes to the conclusion that to the religious Orders are chiefly due the theological quarrels and hatreds, the political intrigues and the party strifes, which have disturbed the State during that period.

After this exordium La Chalotais returns to consider the Jesuits in particular. Their constitutions show that they are a highly-organised body under the despotic control of a General who is responsible to no one save the Pope. Quotations from Jesuit writers are advanced to prove that, according to the official view of the Society, the ecclesiastical authorities are superior to the temporal. But, rejoins La Chalotais, "the Pope himself is not the absolute master of the Church and the Church herself has no power over temporal matters; she exists inside the State[3]." This thesis has been maintained by many different statesmen and at many different periods of history and it is a question which admits of endless debate; but La Chalotais makes it clear that if the Jesuit General is above the laws of the State in which his society is domiciled, there must arise a "choc des deux pouvoirs" which is inevitably a menace to good government. Because the Society of Jesus is a powerful body, ultramontane in outlook, and has used its power to stir up strife and to gain its ends by force, persecution and intrigue, its continued existence is a serious danger to the state. "After all these details it is not necessary to ask if

[1] *Compte Rendu*, p. 4.   [2] *Op. cit.* p. 8.   [3] *Op. cit.* p. 25; see also p. 72.

LOUIS-RENÉ DE CARADEUC DE LA CHALOTAIS

(1701–1785)

the Order and the regulations of the Jesuits are compatible
with civil government. If an Order is to be in harmony
with the principles of government we must not be able to
draw from its constitutions principles which contradict the
laws[1]." La Chalotais claims then, not that the Jesuits should
be banished from the country, but that their association
should be disbanded and that they should become ordinary
citizens, amenable solely to the law of the land. In a second
Compte Rendu, read to the Parlement of Rennes in 1762,
he elaborates his original theme. He draws a distinction
between the secular clergy, who are Frenchmen and citizens,
and the regulars, who too often are ultramontane and whose
patriotism is therefore suspect. He quotes once more from
Jesuit writers who have exalted the ecclesiastical power at
the expense of the civil authority, and again he demands
the dissolution of the Society.

At the time when La Chalotais drew up his two *Comptes
Rendus* the Jesuits had been for more than a century and
a half the foremost educators in France. As we might have
expected, their methods had not escaped criticism. La
Chalotais complains that these are prejudiced and tinged
with "the spirit of ultramontanism and of the Inquisition[2]."
Their teaching is based on the *Ratio Studiorum* which dates
from the sixteenth century and has never been revised; the
driest and narrowest classical curriculum is in vogue, while
scientific or historical enquiry is discouraged. The result is
an "éducation pédantesque et monastique." Yet, in spite
of this inadequate system, each Jesuit college is erected into
a university, conferring degrees in opposition to the ordinary
universities and forbidding Jesuit students to graduate
elsewhere. La Chalotais realises that the schools of the
Society of Jesus were not unique in giving a type of education which was obsolete and inadequate. He concludes
his first *Compte Rendu* with an appeal to the king, part of
which merits quotation. "Reform, Sire," he says, "the
education of youth in all the colleges (*i.e.* secondary schools)
of your kingdom; it is faulty and barbarous, especially in
the Jesuit colleges. All men of sense and education are

[1] *Compte Rendu*, p. 102.　　　[2] *Op. cit.* p. 214.

agreed on this point. Encourage literature and the sciences; from them are derived the glory and happiness of kingdoms and the honour of sovereigns....Grant us, Sire, teachers who will be loyal to your Majesty and the State through a sense of duty, of principle, and of religion. Your Majesty has in his universities and academies men of conspicuous merit and ability. They are Frenchmen by birth and choice; they are also Frenchmen by conviction. They know well the principles upon which your government is based and give them their strongest support. Bid these men draw up a scheme of education for all ages and for all callings, and let them compose elementary books to carry out this plan. You will supervise their publication and will have them taught in all schools by masters whom you consider worthy of these duties and of your choice[1]."

While La Chalotais was presenting his *Comptes Rendus* to the Parlement of Rennes similar documents were being prepared by lawyers of eminence in many parts of France and were being laid before the provincial Parlements. All alike agreed in regarding the continued existence of the Society of Jesus as a menace to the State. The Jesuits, on their side, naturally did not remain idle but defended themselves with vigour. Books and pamphlets innumerable were put forth by both parties and the Jansenist periodical *Nouvelles ecclésiastiques* performed prodigies of valour in an attempt to avenge ancient wrongs. As has been indicated, the Jansenists, "philosophes," and Parlements were backed by a strong body of public opinion and against that opinion not even the Jesuits could stand. The Parlement of Rennes published an *arrêt*, dated May 27th, 1762, which ordered the dissolution of the "Society of the so-called Jesuits"; and at the beginning of the following August the Society left Brittany. A similar decree of the Parlement of Paris was issued on August 6th, 1762, and this example was followed by the provincial Parlements. Finally, in November, 1764, a royal order confirmed the abolition of the Society throughout France. Thus the Society of Jesus passed from the country; it had already been exiled from Portugal and now Spain,

[1] *Compte Rendu*, pp. 165–7.

Naples, and Parma also dispersed the unfortunate Jesuits. In 1773 the Pope himself—Clement XIV—suppressed the Society. Thirty years later it came into existence again, but although its influence is still great it has never regained its former power.

The reasons for the downfall of the Jesuits were many and they cannot be discussed in detail here. But for our particular purpose it is desirable to examine the strictures which La Chalotais passes upon the education given by the Society of Jesus. Unfortunately there seems to be no human (or divine) institution about which it is more difficult to hold an unbiased view. Among the champions of Protestantism the word "Jesuit" has become a convenient summary for all that is dishonest and superstitious; while in the eyes of their partisans nothing that the Jesuits have ever done may be adversely criticised, and the most serious charges which have been brought against the Society are summarily disposed of as calumnies. La Chalotais, for all his legal training and parade of impartiality, can hardly be regarded as an unbiased critic. The opening paragraphs of his first *Compte Rendu* make it quite clear that he is the counsel for the prosecution. Let us then, who have no *parti pris*, endeavour to estimate more calmly the character of the education which the Jesuits had been giving with conspicuous success in all parts of France for more than a century and a half.

The school system of the Society was highly organised. Every detail of teaching method and school routine had been carefully thought out and tested in practice. The teachers were, on the whole, men of ability who had been prepared for their duties by a rigorous system of training. The keynote of the school-work was thoroughness; every point was driven home and made fast by frequent repetition. Interest in the lesson was fostered by appeals to emulation and the pupil's own sense of *amour propre*. The hours of work were shorter than was usual in other schools and the methods of discipline were commendably mild when compared with those in general use elsewhere. Nor was provision made for intellectual education alone; bodily health was regarded as of great importance and many kinds of physical exercises were held in honour. A school which can combine advantages such as these can hardly fail to be efficient, and when we add that no fees were payable, it is not difficult to realise why the Jesuit colleges won an immediate and continued success. Throughout its sojourn in France the Society of Jesus controlled a large and important part of the secondary education of the country. At the time when La Chalotais made his attack there were more than 150 Jesuit institutions in France and the members of the Society numbered over three thousand. It was estimated that since the Jesuits had been domiciled in France more than two million pupils had passed through their colleges. In the single Collège de Clermont at Paris in the year 1729 there were some 500 boarders; and the popularity of the school was such that it was necessary to enter the names of intending pupils a year in advance. In Rennes itself the Jesuit college, founded in 1603, educated in the course of its career more than 4000 boys.

The curriculum of these schools, which was so adversely criticised by La Chalotais, was based on a document called the *Ratio Studiorum*. This had been drawn up in 1599 and remained the authoritative plan of studies until the suppression of the Society in 1773. In it everything was carefully mapped out and correlated so that the teacher had a code of instructions which was his constant guide. The classical languages naturally formed the basis of the curriculum. Latin was to be the medium of instruction and even of conversation and the use of the vernacular was, as far as possible, discouraged. The methods of teaching philosophy were scholastic and there was no scope allowed for independent enquiry. This scheme, though it stands self-condemned when judged from a twentieth-century standpoint, was normal in the secondary schools of the period when the *Ratio Studiorum* was drawn up. We have already seen it at work in the University of Paris. But during the seventeenth and eighteenth centuries real progress had been made in the content of the curriculum. The Port-Royalists and Oratorians had successfully introduced the use of the mother-tongue, as well as the study of French literature and history, of mathematics and the sciences. Scholasticism had gradually disappeared; under the inspiration of Descartes independence of mind and a love of truth for its own sake had not only been welcomed at Port-Royal and in the Oratory but had even made some headway in the colleges of the University. Amid all this real advance the Society of Jesus remained immobile, still tied fast to the *Ratio Studiorum*. The various *comptes rendus*, of which that of La Chalotais is the most important example, are full of complaints on this head. French authors are neglected; classical or biblical history may be taught but the pupils learn nothing of their own country's past; philosophy consists merely in copying down and learning by heart a number of empty phrases and formal arguments. There is indeed considerable justification for La Chalotais' complaint that the education given by the Society of Jesus was "pedantic and monastic."

The efficiency of the Jesuit colleges, in spite of the inadequacy of their curriculum, continually aroused the opposition and jealousy of the universities. One of the chief grievances alleged against the Society was that its colleges granted degrees to those who had passed through the prescribed course. As we have seen, La Chalotais also complains of this practice. Yet the Society had a real right to the privilege. It has been pointed out in a former chapter[1] that the power of granting degrees to students of the University of Paris was held by a chancellor to whom this authority had been committed by the Pope himself. In theory the Pope was the ultimate "fountain of honour," although he might delegate his functions to a chancellor or bishop or other ecclesiastical dignitary. The right to confer degrees which the Archbishop of Canterbury still possesses, is a post-Reformation survival of this practice. But the General of the Society of Jesus, as we have seen, was responsible directly to the Holy See and from it he had obtained amongst other privileges that of granting degrees. In this respect his position was similar to that of the

9   [1] See *supra*, p. 1.

Chancellor of Notre-Dame. When therefore La Chalotais suggests that in exercising this power the Society of Jesus is infringing a prerogative of the universities, he does the Jesuits an injustice. At the same time it must be confessed that the right had not always been exercised with due discretion. Persons of mediocre attainments were sometimes admitted to the status of master of arts without being compelled to submit to any kind of examination. Similar complaints are heard from time to time about the University of Paris[1]; at Oxford it is only within the last hundred years or so that the general standard for degrees has been to any extent rigorously enforced. Such facts, although they do not excuse the shortcomings of the Society of Jesus in this respect, do at any rate afford some kind of explanation.

The most serious charge which La Chalotais brings against the Jesuit system of education is that of being "tinged with the spirit of ultramontanism and of the Inquisition." It cannot be denied that the Jesuits were what may be called an "international" Congregation, and therefore an enthusiastic patriot might excusably regard them as anti-national. The motto of the Society was "Ad Maiorem Dei Gloriam" (A.M.D.G.), and as Quick[2] well points out, the Jesuits too often regarded the glory of God and the success of their Society as convertible terms. The fault which vitiated the Jesuit educational system from beginning to end was that its aim was not primarily and above all things the best intellectual and moral development of the individual pupil; it was rather the advancement of the Society as a whole and the extension of its influence. No doubt it is quite possible to achieve the highest interests of the individual in securing those of the institution to which he belongs; but in education we must aim first at the former and acquire the latter as a by-product. The Jesuits tended to reverse the process. Their

[1] For example, from 1395 to 1500 no candidate for a degree in the University of Paris was rejected. See also Gaston Boissier, "La Réforme des Études au XVIᵉ Siècle" in *Revue des Deux Mondes*, vol. LIV., Dec. 1882.

[2] *Educational Reformers*, chap. IV. Quick's chapter on Jesuit education is still the best short account of the subject and the fairest estimate known to the present writer.

political and ecclesiastical activities often reacted adversely
on the spirit of their schools. Originality of thought,
initiative, pursuit of truth for its own sake—all these might
be subversive of a cast-iron system and they were therefore
ruthlessly suppressed. Up to a point the teachers of the
Society of Jesus were marvellously effective and among
their educational methods there are many worthy of
admiration and imitation. Yet one is forced reluctantly to
agree with La Chalotais in thinking that their system was a
bad one because it missed the true aim of education; it was
not disinterested. The growing realisation of this fact had
contributed to the increasing unpopularity of the Society in
France. The Oratorian schools had offered an example of
an enlightened and progressive system, interpreted by
teachers who were Frenchmen not only by birth, but also
by allegiance, and who cherished no political aims which
might conflict with those of the State. Thus the Jesuits had
begun to suffer an eclipse. Men were coming to realise that
in education there are factors of greater importance than
mere efficiency of teaching and organisation, or even the
absence of school fees. The spirit of the times demanded a
training which would produce citizens well-equipped to play
their part in the State to which they belonged, free from the
trammels of prejudice and tradition, and ready to welcome
new ideas in a spirit of tolerant criticism. The distant
thunder of the Revolution can already be heard.

The Jesuits, then, after having made so striking a contribution to the secondary education of France, disappeared
from the country and their colleges ceased to exist. But it
was easier to put an end to a great teaching institution than
to find a newer and more suitable educational system ready-
made to take its place. In La Chalotais' own city of Rennes,
for example, the departure of the Society left a gap which
was very difficult to fill; a staff and an organisation were
improvised, but it proved impossible to offer any longer a
gratuitous education, and a fee of twelve livres for each
pupil was levied until other arrangements could be made.
All over France, in fact, a "kind of anarchy[1]" reigned in

[1] Cf. Rolland, *Recueil*, p. 429.

the schools and there was a general outcry for the immediate institution of a new, efficient and reformed system of education. It was to the Parlements that the situation was due, and it was to the Parlements therefore that the public looked for schemes of reorganisation. Thus it came about that those who had but recently been examining the Jesuit constitutions and straining every nerve to secure the dissolution of the Society, now turned their attention to the problem of national education; and in this movement La Chalotais played a valuable and conspicuous part. In February, 1763, appeared a royal edict laying upon the *procureurs généraux* of the Parlements the duty of drawing up schemes for those colleges "which do not depend on the Universities"; and it was on the twenty-fourth of March in the same year that La Chalotais laid before the Parlement of Rennes his *Essai d'Éducation Nationale, ou Plan d'Études pour la Jeunesse.* The keynote of the author's proposals is sounded in the title; with him education is a national affair—the concern of the State—and therefore it must not be entrusted to any body which is not directly under governmental control. The idea was not essentially a new one. It had not only been advocated but also put into practice in ancient Greece; but in La Chalotais' own century it is found, for example, in the educational writings of the Abbé de Saint-Pierre who wrote *Paul et Virginie*, in the *Considérations sur les Mœurs de ce Siècle*[1] of Duclos, and more generally in Voltaire and even Rousseau. In fact, the proposal to nationalise education was "in the air"; but the *Essai* of La Chalotais none the less stands out in the history of educational thought because it gives to this idea its first full and detailed exposition.

With the first edition of La Chalotais' scheme, which was given to the public in printed form in 1763, there is bound up another pamphlet. It is entitled *De l'Éducation Publique* and had been first published at Amsterdam towards the end of the previous year[2]. It was an anonymous work and its

---

[1] See especially Chapter II.
[2] The date on the title-page is 1762, but it is possible that the book did not appear until early in January, 1763.

authorship has been attributed to various contemporary *littérateurs*[1]; but we shall probably be right in ascribing it to Diderot, whose views on education are better known not only from the *Encyclopédie* but also from his *Refutation of Helvétius* and the plan for a Russian University, which he prepared for the Czarina Catherine II. The *Essai* of La Chalotais deals broadly with the administrative side of a national system of education; but in the *brochure* attributed to Diderot we find detailed regulations for the interior organisation of schools, including programmes of study and recommendations on the subject of discipline. Thus the two pamphlets are complementary; what the one lacks the other supplies, and the two are bound up together because La Chalotais explicitly takes the responsibility for most of the recommendations made by the author of the second treatise. In a postscript to the *Essai* La Chalotais refers to the *De l'Éducation Publique* in terms of high praise and says: "I believe that our plan is good and may prove useful; I say *our* plan because his is almost the same as mine." The few points upon which the two authors disagree are specified by La Chalotais; they are few in number and are not really essential to the general scheme. In outlining, therefore, the proposals which La Chalotais makes, we shall include those set forth in the *De l'Éducation Publique*, distinguishing only such details as would not commend themselves to the author of the *Essai*.

La Chalotais opens with a description of the existing situation and a criticism of contemporary methods of education. The Jesuit colleges have been destroyed and now a constructive policy is imperative. "Let us therefore endeavour to impress on the minds of the young those kinds of knowledge which they will find necessary for filling the various professions, for working in them to their own happiness and to that of others, and for contributing as a result to the general well being of society[2]." To La Chalotais

---

[1] This question is fully discussed in the *Revue Internationale de l'Enseignement* of Oct. 15th, 1892: E. Dreyfus Brisac: "Petits Problèmes de Bibliographie pédagogique."

[2] *Essai*, pp. 3–4.

school education is a matter of the greatest importance; but he does not, like Helvétius, unduly emphasise it, nor does he, like Rousseau, regard "les sciences" as dangerous or useless. "Nature," he says, "makes differences between men, but education makes perhaps even greater differences[1]." The literary curriculum of the day is not to be entirely condemned; "literature is at once the food of the mind and also the enlightenment and adornment of the world[2]." But the contemporary *collèges* have interpreted the subject in a barren and narrow spirit. "What does the pupil know after ten years spent in either getting ready to enter a college or in wearing himself out in passing through the various classes[3]?" The education which is given leaves most pupils unable to distinguish a good reason from a bad one—or even to write a simple letter without committing glaring errors. La Chalotais goes on to criticise the teaching personnel of the colleges which are administered by the various Congregations. It is a strange paradox that those who are responsible for the upbringing of the children of others should be condemned to have none of their own. Moreover if all schoolmasters are ecclesiastics purely dogmatic instruction tends to be overdone, while there is a most conspicuous absence of instruction in the civic and political virtues. The care of the body is neglected (this was not true of the Jesuits), while "modern" studies such as geography and the natural sciences play far too small a part in the curriculum even if they are included at all.

La Chalotais ends the opening section of his *Essai* with a warning which at first surprises us when we remember from whom it proceeds. It is not for everybody that the national system of schools is to be prescribed. There are already, our author complains, too many *collèges* in the kingdom, and the remedy is to have fewer schools and better ones. Working-class parents, tempted by the cheap or gratuitous education offered, send their children to secondary schools, and in consequence there is a shortage of entrants into the manual trades, while the recruitment of the navy also proves difficult—a serious matter in view of the wars with

---

[1] *Essai*, p. 4.   [2] *Op. cit.* p. 10.   [3] *Op. cit.* p. 11.

England. Even elementary education is overdone. The Brothers of the Christian Doctrine, "who are called *Igno-rantins*[1]" are the chief offenders. "They teach reading and writing to people who ought to learn nothing beyond how to use a plane or a file, but who are no longer willing to do this." Remarks such as this remind us that La Chalotais, in spite of the "modern" character of many of his theories, is still the representative of his epoch. In pre-revolutionary France the ideal of an education provided by the State for every citizen was not generally held even among the "philosophic" party. Voltaire in a letter[2] to the author of the *Essai* thanks him for having forbidden studies to the working-classes. The author of the *De l'Éducation Publique*, on the other hand, does not take up this attitude, and this question of universal education is one of the few upon which he and La Chalotais joins issue. Diderot—if indeed he was the writer—estimates that the total population of France in his day was 18 millions, of whom some 2 millions were boys between the ages of seven and sixteen. If an average of 500 students were allowed for each of the existing 300 *collèges* in the country (this seems a very liberal estimate), a total of 150,000 is reached. Add to this some 30,000 children who are receiving education in the "little schools" and there still remain 1,820,000 boys of school age who are receiving no education at all, or at best "arbitrary, defective and irregular instruction." Many of these children live in the small country towns and villages where school facilities are few or entirely lacking. Yet the smallest hamlets of France are none the less part of the State and the poorest children are still "children of the motherland." They are the future artisans, labourers and soldiers, whose existence is necessary to the country. It is lamentable therefore to see so many children, "our compatriots and brothers so neglected, so deprived of help to which, because of their needs, they have just as much right as others—nay, more than others,

---

[1] Or *Doctrinaires*. They were founded by César de Bus in 1592. Their original aim was the instruction of poor children in country districts, but they also opened secondary schools.

[2] Dated Feb. 8th, 1763.

because they have less opportunities[1]." But La Chalotais does not trust education so completely as this; he cannot—like the author of *De l'Éducation Publique*—rise to the view, already foreshadowed by Comenius and other Protestant educational reformers, that to every member of society is due an education which will enable him efficiently and completely to play his part as a citizen and as a man. Experience has proved perhaps that the danger lest schooling may unfit the cobbler for his last is not so great as has sometimes been anticipated. There may lurk a grain of truth in what La Chalotais says; but no truly national system of education will make a full school course the prerogative of a privileged class, or deny instruction to any individual group in the community, simply for fear lest they may rise above that state of life to which it has pleased God to call them. It is this essentially false conception of the problem which is to be deplored. Rather should every member of the State have the fullest opportunity to profit by the best kind of education of which he is capable; the selection should not be one of class but of ability. It is easy to criticise La Chalotais; but in spite of our modern continuation schools and free secondary education the ideal is not even yet fully realised.

The second section of the *Essai* deals with the education of children up to the age of ten. It opens with some general remarks on educational theory in which we can trace the deep and widespread influence of the sensational philosophy of Locke. The mind is described as a "capacité vide," which is apparently nothing more than a French equivalent for the familiar *tabula rasa*. If everything comes to the mind through the medium of the senses we must in the education of the child begin with the simple and concrete and lead on later to the complex and abstract. The learner must first be familiarised with things that he can see and touch; and the contemporary type of primary education which deals too exclusively with words and abstractions stands self-condemned. In making these statements La Chalotais does not show any originality; they were already commonplaces

[1] *De l'Éducation Publique*, p. 160.

in the educational theory of the day. We find them not only in Locke's *Essay*, but also in the writings of the Port-Royalists and of Helvétius, and in the *Émile*. La Chalotais is an eminent lawyer with a deep interest in education, but on the philosophical bases of the subject he has nothing new to tell us. In fact, later in his *Essai* he seems to some extent to abandon the theory of the *tabula rasa*, for he speaks of the mind being already capable of an infinite number of "combinaisons" when first it applies itself to sensible objects. It remains true that La Chalotais sees clearly the inherent fault of the education which was given in the secondary schools of his day, and with characteristic practical common-sense he indicates the true principles upon which the teaching process should be based.

The question of learning to read and write is not discussed in any detail. The latter subject goes almost unmentioned and, as regards the teaching of reading, La Chalotais is of opinion that no really satisfactory method has yet been invented, and that it is the business of the government to discover and enforce one. The problem had been perplexing educationists in France for the past hundred years and more. The method invented by Pascal and put into practice at Port-Royal had been applied elsewhere, often with modifications and improvements. Regents and *maîtres-d'école* alike had put forward their various schemes, some advocating the spelling out of each letter, others preferring a syllabic method. La Chalotais, applying his general principle of governmental control to this detail of teaching practice, wishes these methods to be examined and standardised by a central authority.

At the age of six, when the pupil should already have learned to read and write, he must be introduced to the study of history—a subject most suitable for children. They have a natural love for hearing stories; if they are interested in the adventures of Hop-o'-my-Thumb or Bluebeard, are they not capable of appreciating the story of Romulus or of Clovis? Above all, the history of the child's own country should be learnt; it would be shameful for the future citizen to be ignorant of such a subject. But there is a lack of text-

238 A PLAN OF NATIONAL EDUCATION [CH.

books on history suitable for young children. La Chalotais
therefore expresses a wish for elementary treatises on the
history of special countries and special periods, and for
biographies not only of famous men but also of "femmes et
enfans célèbres." In default of such books the teacher should
tell the children what is necessary and then make the
members of his class reproduce the stories orally.

Like Nicole, La Chalotais realises that the teaching of
history must be continually illustrated by pictures of the
people and places of which mention is made. The study of
geography must therefore be correlated with that of history.
Geography, of course, is not regarded as a science or as a
school subject which develops the reasoning powers; that
conception is essentially a modern one. To La Chalotais, as
to his contemporaries, it is "an affair of the eyes and the
memory," and therefore it is particularly suited to young
children. It can be imparted to some extent by the reading
of accounts of voyages and descriptions of foreign countries.
Nature study is another subject of value in the education of
the child whose main concern is still with "things." The
properties of familiar minerals and plants, the life-history of
animals or birds which can be easily observed—these attract
the curiosity of the child and he finds pleasure in the study
of such subjects. At this stage there is no question of the
exercise of reason; it is merely a matter of observation and
remembrance. At the same time the interest of the young
child can be awakened by "récréations physiques"—elementary experiments which will show the general principles
of simple machines. The lever, the pulley, the balance, can
be made the subject of easy lessons. The study of mathematics also is suitably begun at this stage. Elementary
astronomy, again, and the wonders revealed by the micro-
scope not only fascinate the child, but may be made the
basis of much moral and religious teaching; the question:
"Quis est qui creavit hæc?" will lead on to a knowledge
of the great First Cause underlying all nature.

We pass now to the third section of the *Essai*—that which
deals with the education of the child who has passed the age
of ten years. It is at this stage that Latin is begun; Greek

will be reserved only for such pupils as show a decided bent for classical studies. But it is not the Latin teaching of the Jesuit *collège* that La Chalotais advocates; the study of French—"the mother-tongue, the most necessary during the whole course of life[1]"—must precede and accompany that of Latin. Here again La Chalotais merely re-echoes the recommendations of the Port-Royalists, and he prescribes as a text-book the *Grammaire générale* of Lancelot and Arnauld. This work was a well-meant, but not very successful attempt to set forth the general principles which are common to all languages, and in particular to French, Latin, and Greek. Although the book is not infrequently recommended by eighteenth-century educationists for the use of schoolboys, anyone who will take the trouble to examine the *Grammaire générale* will probably agree that it is far more suitable to those who have already made some considerable progress in the study of the languages with which it deals. Moreover, in prescribing such a work for the needs of the child of ten who is beginning Latin, La Chalotais is inconsistent with his own postulate that in the educational process we must pass from the particular to the general. He is better advised in his strong recommendation that the reading of authors should come before the writing of "themes." The experienced teacher of Latin will doubtless urge that in the earliest stages translation of simple sentences from Latin into the vernacular and from the vernacular into Latin must proceed *pari passu*. But La Chalotais is here protesting against the too common contemporary practice of giving the writing of Latin prose an unduly important place in the curriculum, and consequently of neglecting the study of classical authors. But in any case French and Latin authors and French and Latin composition are to be studied side by side. Phædrus may be compared with La Fontaine, Horace with Boileau. Another point upon which the author of the *Essai* lays the greatest stress is that "schoolchildren should never be set to write any composition except upon subjects about which they already have a sufficient knowledge[2]." Instead of setting the pupil to give his idea of "Cæsar's harangue to his

---

[1] *Essai*, p. 71.   [2] *Op. cit.* p. 85.

soldiers at Pharsalia," La Chalotais would prefer as subjects
for an essay a description of a plant or flower, of a wind-mill
or a watch. Yet to him the ultimate aim of the study of
language and literature is the development of "taste"; this
he defines as "a quick, lively and delicate power of appreciating the beauties which should form an essential part of
a work[1]." In origin taste is a natural gift, but it can be
improved by study and practice. It is formed by careful
examination and comparison of classical authors—whether
Latin or French—who are masters of style, and by reading
the works of capable literary critics. La Chalotais recommends, amongst other works, the *Conseils à un Journaliste*
of Voltaire.

But a purely or mainly literary education is essentially
one-sided, and La Chalotais therefore returns to sketch in the
rest of the curriculum. Geography and history at this stage
again are of paramount importance. But by geography now
is meant not a mere collection of "tedious details" as to the
whereabouts of certain towns; it rather leads up to the study
of the economic life of the nation as a whole. It must aim
at showing how the different classes of society live—"what
kind of bread a workman, a day-labourer, an artisan, eats;
on what kind of bed he sleeps[2]."

History also must no longer be confined to isolated
anecdotes. The story of the mother-country is still the subject
of greatest importance and La Chalotais expresses the desire
that a "French Plutarch" may arise to do justice to the
theme. But it should be studied critically and not by rote.
This leads our author to point out the inadequacy of the
logic course given by the schools of his day. The advancing
and rebutting of formal syllogisms do not really train the
faculty of judgment. Logic is never taught to women or to
boys in the early years of school life, and yet they can reason
as clearly as those who have passed through the philosophy
form of a *collège*. These barren methods must be cleared
away; the pupil must learn to think things out for himself
and never be content with *a priori* rules. He must examine
carefully the exact meaning of the terms which he uses; he

[1] *Essai*, p. 145.   [2] *Op. cit.* p. 149.

must endeavour to trace causes and verify his conclusions. The influence of Descartes and his followers is manifest throughout this part of the *Essai*, and La Chalotais is recommending principles which had already been applied in school practice by the Port-Royalists and Oratorians, and even to some small extent in the Universities. But at the same time he is giving expression to the characteristic spirit of his times—the period of the "philosophes" and the *Encyclopédie*. For La Chalotais the aim of the upper part of the school course should be to impart to the pupil some measure of the true philosophic spirit which is not mere erudition but rather an attitude towards life in general. To use his own expression, "it is a spirit of illumination, useful for everything, applicable to everything, which relates each thing to its principles without reference to current opinion or custom[1]."

Closely related to philosophy, thus interpreted by La Chalotais, is his conception of ethics. All vices, he says, are based on false opinions or mistakes; if we endeavour to foster accuracy of judgment in our pupils, we shall help them at the same time to lead moral lives. La Chalotais is no opponent of religion, although he believes that the teaching of Christianity is the business of the family or, more especially, of the churches, rather than of the school. But behind the various religions there are certain great principles of morality which existed before revealed religion came into being, "although they draw their chief sanction and their strongest influence from the confirmation which revelation bestows upon them[2]." For example, the distinction between good and evil is anterior to revealed religion; it is external and unchangeable and part of the very nature of things. Instruction in these fundamental ethical truths La Chalotais claims to be the definite duty of the State, and this subject must therefore take its place in the curriculum of the schools which he advocates. Religion may be left to the churches, for if the heathen nations of old were able to distinguish ethics from religion, we moderns may well do the same. La Chalotais does not wish to suppress

---

[1] *Op. cit.* p. 156.   [2] *Op. cit.* p. 132.

the Church or to proscribe religious exercises; rather would he advocate a *concordat* between the various churches and the temporal authorities, because after all the true aim of both should be one and the same, and the same ethical principles ultimately underlie the training of the good citizen and the training of the good Christian.

La Chalotais gives few recommendations as to the administration and internal organisation of individual schools, but we can fill the lacuna from what is said in the *De l'Éducation Publique*. As the schools are a national concern it is desirable that a board of governors, representing the public, should have the rights of inspection and control. It is suggested that this board should consist normally of three persons—a lawyer, an ecclesiastic, and "one of the principal inhabitants" of the town in which the school is situated. These governors are to be given extensive powers and it seems almost as if they are to discharge the duties usually undertaken by the head master. They are to regulate the studies and organise the school; they will appoint the masters and have charge of the fabric of the school-buildings; but they are enjoined always to consult the opinions of the staff on such matters "because no one knows better what is desirable for a school than those who teach in it and whose honour is concerned in it[1]."

The subjects of study are to be those which have already been indicated in the *Essai* of La Chalotais. If a boy is not fit for promotion, he must spend another year in the same form. Discipline is to be enforced with an eye to strict regularity rather than to severity. The sting of a punishment should lie chiefly in the disgrace and not in the physical discomfort which it brings. Prizes have their value. The writer of the *De l'Éducation Publique* gives rein to his imagination on this point. Silver medals of various sizes should be awarded. On one side will be a cross with the *fleur-de-lis* and the name of the King and of the town in which the school stands; on the other, the figure of a book with a half-open compass lying upon it and an inscription giving the title of the form and the name of the prize-winner.

[1] *De l'Éducation Publique*, p. 190.

These distinctions are to be awarded not only for success in class-work, but also for good conduct. In the former case the ribbon for the medal is blue, and in the latter gold-coloured. The pupil who distinguishes himself in both categories receives only one medal, but its ribbon is striped with blue and gold and the wearer is given some prefectorial authority over his fellows. For boys of outstanding ability a system of state scholarships is proposed.

Such, then, in its essentials is the scheme put forward for the intellectual and moral education of the future citizen. La Chalotais claims that those who have undergone such a training will have "un esprit solide." If they are of noble birth they will not follow the evil example of so many of their contemporaries, by leaving their estates and wasting their patrimony at the Court. This custom which had been encouraged by Louis XIV, because it weakened the nobility and added to his own grandeur, had persisted into the eighteenth century and is deplored by several observers of the period. La Chalotais believes that those nobles who have learnt to be true citizens and to understand and work for the welfare of the State will remain in the country and develop its resources, while at the same time not neglecting their own intellectual interests. Again, the State consists not merely of men; women are citizens and therefore a national system of education must make provision for them also. Re-echoing the opening words of Fénelon's *De l'Éducation des Filles*, La Chalotais exclaims: "It is inconceivable that the education of women in France should have been so much neglected[1]." There is no reason therefore why the scheme which is outlined in the *Essai* should not be applied to girls' schools also, although the author seems to indicate that instruction in Latin might be omitted. Not only would the future mothers of the race be better instructed, but the men of the next generation would benefit because they would have received a better home education. La Chalotais' discussion of the education of girls is supplemented at some length in the treatise *De l'Éducation Publique*. Its writer points out that "it is useless to strive to improve the

[1] *Essai*, p. 142.

education of boys if we do not consider how effectively to reform that of girls[1]."

Owing to the neglect of women's education girls grow up to be frivolous and empty-headed; they are not a help but rather a hindrance to young men and they have won for the Frenchwoman a bad reputation in foreign countries. The same criticisms are passed on the content of female education as had been made by almost every writer on the subject for the previous century and a half; and it seems obvious that, in spite of the revival of conventual education during the seventeenth century and the success of isolated institutions such as St Cyr, very little progress had been made in the education of the average French girl. At the end of the seventeenth century in the whole of France, excluding Paris, only 13·74 per cent. of brides were able to sign their marriage certificate. "Dress, music, and the dance," writes the author of the *De l'Éducation Publique*, "are almost the sole pre-occupation of girls. If we add a small tincture of geography, mythology, and history, their education is complete[2]." They know nothing of the sciences and cannot even write or spell correctly. The solution is practically that which La Chalotais himself suggests; girls must be educated in much the same way as boys, with the substitution of needlework and other handicrafts for those studies "which are suitable only for our sex." The *régime* of the convent is the very "antipodes" of the educational system best suited to girls; and the writer concludes in a passage full of the spirit which animates La Chalotais also: "Let us raise ourselves courageously above blind routine and evil prejudice, and by wise endeavour let us dare to aim at perfection[3]."

The *Plan d'Études* which La Chalotais and his fellow author set forth is a real advance upon the general school practice of their day; it is of particular value because the principles upon which it was based, although familiar enough in modern times, were not those usually accepted in the middle of the eighteenth century. As a scheme of educational organisation, then, the *Essai* had a real value; but to

[1] *De l'Éducation Publique*, p. 227.   [2] *Op. cit.* p. 229.
[3] *Op. cit.* p. 231.

complete this it was necessary to show how it could be put into practice. The great difficulty with which La Chalotais was confronted was a shortage of teachers. The departure of the Jesuits deprived France at a single blow of some hundreds of well-trained professional schoolmasters and it was impossible to replace them by other teachers of equal ability. The universities had no available "pépinières de régents." Some of the vacant colleges of the Society of Jesus were given over to other teaching societies; but, as we have seen in the case of the Oratorians, they were unable to cope successfully with the new situation and really weakened themselves in attempting to do so. Until the new order of things is firmly established and sufficient teachers are forthcoming, La Chalotais sees that temporary expedients must be tried. The existing masters must avail themselves of the assistance of the more advanced pupils who will teach their younger schoolfellows. But it is upon the provision of suitable text-books that La Chalotais relies chiefly for the solution of the difficulties; he even seems to think that such books, put into the hands of a child who has already learnt to read, will to some extent dispense with the necessity for a teacher. We have here repeated the recommendation which La Chalotais makes at the end of his first *Compte Rendu*. If only the king—the mouthpiece of the State itself—will order these proposals to be carried out, then everything is possible; the projected text-books could be printed at the *Imprimerie Royale* and if they were sold to the schools no expenditure of public funds would be entailed. If such books were used it would be sufficient that the teachers who were still retained should be able simply to read, so long as they were persons of good character; "this will bring us back to domestic education which is the most natural and the most conducive to the inculcation of morality and the welfare of society[1]."

So ends the *Essai* and one can hardly suppress a feeling of disappointment that so well-conceived a scheme of educational administration should be so inadequately enforced. After all, a plan of national education, resting on the

---

[1] *Essai*, p. 149.

assumption that the training of the future citizen is the concern not of the Church but of the State, is not likely to be realised when teachers of the most meagre attainments read out to their pupils passages from text-books, even though these be "faits avec un esprit philosophique" and prescribed by a paternal government. Still less will the end be achieved if the children are left to spell out their inspired lesson-books unaided. But perhaps it is hardly fair to judge La Chalotais thus, because he is admittedly legislating for abnormal conditions. He recognised quite clearly that in a complete and adequately organised system of national education properly qualified teachers would be necessary. This is made evident by a passage in the *De l'Éducation Publique*. There it is laid down that masters must have the requisite knowledge, irreproachable character, and a free hand in their own sphere. They must be spared financial worries; "men wholly devoted to study ought to have the ease which rules out care for the present, and the security which spares them anxiety as to the future[1]." The average salary of a regent in the highest forms of the colleges of the University of Paris was about 1500 livres[2] in the middle of the eighteenth century. It must be remembered however that these men were celibates and were usually provided with rooms in college and often made profits on taking boarders. In those days, also, it was possible to be "passing rich on forty pounds a year"; and any sum would have to be multiplied several times to produce its modern equivalent. It is suggested in the *De l'Éducation Publique* that the salary paid to contemporary secondary schoolmasters in Paris should be taken as a standard wage under the proposed national system of education; but that in the provinces a slightly smaller amount should be given. It is obvious therefore that La Chalotais and the writer of the *De l'Éducation Publique* would agree in advocating that under normal conditions a well-trained and suitably-paid teaching staff should be provided for the State schools. The great obstacle is the

---

[1] *De l'Éducation Publique*, p. 196.
[2] It had been fixed at 1000 livres in 1719, but since that date had been increased.

difficulty of obtaining such men and of financing them adequately. In the *De l'Éducation Publique* the knot of the difficulty is cut by a proposal that the necessary teachers shall be drawn from the ranks of the secular clergy. "Can we doubt," says the author[1], "that the secular clergy, who have always been so diligent in retaining their just prerogatives, would ever hand over to others, save with the deepest regret, a duty so noble as that of public instruction." To finance these new teachers, taxes should be levied on the districts in which the schools are situated, and useless abbeys and prebends should be suppressed and their revenues devoted to educational purposes. These proposals did not commend themselves to La Chalotais and they constitute one of the only two important points upon which the two authors do not find themselves in agreement.

The *Essai* of La Chalotais has been overshadowed by the numerous other treatises on education which appeared at about the same date, and notably by Rousseau's *Émile*. But the pamphlet has a value all its own; it is no chimerical work of fancy, but a plan of practical politics, full of common-sense. Its short-comings are obvious—its fear of an "educated proletariat," its parroting of the catch-words of contemporary philosophy, its exaggerated estimate of the power of the text-book. But behind all this there are proposals which were eventually put into practice and have since had a profound influence upon education in France. But this influence was not immediately felt; on the downfall of the Jesuits the old College of Clermont in Paris was made over to the University; all the smaller colleges which were not "de plein exercice[2]" were amalgamated with this institution which in 1682 had been renamed the Collège Louis-le-Grand. Thus the University of Paris regained, for the first time since the advent of the Jesuits, complete control of the secondary education of the city. But the University was destined to last for less than another thirty years; and it is the lawyers and statesmen, following the lead of La Chalotais and his contemporaries, who now evince the most progressive spirit in regard to educational matters. The *Plan* of Rolland,

---

[1] *De l'Éducation Publique*, p. 198.   [2] See *supra*, p. 5.

dating from 1768, the proposals of Talleyrand and Condorcet in the revolutionary period, all show the influence of the movement of which La Chalotais is the chief exponent. Education is no longer regarded as an instrument for securing the everlasting salvation of the soul of the individual; it is now the chief means of ensuring the well being of the State and for that reason public instruction must be the direct concern of the State itself. When the upheaval of the Revolution had cleared away existing educational institutions, the work of reconstruction began and the schemes of La Chalotais and those who co-operated with him were realised almost in their entirety. The constructive genius of Napoleon gave birth to a system of national education characterised by extreme centralisation. There was a subsequent reaction and retrogression, but this was not permanent. It remains true that we can trace back to La Chalotais the main principles upon which is based the school-system of the French Republic at the present day.

In another respect La Chalotais anticipates a modern French practice. As we have seen, he regards the teaching of religion as being outside the purview of the State school, but he advocates strongly what would nowadays be called "direct moral instruction." To an English observer one of the most interesting phases of the life of a modern *lycée* is the instruction in *morale*. This subject is studied once a week in the fourth and third forms (boys aged about 13 or 14) and it includes lessons on individual and social morality, which consist mainly of anecdotes with a didactic aim. With such a subject the effect produced on the pupils must depend even more than usual upon the personality of the teacher. A writer in the Board of Education *Special Report on Secondary Education in France*[1] says of the lessons in *morale* which he had witnessed: "It seems to me that they lead children to think of moral questions from the healthy intellectual point of view rather than from the emotional, and thereby avoid a danger on the one hand of cant, and on the other of taking the edge from real moral sensibility which a child ought never to be asked to display." None

[1] Vol. xxiv.

the less, there is a wide diversity of opinion even in France itself as to the value of the lesson in *morale*; and it does not seem easy to impose upon boys of thirteen and fourteen an ethical code, based on pure reason, which shall serve them as a criterion of conduct throughout life. It may be doubted whether the average English boy, at any rate, would normally benefit greatly by this kind of instruction. We can hardly blame him for his instinctive dislike of the occasion being "improved" or of having his deepest sensibilities publicly played upon. Readers of Kipling's *Stalky and Co.* will remember the unfortunate impression created by the well-meaning lecturer who harangued the school on the subject of patriotism. The writer ventures to assert that the experience of most schoolmasters in this country would bear out his own feeling that the virtues of public service, patriotism, honour, and purity are more easily and effectively inculcated by fostering a feeling that certain things are "not done" by a decent person or in a decent school, than by asking boys to consider such subjects from a purely intellectual point of view. This does not mean that the moral lesson must be entirely neglected. On the contrary, the conscientious teacher will not fail to make the most of any opportunity that may arise in class-work or in the ordinary course of school life. By so doing he can raise the pupils' outlook for the time being to a higher plane, and the effect produced is the more valuable and lasting because it is unexpected. The history lesson will afford many and conspicuous examples of civic and personal virtue; the heroism of an "old boy" will appeal with peculiar force to the present members of the school to which he used to belong. But so soon as a definite hour is set apart for moral instruction, of whatever kind it be, there is a danger that an atmosphere of artificiality and restraint may be created and thus the desired end is not always attained. It would seem, therefore, that the development of character, which our Gallic neighbours seek to inculcate to some extent by direct moral instruction, we would more wisely leave to indirect methods, and chiefly to that sense of public spirit and tradition of personal service which is the peculiar glory of our English schools.

CHAPTER VIII

THE EARLY EDUCATION OF CHILDREN—
MADAME NECKER DE SAUSSURE

UPON our conception of the nature of the child depends the character of the education which we give him. The great change which in comparatively recent years has come over the aims and ideals of the educator and the teaching methods and other means by which he seeks to achieve them, is due to the fact that the current estimate of child nature has been profoundly modified. The process of change has been more marked and more rapid within the last few decades owing to the growth of psychological study and the application of it to the nature and development of the child's mind; but we can trace the movement back for several centuries.

Not only during the Middle Ages but also under the inspiration of the Renaissance it had been very generally taken for granted that the child is a *homunculus*—a man writ small. His education therefore aimed at assisting him to mimic the ways of an adult. He studied the same subjects as did his seniors; he began to learn reading by spelling out Latin words, and his immature mind was exercised with formal grammar mastered by brute force of memory. The proud father of an intelligent child strove hard to turn him into a premature adult. This practice is even yet not quite obsolete among us, but the career of Richard, son of John Evelyn the diarist, will serve to illustrate the point. At the age of two and a half this infant could "perfectly reade any of the English, Latine, French, or Gottic letters, pronouncing the three first languages exactly[1]." By his fifth year he could decline all the Latin nouns and conjugate the verbs both regular and irregular; he had a large vocabulary, could

---

[1] Evelyn, *Diary*, 27 Jan., 1658.

make "congruous syntax," turned English into Latin and *vice versa*, and "did the government and use of relatives, verbs, substantives, elipses, and many figures and tropes." He could recite innumerable verses, had a strong passion for Greek and a wonderful disposition for mathematics, besides displaying many signs of precocious piety. Richard Evelyn died three days after his fifth birthday, to his father's unspeakable grief[1]. The story of the dearly-loved child's promise so tragically unfulfilled, and of the stricken father's sorrow arouses our sympathetic response across the ages; but our present purpose is chiefly to notice the *régime* to which the little boy was subjected. He had merely anticipated by some six or seven years the mental equipment of a boy of eleven or twelve.

The contemporary attitude to childhood is illustrated in many other departments of life. Children were dressed exactly like miniature adults; their manners and behaviour were modelled on the conventions which their elders observed; there were few books prepared for their own special enjoyment, but they were regaled with Plutarch's *Lives* or, at best, Æsop—works which had originally been written for adults. The Latin conversations which they learnt by heart in their Colloquies were to a large extent such as could be put into the mouths of grown-up persons. In short, at every turn an attempt was made to regulate child-life from an adult standpoint and the distinctive characteristics of childhood as such were to a large extent repressed. Little wonder then that the education of young children was concerned not so much with what children actually are as with what, according to preconceived standards, they ought to be.

It is for this reason that throughout the period which we have just been considering little interest is shown in the education of quite young children, as distinct from those of ordinary school age. Comenius was one of the first modern educational thinkers to legislate especially for very young children. In his

---

[1] He ends his account of the child's life and death with the words: "Here ends the joy of my life, and for which I go even mourning to the grave."

system he provides a "Mother School" for the first six years of childhood. He realises the importance of inculcating desirable habits from the first and he advocates the encouragement of play. His curriculum for this home-school includes such subjects as metaphysics, optics, astronomy, mechanics, dialectic, rhetoric, economics, and so forth. But by these imposing titles Comenius means nothing more than that the child's interest in his environment should be met by intelligent response on the part of those responsible for his education, and that he should be given opportunities for self-expression. Still the fact remains that Comenius was one of the first educators of modern times to realise that the child is not merely a miniature adult and that he must be dealt with as a child.

In this country the same truth was clearly enunciated for perhaps the first time by a contemporary of Evelyn's—John Locke. With him the child is the determining factor in the educational process. He concerns himself, for example, with play and playthings; "these I confess," he says[1], "are little Things, and such as will seem beneath the Care of a Governor; but nothing that may form Children's Minds is to be overlooked and neglected, and whatsoever introduces Habits, and settles Customs in them, deserves the Care and Attention of their Governors, and is not a small Thing in its Consequences." The formation of habits of good conduct is with Locke the first object of education; intellectual training is a secondary aim, and since the inculcation of desirable habits, if it is to be effectual, must be begun in infancy, Locke concerns himself with children from their earliest years. He urges that learning should as far as possible be made a "sport"; he advocates picture-books—*Reynard the Fox* is recommended as a reader; and he very sensibly protests against the indiscriminate use of the Bible as a text-book for the instruction of young children. Illustrations such as these, which might be multiplied indefinitely, show that Locke's conception of the child's nature and mental needs was different from that of Evelyn. But Locke was an innovator. The case of little Richard Evelyn, although

[1] Locke, *Thoughts concerning Education*, section 130.

doubtless abnormal and exaggerated, is none the less symp-
tomatic of the general attitude of contemporary educators
towards young children. It was not until the latter part of
the eighteenth century that the reform heralded by Comenius
and Locke received a fresh and vigorous impulse from
Rousseau. The *homunculus* tradition died hard. There were
many traces of it in the nineteenth century—*e.g.* in the
conversations in Mrs Markham's *History of England,* in the
Looking-Glass for the Mind and similar "improving" books
for young people, and in the children's magazines of sixty
or seventy years ago. But in spite of this the movement
inspired by Rousseau widened rapidly during the nineteenth
century and eventually transformed the education of young
children.

Rousseau is doubtless influenced by the "wise" Locke, as
he calls him, but he goes far beyond his predecessor. "We
do not know childhood," he says[1]; "Those who are wisest
are attached to what is important for men to know, without
considering what children are able to apprehend. They are
always looking for the man in the child, without thinking of
what he was before he became a man." Rousseau therefore
has a bitter and undisguised hatred for "those ridiculous
establishments called colleges," in which the traditional
instruction of past ages is maintained. The attack is levelled
chiefly at the Society of Jesus which had for long been the
predominant educational force in France, but which in
1762—the very year in which Rousseau's educational treatise
the *Émile* appeared—had been banished from the country.
It is sometimes, at any rate, true that the "outsider sees
most of the game"; and even if Rousseau had had but little
experience as a teacher and had failed conspicuously when
the opportunity of gaining such experience was offered, yet
he was clear-sighted enough to see some things which were
wrong with contemporary education. In his *Émile,* with all
its paradoxes and extravagances—perhaps because of them
—he drew men's attention to these faults, and by so doing
helped to set them right. To use R. H. Quick's vigorous
metaphor, Rousseau removed the teacher's "blinkers," so

[1] Rousseau, *Émile,* Preface, iii.

that he was enabled to realise the short-comings of the traditional system which he was following blindly and un-questioningly. He saw at last that education must accom-modate itself to the child and that the child must not be accommodated to a predetermined system of education. To make this for ever plain was perhaps Rousseau's greatest contribution to the science of education, and for this reason his *Émile* may justly be regarded as the *Contrat Social* of all subsequent educational revolutions. As Lord Morley says, "It cleared away the accumulation of clogging prejudices and obscure inveterate usage which made education one of the dark formalistic arts; and it admitted floods of light and air into tightly-closed nurseries and schoolrooms[1]." In spite, therefore, of the fact that he had his predecessors, Rousseau was a real and original reformer; by his violent attacks on existing usage, by his wild flights of fancy and his often exaggerated suggestions, he awakened minds which had grown torpid in routine. Even if the solutions which he himself propounded were often ill-judged, those who after-wards attempted to put into practice the theories which he enunciated would have failed of their purpose without his inspiration.

The theory of education—a subject which bulks largely in our modern programmes of professional training for teachers—begins as a serious science with Rousseau. The *Émile* is not merely a teacher's handbook like Rollin's *Traité* or Coustel's *Règles*; it does not sketch a Gargantuan curriculum like Milton's *Tractate*; it is not even, like Locke's *Thoughts*, an acute prescription for the education of the "gentleman," although Émile is confessedly not one of the "common people." It is an attempt to analyse the development of the human soul from the earliest years of life to maturity; and the motive power of the book is the intense feeling which inspires every thought and which contrasts so vividly with the cool-headed common-sense of the English philo-sopher Locke.

It is easy to understand, then, that the education of the young child had a very special significance for Rousseau. It

[1] Morley, *Rousseau*, II, 248.

was to this stage in the development of the soul that the
"natural" and "negative" education[1] which he advocated
applied with most significance. Moreover, Rousseau had a
deep sentimental interest in children which is apparent to
any reader of the *Émile*[2]. His life was full of the strangest
contrasts. Rousseau had never known the joys of happy
fatherhood and tranquil home life. The children born of his
liaison with the inn-servant, Thérèse le Vasseur, were taken
at his suggestion and against their mother's will to the
"Enfants Trouvés[3]." Although he excuses this conduct in
his *Confessions*—and it is worth bearing in mind that we
owe our knowledge of his unnatural behaviour to his own
writings—it seems obvious that he afterwards repented very
sincerely of his action. The old Latin tag "Video meliora
proboque, deteriora sequor" could often be applied to him
with singular appropriateness. His private life was at times
sordid, sensual, and contemptible; yet none more thoroughly
than he could appreciate the best and most beautiful of
human relationships. His treatment of marriage and family
life in the *Nouvelle Héloïse* is unsurpassed, while the responsibilities of a parent are nowhere more eloquently
advocated than in the *Émile*. There is a cry of real remorse
in the words: "Reader, believe me when I predict that
whoever has a heart and neglects such sacred duties will
long shed bitter tears over his mistake and will never find
consolation for it[4]." If therefore we confined our attention
to Rousseau's autobiography alone, we might expect him to
be the last man to have a deep and affectionate interest in
children; as a matter of fact he is one of the first interpreters
of the charm of childhood. In another of his works[5] he says:
"It would certainly be quite incredible that the *Héloïse* and

---

[1] See *infra*, p. 256.

[2] See also the ninth promenade in *Rêveries du promeneur solitaire*.

[3] An attempt has recently been made to prove that this incident
in Rousseau's life is not authentic and that he never had any children
by Thérèse le Vasseur. Higher criticism of this kind seems to be
based on insufficient evidence. Refer to Gran, *Jean-Jacques Rousseau*,
pp. 287 ff.

[4] *Émile*, I, 32.

[5] *Rêveries du promeneur solitaire*, No. 9, p. 164.

the *Émile* were the work of a man who did not love children."
He combats fiercely the doctrine of original sin. He loves
to watch children at play. "If I have made some progress,"
he says[1], "in the knowledge of the human heart, it is the
pleasure that I used to take in watching and observing
children which had earned me that knowledge"; and again:
"I do not think that anybody has been more fond than I
have been of watching little children romping and playing
together." The criticism that Rousseau did not care to watch
his own children is of course obvious; but it has already been
pointed out that he acknowledged that he had committed
a mistake—if not a grievous fault—and the *Émile* itself is to
some extent a kind of reparation for his own short-comings
as a father.

The salient points of Rousseau's system of education are
that it should be progressive—*i.e.* accommodated to the
various stages in the child's development; that in the early
years it should be negative—*i.e.* that no definite and formal
instruction, either intellectual or moral, should be given; and
that, to ensure this, it should be natural. The last-named
characteristic is the most important, for it gives the clue
to Rousseau's whole system. Nature as defined by him is
"primitive dispositions, including our sensations and feelings
of pleasure and pain, together with the judgments founded
on these." The action of man is regarded as something
outside "nature" and often in opposition to it. "Everything
is good as it comes from the hands of the Author of Nature;
everything degenerates in the hands of man[2]." It is not
difficult to pick holes in Rousseau's arguments, to point out
his inconsistencies, and to show that apparently he was
incapable of regarding a case with judicial impartiality.
What Rousseau advocates in his *Émile* is almost the
complete contrary of the ordinary educational practice of
his day. "Take the very reverse of the current custom and
you will nearly always do right[3]." The contemporary child,
regarded as a miniature adult, was set to learn subjects
quite unsuited to his stage of mental development; inculcated

---

[1] *Op. cit.* p. 163. [2] *Émile*, first sentence, p. 1.
[3] *Émile*, p. 140.

by methods equally inappropriate. It was inevitable that Rousseau, fiercely impatient of tradition, should react to the opposite extreme in his protest against the artificial literary education which had been inspired by the Renaissance. The *Émile* teems with exaggerations, but they arrest our attention and make us reflect. Moreover the book has the advantage— of which use had hitherto not often been made by writers on educational matters—of being cast in the form of a novel; and the style of its author entitled him at once to a place among the "grands prosateurs" of a nation which has always shown a keen appreciation of good literature. It is hardly surprising, therefore, that the *Émile*, with all its faults, has had as much influence upon educational thought and practice as any treatise on the subject. The publication of the book was followed by an outpouring of improvements, imitations, and refutations. The followers of Rousseau were innumerable. Some of the greatest educators of the succeed-ing century—Kant, Basedow, Pestalozzi, Frœbel—owe the better part of their inspiration to the spirit which breathes in the *Émile*. It is not too much to say that to the gospel preached by Rousseau are ultimately due the sweetness and light which pervade the modern infant school, and the scientific interest in the development of the child which is displayed by the modern educational psychologist.

As we have seen, Rousseau was able to interpret with wonderful skill the charm of family life and of childhood. It is perhaps for this reason that we find a considerable number of women among those who were greatly influenced by his writings upon education. Mme Roland, the heroine of the Girondist party at the Revolution, was an ardent admirer of Rousseau. "His genius has fired my heart," she says[1]; "I feel that he has elevated and ennobled me. I do not in the least deny that there are some paradoxes in his *Émile*....But how many wise and wholesome reflections! What useful maxims! What beauties to atone for the faults!" Mme de Staël, the daughter of the financier Necker and a well-known authoress, is another disciple of Rousseau, although her admiration is more discerning than that of

[1] *Lettres*, No. 23.

Mme Roland. Mme Necker, mother of Mme de Staël, also owes much to him. Mme d'Épinay, a personal friend of the author of the *Émile*, was considerably influenced by him although she remained essentially a creature of "society," and her education of her own daughter hardly harmonises with Rousseau's theories about Nature.

The follower of Rousseau who with the greatest discernment selects what is admirable in the *Émile* and rejects what is false or extravagant is Mme Necker de Saussure. She realises clearly that Rousseau is "sometimes a dangerous guide, but often an excellent observer[1]," and so with consummate judgment she corrects his extravagances and restores balance and sanity. Her educational writings are far less vivid and arresting than those of Rousseau, but they are infinitely more judicious and scientific. It is the peculiar glory of France to be able to boast a succession of women educators and writers on education such as no other nation can show. Some of those who owed their inspiration directly to Rousseau have already been mentioned; but the names of Anne de Xainctonge, Jacqueline Pascal, Mme de Maintenon, and the Marquise de Lambert remind us that the phenomenon is not due to the writer of the *Émile*; while in more modern times the succession is worthily carried on by Mme Campan, Mme de Rémusat, Mme Guizot, Mme Pape Carpentier, and many another. In this brilliant company Mme Necker de Saussure occupies a prominent place. She is not concerned with the formal education of the class-room, but she has left us a book—*Éducation Progressive ou Étude du Cours de la Vie*—which marks an epoch in the history of education. It is the first great treatise on the theory of education, stated not in a series of recommendations to teachers or parents, nor in the form of a novel with a purpose, but as an acute philosophic analysis of the development of our intellectual powers and our moral nature.

The authoress of such a book is naturally an interesting figure. Adrienne-Albertine de Saussure was not a Frenchwoman for she was born in 1766 at Geneva. But by her education and her tastes she is essentially a product of

---

[1] *Éducation Progressive*, I, 121.

ADRIENNE-ALBERTINE NECKER DE SAUSSURE

(1766–1841)

French civilisation and it is hardly necessary to apologise for including her in a portrait gallery of French educators. She herself says: "I do not separate from the French people the inhabitants of the small neighbouring states in which the French language is spoken. There are many noticeable differences in small points and some of these states have a very marked national individuality; but as regards intellectual matters their education and civilisation are similar. As these small states have no arts or literature of their own, their men of genius have perforce followed—in spite of innumerable obstacles—the way traced out by the great French models[1]." Intellectually, therefore, the authoress of the *Éducation Progressive* is a Frenchwoman. Her father, Horace Bénédict de Saussure, was a scientist of considerable eminence; he was professor of Physics at Geneva, he had invented several meteorological instruments, and he was a recognised authority on the geology of the Alps. It was to him that Albertine owed her education, for she never attended a school of any kind. As we might have expected, her range of study was wide and went far beyond that allowed to most girls of the period. She learnt from her father the value of the scientific method of observation and experiment, but her education was never narrowed down to a merely formal study of natural phenomena. At the age of about seven she travelled with her family to Italy; but the eminent scientist did not for all that relax his care of his little daughter's education. Wherever they went, in inns and diligences, M. de Saussure was always ready to continue her lessons if there were but a few minutes to spare. Such an education, unique of its kind, made a deep impression on the child, who was already of precocious intelligence. At Rome the Pope, Clement XIV, granted a private audience to the Saussures. He was so charmed with their little daughter Albertine that he not only blessed but also kissed her, remarking as he did so: "I must go to confession, for I've just kissed a pretty girl!" On arriving at Naples M. de Saussure, in consideration of his fame as a scientist, was invited to the court, and he took Albertine with him. There the child recited fables and

10   [1] *Op. cit.* I, 289 n.

was plied with questions to which she replied with such
intelligence that she was acclaimed as a prodigy and became
a nine-days' wonder. One is reminded of Jacqueline Pascal
—herself the daughter of a distinguished scientist and
educated by him at home—making her extempore verses
at the court of Louis XIII. On returning to Switzerland
Albertine continued her tranquil life at home under the
watchful care and expert tuition of her father. It was
perhaps to her early visit to Italy that she owed her life-
long love for the Italian language. She also studied Latin
and became proficient in both English and German. Many
branches of natural science interested her—in particular
astronomy, botany, and geology. She is described as having
"regular and finely modelled features; her eyes, large and
dark, threw up the whiteness of her complexion; her hair,
which was brown, she wore powdered in her youth; she was
short, but with a perfect figure which she preserved to an
advanced age." We can picture her as a quiet, thoughtful
girl, widely read in the best literature of several great nations
and deeply interested in the workings of nature—appreciating
to the full the glories of sky and lake and snow-crested
mountain; and with all this deeply imbued with the
doctrines of Calvinistic Protestantism which had flourished
vigorously in Geneva ever since it first made its home
there.

In 1785, at the age of nineteen, Albertine de Saussure
married Jacques Necker, nephew of his more famous name-
sake the financier of the Revolutionary period. He had been
a cavalry officer but left the service at his marriage and—
perhaps under his wife's inspiration—applied himself to the
study of plants. He did this with so much success that he
was afterwards elected to a professorship of botany at
Geneva. His other interests included applied chemistry and
politics; he introduced improvements into lithographic
printing and took an active part in the political life of his
city, profoundly influenced as it was by the French Revolution and the events which followed thereupon. In short, he
seems to have been a man in whom Albertine de Saussure
would find many common interests and we are not surprised

to learn that the marriage was a happy one. Her life continued to be tranquil and uneventful in spite of the storms which raged outside. Her home became a centre of the intellectual life of Geneva. One met there scientists like De Candolle, the botanist, and Pictet, the meteorologist; politicians like Dumont, who translated into French the works of Jeremy Bentham; historians like Simonde de Sismondi, whose work on the Italian republics has not yet been forgotten. Distinguished foreigners when visiting Geneva did not fail to call upon Mme Necker de Saussure. On one occasion Miss Edgeworth came to visit her fellow-educationist and records the event thus: "Met Mme Necker de Saussure—much more agreeable than her books. Her manner and figure reminded me of our beloved Mrs Moutray; she too is deaf and has the same resignation void of mistrust in her expression when she is not speaking, and the same gracious attention to the person who is speaking to her[1]." At another time the visitor was Sir Humphry Davy who was accompanied by his assistant Michael Faraday—destined before long to become famous. But Mme Necker de Saussure's closest friend was her husband's cousin, the famous Mme de Staël, who frequently came over from her château at Coppet, on the shores of Lake Leman, to see her relatives at Geneva. Thus Mme Necker de Saussure gathered round her what in an earlier age and at Paris might have been called a *salon*; though it was rendered eminently serious and respectable by the influence of one of the strictest forms of Protestantism, and the topics of discussion were by no means mainly literary. In such a centre of intellectual activity the life of Mme Necker de Saussure was spent, and in considering her writings upon education it is well to bear this fact in mind.

Bénédict de Saussure died in 1798 and it may be imagined how deeply his daughter felt her loss. Her friendship with Mme de Staël grew and the two women interchanged, with mutual profit, their views on subjects which interested them. As she drew on towards middle age Mme Necker de Saussure became afflicted with deafness, which must have been

[1] *Life and Letters of Maria Edgeworth*, ii, 14.

singularly trying to one who formed—as she did—the centre
of an intellectual circle. Not unnaturally she sought relief
in literary work. She prepared a translation of Schlegel's
Treatise on Dramatic Literature; but her first work of real
importance is a *Notice sur Madame de Staël*—her tribute to
the memory of her friend whom she lost in 1817.

Meanwhile a young family—two sons[1] and two daughters
—had been growing up around her, and we can realise how,
with her strong traditions of the value of home-ties and
her deep interest in matters intellectual and spiritual, the
problems of education would present themselves to her with
a special insistence. Her greatest literary achievement therefore is the treatise on this subject, to which reference has
already been made. The first volume of the *Éducation Progressive* appeared in 1828 and the third and last ten years later.
The importance of the book was at once recognised and it
was crowned by the French Academy in 1832. It was the
last of Mme Necker de Saussure's works, for she died in 1841.
The *Éducation Progressive* errs, it must be confessed, on the
side of length and at times betrays a lack of coherence and
unity; but in originality and philosophic insight much of it
is of the highest value. The book appeared originally in three
parts. The first deals with the period of infancy up to the
age of five; the second with childhood from the fifth to the
fourteenth year; while the third is a special study of the
education of girls and women. The first and third parts
of the treatise are perhaps the most valuable; but for the
purposes of the present chapter it will be necessary to confine
ourselves mainly to part of the first volume of the *Éducation
Progressive* and to limit our discussion to what it has to say
concerning the education of young children during the first
three years of their life.

As the title of her treatise indicates, Mme Necker de
Saussure takes up the standpoint of what would nowadays
be called genetic psychology. Doubtless she borrows the
principle from Rousseau, but in her application of it to

---

[1] The eldest son, Louis, followed in the footsteps of his maternal
grandfather as an Alpinist and a geologist. He was educated for a
while at Edinburgh, and in his old age returned to settle down there.

education she shows a far juster appreciation of facts than
did her predecessor. The author of the *Émile* had divided
progressive—or, as he termed it, "successive"—education
into three clearly-marked periods. First comes the education
of the senses up to the age of twelve; this is followed, from
twelve to fifteen, by a period of intellectual education;
finally, between the ages of fifteen and twenty, comes the
education of the will—moral and religious education. Mme
Necker de Saussure clearly sees that this artificial division
of childhood and youth into clear-cut periods is clean
contrary to Rousseau's own principle that we must follow
Nature. "With Nature"—to quote the *Éducation Progressive*[1]—"one can nowhere lay hold on a beginning; she
is not to be surprised in the act of creation, and it seems that
she is always developing." The principle of evolution is as
true of the development of the individual mind as it is of
the human race as a whole, and Mme Necker de Saussure,
realising that the soul is a unity, sees clearly also that it
must develop as a unity. Senses, intellect, will—all alike
are present from the first and all must progress concurrently.
"If the work of education lies in developing the faculties, we
cannot assign any fixed limits to it. It is always possible to
expand the mind and to make the heart better....How then
can we assign a limit to the duration of education[2]?"

Mme Necker de Saussure therefore realises that from the
outset education must concern itself with every side of the
child's being; it must co-operate with nature in the development of the young soul just as the gardener co-operates
with nature in the development of the tender plant. But
what is to be the ultimate aim of the process? In her first
chapter Mme Necker de Saussure gives her answer to this
question: it is to enable the child to fulfil one day his
highest destiny. What then is that destiny—the *summum
bonum* of the early philosophers? Most of them had answered
"happiness," giving the term many and varied meanings;
but to Mme Necker de Saussure the highest good in human
life is what she calls "self-perfection"—so to pass through
things temporal that we finally lose not the things eternal.

[1] I, 163.   [2] *Op. cit.* I, 2.

Hence she concludes that the aim of education is "to give the pupil the will and the means to attain to the perfection of which he will one day be capable[1]." With her, religion is the mainspring of the whole educative process. Man's life here is but a preparation for the life to come and education is therefore an aid to the achievement of eternal life hereafter. In the Scriptures the word "glory" is often employed to denote not only the Christian's recompense in the next world but also his upward progress—*i.e.* his religious development—through this present life[2]. The process of perfectionment is one and continuous; and even though in its fulness the attainment of perfection is an ideal, yet education, to be effective, must be governed and inspired by ideals. But Mme Necker de Saussure is not merely a religious sentimentalist; her lofty aims do not prevent her from being practical. "Education, which is concerned with all the relationships of a man, should be directed towards God. But while relating all earthly matters to their centre, education does not neglect to make them valued at their proper worth. Its ultimate aim is the life to come, but its immediate aim is the complete realisation of this present life[3]."

With this outline of Mme Necker de Saussure's general conception of the scope and aim of education, let us proceed to consider in greater detail how she applies it to the special needs of children in the first three years of their life. She begins by calling attention to the fact that the human race possesses no implanted instincts as to how children should be educated. In different countries and ages there are a thousand conflicting customs and theories. Hence the need of child-study. At her home in Geneva Mme Necker de Saussure was continually meeting men who had devoted their lives to the patient investigation of natural phenomena; but it had apparently occurred to no one to observe methodically the development of the young child and to mark the character and gradual evolution of his mental powers. "In my opinion," she says[4], "it is astonishing that

[1] *Op. cit.* I, 27.　　[2] See *op. cit.* I, 24, and cf. 2 Cor. iii. 18.
[3] *Op. cit.* I, 77.　　[4] *Op. cit.* I, 80.

although such admirable patience has been devoted to the natural sciences, yet childhood has never been systematically studied"; and again: "Cannot education be raised to the rank of a science—that is to say, can we not arrive at definite conclusions when the facts of childhood have been methodically examined and classified[1]?" She recurs several times to the possibility of observation, classification and scientific method in education. Women in view of their special natural gifts are most suited to carry on this work. "It is necessary to have the flexibility of spirit of a woman to follow these mobile beings in their perpetual variations.... Such a study does not consist merely of observation; if one has not the flexibility of imagination which enables one to assume a new nature and to be oneself and another person at one and the same time, one will never know these young creatures. Moreover, it is necessary to love them in order to understand them, for they are divined less by the intelligence than by the heart[2]." These observations, made by women with the seeing eye and the sympathetic imagination, must be carefully recorded; and for this reason Mme Necker de Saussure recommends that every mother should keep what nowadays is sometimes known as a "Progress Book." The development of the physical, intellectual, and moral nature of each child should be noted down in a dated journal and the growth of sentiments and ideas duly chronicled. Not only should this be done for isolated children by their mothers, but teachers also should make similar records for the pupils who are entrusted to their care. The data thus chronicled might be submitted to an association formed for the special study of child-psychology and its application to teaching. "At this time when so many splendid enterprises are being undertaken in the cause of religion and humanity, why should we not hope that an important association will be formed to undertake to solve the great problems of education by the examination of these data? What more important research could ever be the object of human thought[3]?" Finally—one feels at first that it is almost an anti-climax—Mme Necker de Saussure

[1] *Op. cit.* I, 85.   [2] *Op. cit.* I, 86.   [3] *Op. cit.* I, 89.

recommends that the educational experiments, designed to test the theories promulgated by the experts of the association, should be performed upon the *vile corpus* of an establishment for "enfants trouvés." But the prime reason which she gives for such action shows the scientific spirit: "With them there would be the least fear of complication due to antecedents, for one would reap nothing but what one had sown oneself[1]." The possibility that experiments might be complicated owing to the influence of heredity does not seem to have presented itself to her.

The value of Mme Necker de Saussure's contribution to educational thought is nowhere more clearly seen than in this insistence upon the scientific study of childhood. She is the forerunner of a widespread movement which in modern times has rendered inestimable service to the parent and the teacher; and her "important association" has been realised in the London Child Study Society and many other learned bodies with similar aims. But while we recognise to the full the value of the work which they do, let us not forget the Swiss lady who nearly one hundred years ago pointed the way, and let us not grudge to her the honour which is her due.

Mme Necker de Saussure's own acute observation of child life led her to abandon the faculty psychology which had hitherto dominated educational theory. What were regarded as separate activities of the mind, each distinct and unrelated to the others, she sees to be but different manifestations of one and the same mental life. It is true that in the child these activities develop slowly—more slowly than in many other animals. The young chick can run, scratch, peck, and distinguish corn from sand almost as soon as it has emerged from the egg, whereas the child at birth seems to have but one instinct—that of sucking—and for the first few years of his life his activity is governed almost entirely by his sensations and desires. His power of reasoning is as yet latent; but it *is* latent—it is not something superadded *de novo* at a later stage. Thus education can start from the earliest days of the child's life. "Intellectual education in

[1] *Op. cit.* I, 90.

the first stages can as yet consist only of a preparation for the future exercise of the reason. The secret, in this respect, lies in fixing on the infant's mind the too fleeting impressions by means of the interest which one ought to learn to stimulate. The essential thing is that he should remember facts which are stored up in his memory and which can one day furnish points of comparison for his judgment[1]." Although this process is rendered difficult by the fact that the child's attention is so easily distracted, much can be done even in the earliest stages to emphasise the desired impressions. For example, "to caress a dog or a cat, while he is watching you, is to develop in him that sympathy which young children so easily feel for animals; to show him a pretty object and let him examine it in detail is to strengthen his attention and at the same time to excite in him admiration—one of the most beautiful emotions of the soul; to give him pictures to recognise is to awake in him imagination. In short, there are a thousand ways in which to appeal to his growing faculties[2]." The germ of this doctrine had, doubtless, been propounded already by Rousseau. Early in the *Émile*[3] he had said: "The education of man begins at his birth. Before he can speak, before he can understand, he is already instructing himself." Rousseau's recommendation that the young child should be accustomed to see and touch spiders, toads, snakes, and crabs, and to see hideous masks, so that never thereafter may such objects cause him fear or disgust, is for all its grotesqueness at bottom similar to the advice which is given by the authoress of the *Éducation Progressive*. The different ways in which the two thinkers develop the same theme is characteristic of the contrast between them.

In her remarks on education during the first year of the child's life, Mme Necker de Saussure has much to say on the subject of habits, and here she joins issue with Rousseau. Realising that the formation of habits begins at the earliest stage, she sees also that they must be guided and controlled from the very first. "To leave this entirely to nature is to allow whatever she has sown to grow at random. This is the great objection to that negative education which it is so

---

[1] *Op. cit.* I, 104.   [2] *Op. cit.* I, 104.   [3] I, 13.

fashionable to applaud. If we decide to do nothing and to
prevent nothing—'que rien ne soit fait,' as Rousseau says—
then habits will be formed before we are aware of them, and
we shall find that things which we did not look for have
overtaken those which we hoped to obtain. We shall then
all the more promptly be compelled to resort to correction
and constraint—the very methods which we had hoped to
avoid. We shall enter upon a *régime* of prohibition which is
most undesirable and rarely effective[1]."

Our authoress proceeds to consider the tendency which
young children have to cry. Like Rousseau, she realises that
the arts of the inefficient nurse, who gratifies every passing
desire and whose sole aim is to keep the baby quiet, must
in the end fail of their purpose because they tend to engender
an undesirable habit. The child will not be long in perceiving
that he has only to cry loud and long enough in order to
have any wish gratified. Both writers see clearly that to
deal successfully with this problem—and all those who have
been intimately associated with young children will acknowledge that it is an extremely important one—we must first
discover and deal with the cause of the tears. But whereas
Rousseau makes the subject an occasion for a tirade against
contemporary practice, Mme Necker de Saussure discusses it
with a sanity and a sympathy which give her remarks a real
practical value. For Rousseau "the long crying-spells of a
child who is neither swaddled nor ill and who is left in need
of nothing, are but cries of habit or of obstinacy. They are
not the work of nature but of the nurse who, not being able
to endure the trouble caused by them, increases the difficulty,
without thinking that by causing the child to keep quiet
to-day she encourages him to cry all the more to-morrow. The
only way to cure or to prevent this habit is to pay no
attention to it[2]." Mme Necker de Saussure rewrites the whole
passage from the standpoint of preventive moral education.
She lays it down that: "the most certain fact for an observant
mother is to take it for granted that tears have a reason;
if she looks carefully for the cause, she will find foundation
for far more griefs than she imagines. Little children, in

---

[1] *Éduc. Prog.* I, 106.   [2] *Émile*, I, 82.

spite of what is said, have no caprices; a hope unfulfilled, a pain felt or anticipated, are nearly always the causes of their cries[1]."

The treatment of those griefs which are due to physical pain lies largely outside the scope of education; but those which arise from mental causes are discussed in the *Éducation Progressive*. If we are to anticipate them, the surest safeguard will be to develop regular habits. This is true of young children at almost every stage of their career. The baby who has not been accustomed to be rocked to sleep or to be provided with that unhygienic abomination known as a "comforter," will not howl lustily until someone, in sheer desperation, provides the desired solace. The child who has learnt to behave politely as part of the natural order of things will not need bribing with sweets in order to show respect to a visitor. And because tears are often a result of over-excitement—another infringement of the law of regularity in the conduct of the child's life—Mme Necker de Saussure lays great stress on serenity—"mot charmant," she calls it. "We shall maintain in our children an habitual tranquillity of soul, an untold blessing and one easy to lose, but the most necessary perhaps to their moral nature which is as yet so weak and unstable....But I am concerned not merely with preventing the evil of which I am speaking. There is a whole group of characteristics—perhaps the highest of all—which grow and mature only in the protective shade of tranquillity[2]." There are few passages of the *Éducation Progressive* which are more full than this of mature wisdom. We are all ready, no doubt, to recognise the moral value of the cultivation of the "quiet mind"; and its physical implications are emphasised by every writer on how to be healthy and live long. But the realisation of mental serenity is probably as rare and as difficult under modern conditions as it has ever been in the past. It is surely worth our while to consider what Mme Necker de Saussure has to say on a subject of such real importance to the well being of mankind.

She points out that this serenity of mind is naturally found in the young child. "It shines with a clear light in

[1] *Éduc. Prog.* I, 108.   [2] *Op. cit.* I, 109.

his eyes, it sits upon his open countenance." We must therefore guard against intruding too roughly and too readily upon his mental life. We are too fond of interfering with the child's own interests. We delude ourselves into thinking that he continually needs "amusing," and so we supply a series of mental stimulants which excite his mind, but ultimately weaken and unsettle it. As a corollary, Mme Necker de Saussure lays it down that "it is better to occupy very small children with things rather than with persons. As I have said, it is not that the distinction is very clear to their eyes, but at any rate things are peaceful objects and do not tend to excite them. With things they make experiments without realising it, and their judgment develops by involuntary observation. But with persons they live either in sympathy or antipathy. The influence which human beings exercise one upon the other sets all the emotions in movement, and this action is all the more vigorous in the case of infants because they cannot communicate their thoughts and everything takes place on the emotional plane[1]." This observation again is strikingly true to facts, although Mme Necker de Saussure seems to have been one of the first educational thinkers to realise it. The writer—if he may be allowed a personal reminiscence—well remembers a "brave, sweet babe" who used to lie serenely wide awake in his perambulator under a tree, watching for an hour or more at a time the play of light and shadow in the rustling leaves above his head. It was perhaps not unreasonable to feel that, like the young men in Plato's *Republic*, he was "dwelling in a healthful region and drinking in good from every quarter whence any emanation from noble works might strike upon his eye...and win him imperceptibly from his earliest childhood into resemblance, love, and harmony with the true beauty of reason[2]." Such lessons in the first years of life are learnt from inanimate objects. The parent of any child who is of what is called a "nervy" disposition and who therefore is most easily affected by the stimulus of other individuals, will have noticed that any breaking of routine, which involves the intrusion of some new and

---

[1] *Op. cit.* I, 110.   [2] Plato, *Republic*, 401 c.

striking personality upon the child's mental life, has very
marked effects; and that these effects may persist for some
time and, if undesirable, are often difficult to check. The
moral is that, within limits, the more a child is left to himself
and his normal surroundings, and the less his natural mental
tranquillity is disturbed, the better will it be for him. Let
the child amuse himself. "It seems to me," said a German
physician whom Mme Necker de Saussure quotes, "that
mothers play too much with their children in the first stage
of life and that they stimulate their vivacity too soon." At
the same time, the educator must keep careful watch and
be ready to give the child any help that he may need. If
that is done, the child's gradually-realised sense of trust and
security will develop in him "bienveillance"—good-will—
which in time will in its turn engender a kindly disposition
and a habit of consideration for others; so far-reaching are
the effects of impressions received in the earliest years of
life.

By the beginning of the third year the child has already
made some progress in the art of speech. In the sixth
chapter of her second book Mme Necker de Saussure treats
of this topic at some length and records the result of her
own observations on the growth of language in the child.
What she says is of interest as indicating the scientific
attitude towards education which characterises our authoress;
but otherwise the subject need not detain us. There are
many modern books[1] which include all her investigations
and go far beyond them; but we may stay to notice Mme
Necker de Saussure's remarks about the results of learning
to speak upon the child's own mental development. With
the beginnings of language there is forged a new link of
sympathy between the child himself and those who surround
him; and from this sympathy arises a tendency to imitate.
"After having shared our emotions the child wants to act
as we do. He thinks that he can achieve whatever he sees
us do and his attempts, sometimes skilful, sometimes clumsy,
are a great source of amusement to us[2]." But to the child

[1] Sully's *Studies in Childhood* (ch. v) is one of the most instructive.
[2] *Éduc. Prog.* I, 122.

they are matters of deadly earnest. There is perhaps no one who is seriously interested in the good education of young children, who has not at some time or other been irritated by the outburst of unthinking laughter which greets the attempt of a little child to copy his elders, and who has not noted with sympathy the look of wonderment upon the face of the young experimenter. But Mme Necker de Saussure fully realises the importance of the part which this tendency to imitate plays in the development of the young soul. Hence she sees that to adopt the "negative" education of Rousseau is to run untold risks. We must give "some kind of positive education at the earliest stages. This means that we must not only remove bad examples from the child but must also stimulate in him a gentle movement towards the good and thus make him enter upon life with an inclination in a desirable direction[1]." How then can we ensure that, if we supply the required good examples, the child who is under our charge will imitate them rather than any other? Mothers, says Mme Necker de Saussure, have the key to the secret; to influence children it is necessary first of all to love them. Love begets love. As the Port-Royalist Coustel pointed out, the heart is the spring of all the actions and when once you are master of it you can straightway do whatever you please. This does not mean that caresses must be overdone; on the contrary, they must be kept strictly within bounds. Mme Necker de Saussure does not go so far as Jacqueline Pascal and Maria Edgeworth who forbade them altogether; but she does realise that they may tend to disturb that serenity or tranquillity of mind which she prizes so highly. "Let your caresses then have in them something encouraging—something strengthening, if I may say so. Infuse them with cheerfulness without excess, and above all banish from them any kind of weakness. The more you can make them a mark of approval, the sooner will you render them a useful instrument[2]."

Equally important is it to avoid outbursts of anger against the child or in his presence. Even "righteous indignation" must not be exhibited before him because he judges of

[1] *Op. cit.* I, 128.   [2] *Op. cit.* I, 132.

wrath by its manifestations rather than by its causes. It is
essential that he should never imitate habits of this kind.
"When we reflect upon the immense advantage which
unexcitable people have over others in life, how can we fail
to do our best to obtain this superiority for our children[1]?"

The desire to imitate, which becomes pronounced at about
the third year of the child's life, has many other important
implications. "In poor families," says Mme Necker de
Saussure, "when the mother is sensible and kind, the
children are perhaps more intelligent and advanced than in
other families, because they enjoy a peculiar advantage.
They are interested in everything that they see. They
understand it and take part in it[2]." This is without doubt
a real gain. Children who lead a life apart from that of their
family, knowing nothing of the interests and occupations of
their parents, and who are isolated in a nursery under the
care of a hired nurse, may miss many advantages even
though they be supplied with the most modern and elaborate
toys. But those who are allowed to take their part in the
life of the household, learning its routine by imitation,
develop their intellects and ultimately acquire a habit of
being useful while amusing themselves at the same time.
For such babies their very nursery rhymes have an inward
significance which is denied to the denizens of an elaborately-
equipped nursery situated at the top of the house. The child
for whom "Pat-a-cake, pat-a-cake, baker's man" was
written was not excluded from the kitchen where a professional cook reigned supreme; he had no doubt watched his
mother as she performed all the processes of preparation—
the "patting and pricking and marking with B"—and had
personally witnessed the arrival of the cake piping hot from
the oven "for baby and me." It is not too much to say
that such an experience has a very real educational value[3].

The child's tendency to imitate can be employed not
merely to encourage him, as he grows older, to become

---

[1] *Op. cit.* I, 134.   [2] *Op. cit.* I, 169.
[3] Cf. an article on "Baby Week" in the *Daily News* of July 3rd,
1917.

useful and to enter into the life of the family of which he forms part. It can also be a means of direct moral education. Suppose that a new baby arrives in a family where hitherto there has been but one child; the elder may be inclined to feel jealous when he realises that he is no longer the sole object of interest. But if you can stimulate his imitative activity by encouraging him to do small services for the new arrival, he will take great delight in thus copying his elders and at the same time will conceive a deep affection for the object of his care.

In this all-important third year of the child's life we are still "governing him by habits, the natural result of our care and our regularity[1]." The most necessary of all such habits is that of obedience because by its means we can control the formation of all other kinds of desirable habits. For-tunately we are aided by an instinctive docility on the part of the child towards his parents. There is nothing degrading in such a relationship; it is the outcome of the already existing "sympathy" which exists between the child and those to whom he looks for protection and help; one day it will blossom into filial piety—"vertu sublime et touchante." This feeling is the "distinctive characteristic of the intimate relationship between father and son—a relationship unique in this world by virtue of its sanctity, its depth, and the disinterestedness of the sentiments which it evokes[2]."

To ensure this habit of obedience we must set to work long before the child has begun to reason; the means of securing it is the natural bond of sympathy to which allusion has just been made and the avoidance of occasions which might give rise to contrariance. Discipline therefore must err neither on the side of leniency nor of severity, and it is better to prevent disobedience than to endeavour to cure it. It is, however, a grave mistake to follow the advice of Rousseau and to refrain from exacting obedience or imposing duties upon the child before he is able to appreciate the various social relationships upon which those duties are based. If this were done it would atrophy the feeling of sympathy—the realisation that protection is afforded on the

---

[1] *Éduc. Prog.* I, 151.   [2] *Op. cit.* I, 158.

one side and received on the other—which is the foundation
of the child's obedience towards his parents. For by the
time that the social implications of this relationship are
realised the child is no longer a child; he is a young man,
practically if not entirely independent of his parents and no
longer bound to them by this tie of dependence. Moreover,
it is nature's own method that the affections should mature
more quickly than the reasoning powers, and for this cause
again the habit of obedience must be grounded on affection
and not on argument.

Mme Necker de Saussure proceeds to give some practical
hints as to "the most gentle means of obtaining obedience
at an early stage." Regularity and consistency of treatment
are indicated; and, as has been said, for the young child the
habit of obedience comes most easily when it is associated
with pleasing or avoiding displeasing someone who has won
his love. At the same time a command is a command;
"when once obedience has been demanded, do not laugh or
caress or even request any longer[1]." Our authoress appends
the following "penal code" for children who are in the
second and third years of their life:

Disobedience caused by forgetfulness: Show that you dis-
approve of a repetition of the act by renewing your prohibition in a friendly way.

A rather more voluntary relapse: Assume a serious air and
warn the child that if he offends again the means of dis-
obeying will be taken from him.

A second and entirely voluntary relapse: Put your threat
into execution by silently taking such steps as will effectively
render disobedience impossible.

If, in the last-mentioned case, the child resorts to other
forms of naughtiness in order to express effectively his
sentiments, it is wise to show as little emotion as possible.
Anger not only sets him a bad example, but it may awake
in him an undesirable feeling of triumph that he has
succeeded in rousing you. Mme Necker de Saussure therefore
advises the mother to continue her work as calmly as she

---

[1] *Op. cit.* i, 164.

can, and soon the tears will cease, or will no longer be tears
of anger but of remorse. Then comes the stage when the
child says that he is "sorry" and an affectionate reconciliation is possible. The mother has not in any degree ceded her
claim to obedience and the bond of sympathy upon which
that obedience is founded has been strengthened.

The rapid development of the power of speech during the
third year of the child's life introduces a new subject of the
utmost importance—that of telling the truth. At first the
child has little or no idea of what truth means. The outcome
of that "sympathy" which lies at the base of education may·
sometimes be that he will say what he thinks will give you
pleasure, and not necessarily what is true. The same
phenomenon has been noted among savages and other
peoples who are not far advanced in the moral scale. To
avoid this, it is not sufficient to tell the child that whatever
he says must accord with facts and not with his own desires
or those of other people; this lesson must be enforced by
example. If you are recounting some incident which he has
witnessed or in which he has taken part, and you make
some slight error of fact, he will correct you with that
curious pedantry which is characteristic of young children
at this stage. In that case it is wise to accept his emendation
and thank him for it; he will then appreciate the value
which you set upon exactitude. The habit of truth-telling
may also be fostered by preventive as well as by positive
methods. Encourage children to confess their faults but
grant them full and immediate pardon. Never tempt them
by questions about faults which could easily be denied or
concealed. Never endanger their sense of loyalty and
affection, as well as their regard for truth, by asking them
to play the informer against a servant or a playmate. But
the most important rule of all is that those who deal with
children should set them a consistent example of veracity.
"To deceive a child is not only to set him a mischievous
example, but it is also to lose all our influence with him for
the future....Everything can be repaired in regard to
children except untruth; be impatient, angry, even occasionally unjust—that would be a great pity, but they may

possibly forget[1]." Scrupulous truth-telling on the part of
the educator, therefore, has this double advantage: it sets
an example of the very highest value and it helps to maintain
that influence over children without which a good education
cannot be imparted.

The imagination is another phase of mental activity which
becomes especially prominent at about the third or fourth
year. This manifests itself in several ways. For example,
there is a tendency to personify inanimate objects. Not only
do dolls become for the child living beings, but even the
ordinary utensils of everyday use are endued with life and
therefore arouse a sympathy in virtue of their familiarity
and utility. Mme Necker de Saussure quotes an instance of
a child at this stage who, on breaking his cup, cried: "Poor
cup! I was so fond of you." Professor Sully[2] has dealt in
some detail with the same phenomenon. We can understand
the case of the little girl who offered a biscuit to a steam
tram, but the vivification of inanimate objects resulting
solely from familiarity with them is more foreign to the
adult mind. Sully instances a little boy who conceived a
special fondness for the letter W and used to address it as
"dear old boy W."

Realising the power of this imaginative faculty we must
adapt our method to it. The best kind of toys for a child
at this stage are those which give him scope for invention.
Hence the value of plain blocks which can become at will
houses, trains, ships, animals, and a hundred other objects
at the creative fiat of the child's imagination. The writer
remembers the case of a child, well-provided with elaborate
toys by indulgent parents, who greatly preferred to play
with a quantity of clothes-pegs which doubtless underwent
countless metamorphoses not apparent to the uninitiated;
and who rarely used his expensive playthings for the purposes for which the maker had intended them. The power
of the child's imagination is sometimes so strong that no
material medium at all is needed for its exercise. Mme Necker
de Saussure gives several instances of this, and the following

---

[1] *Éduc. Prog.* I, 181.
[2] See *Studies of Childhood*, chap. II.

will serve to show what is meant: "A father heard from his window his children practising archery in the garden. One judged the shots; the rest appealed to his decisions. They disputed and shouted, applauded the winners and jeered at those who failed. The father became uneasy. Whence did they get the bows? Could they shoot at their age? Would they not hurt themselves? Not being able to rest, he went down into the garden and watched them. He saw them rosy, animated, full of that serious enthusiasm which accompanies the deepest pleasures. The whole pantomime was perfect; but there were no bows, no arrows, no target[1]."

This vividness of imagination which can endow with life not only moving objects but also the commonest articles in ordinary use, and can even be quite independent of any of these media, gives a special importance to the subject of story-telling to young children. "The pictures which we conjure up within them," says Mme Necker de Saussure, "are perhaps more vivid, more brilliant, than is the reality itself. A story makes them see a magic lantern show. There is no need therefore to exert one's powers of invention in order to interest them. Take a child as the principal character. Add a cat, a horse—anything which they can easily imagine —and put some enthusiasm into your tale. Your hearer will drink it all in eagerly....Whenever he meets you he will make you tell your tale again. But be careful to make no alterations. He wants to see again the same scene and the least detail left out or added breaks the spell which charms him[2]." If then the child can vivify with an almost supernatural reality the tales which are related to him, it is nothing short of a criminal action to tell him stories of a terrifying nature. He should never hear of ghosts or bugbears or evil spirits. Shocks to the immature nervous system, produced by these means, do incalculable harm and are extremely difficult to counteract afterwards. Rousseau had suggested that if children were encouraged to play games by night, they would become accustomed to the darkness and to the mysterious surprises which it contains; and that therefore a fear of the dark which—in spite of what Rousseau says[3]—

[1] *Éduc. Prog.* I, 190.   [2] *Op. cit.* I, 187.   [3] See *Émile*, I, 141.

is often associated by children with tales of ghosts and goblins, would be eradicated. Mme Necker de Saussure prefers that the child should learn to forget his fear rather than that he should try to brave it out. That, however,— as has been said—is difficult because of the extraordinary vividness of the impressions received when the imagination is so active. The case is one for prevention rather than for cure.

Having discussed the imagination of the child in his third year Mme Necker de Saussure proceeds to trace the awakening of his conscience. The child is largely under the influence of his emotions; his ideas express themselves very simply and directly in action and are but little subject to restraint or inhibition. These emotions are for the most part those which he feels for other people—the "sympathy" to which Mme Necker de Saussure refers so often. Hence early ideas of right and wrong usually resolve themselves into a matter of pleasing or displeasing some definite person or persons. It will therefore be difficult to persuade the young child that petty thefts, for instance, which affect no one in particular and leave no traces, are wrong *per se*. Conscience must develop out of the habit of obedience which, as Mme Necker de Saussure has already pointed out, begins to be formed in the very early stages of the child's life. The child will be led to recognise that pilfering is wrong in itself because to indulge such a propensity would be a direct act of disobedience against one whom he loves. "If by forgetfulness or weakness the child has given way to temptation, it is when he meets his master (*i.e.* normally, his parent) that remorse fills his heart. He can see without a pang the owner of the flowers or fruits that he has stolen; but his cheeks flush with shame when he meets the representative of his conscience. It is to him that the confessions, the tender and touching explanations, are made; it is to him that the child feels the need for making amends, so natural to the guilty heart[1]."

The authoress of the *Éducation Progressive* goes on to discuss whether children have a natural inclination towards

[1] *Éduc. Prog.* I, 197.

evil, and for the first time, perhaps, her doctrinal views colour her general theory of education. Brought up in the strictest school of Calvinistic Protestantism, she could have but one answer to this question. Rousseau had asserted the original goodness of mankind, but for Mme Necker de Saussure "the most sacred authority—Holy Scripture—has pronounced that the heart of man is corrupt[1]." At the same time our authoress has no exaggerated conceptions of infant depravity. As far as her own observation goes, the only definite tendency towards evil normally exhibited by very young children is a "disposition générale à l'égoïsme." Still, love of self may be a root of many evils and therefore the essential work of education, next to the cultivation of good dispositions, is the eradication of bad ones. In this latter class comes that depraved pleasure in breaking a rule merely for the sake of doing so. Another example is wanton cruelty which doubtless often contains an element of laudable curiosity, but which gets its spice from a sense of braving the feeling of pity and realising that one has the power to be cruel. These tendencies are signs of the disposition towards vice which man's fallen nature inherits; but we must deal tenderly with those who show such proclivities. When parents discover them in their children, they must bear in mind the kindly judgment passed upon human weakness by the inspired Scriptures. Instead of having to deal severely with the evil they ought rather to be forewarned and to check these faults in time. Once more the whole problem turns upon the personal relationship which should exist between the child and those who are responsible for him.

But morality cannot remain for ever in the leading strings. Sooner or later conscience must become a personal possession and it cannot always be exercised by proxy. Hence the vital importance of an early religious development. The whole history of mankind from its very beginning shows that man is by nature religious, and the history of the individual repeats that of the race. The child welcomes the idea of God; though it be so lofty, so profound, that the wisest and most experienced thinkers contemplate it with reverent awe,

[1] *Op. cit.* I, 199.

yet it is not beyond the grasp of the child's mind. It is the pure in heart, not the learned in intellect, who see God. But how are we to introduce this conception of God to the child whom nature has made so ready to receive it? It is chiefly in His works of creation that the divine Demiurgos will reveal Himself to the young child. He will easily accept the idea of a bountiful Creator Who makes the roses fragrant and the strawberries sweet, Who is the Architect and Sustainer of the universe and Who yet has bidden us to suffer the little children to come unto Him. Simple stories from the Old and New Testaments—and especially incidents from the life of our Lord—are well within the comprehension of quite young children, and the truths of revealed religion may thus be imparted through a medium which arouses the child's deep interest and impresses itself on his memory. For this reason Mme Necker de Saussure has little sympathy for "la doctrine sèche des catéchismes," where phrases are repeated by rote and awake no response in the mind of the child.

Thus a knowledge of God and of His attributes is in some measure possible to the little child; and the birth of religion in his heart comes when that *pietas* which he has already learnt towards his parents, is translated into *pietas* towards the God Whom he has learnt to recognise. To revert once more to the words of our authoress: "What is the true object of religious education? It is to teach the young soul to hold communion with God, since the realisation of that communion—however much it may be misused by fanaticism—is none the less of the very essence of religion[1]." When this is realised morality is no longer a duty towards a parent; it becomes a duty towards God and conscience is now raised to the higher plane of religion. Wrong doing is recognised as an offence against divine and eternal law; repentance is seen to be reconciliation with the heavenly Father through the merits of His Son; good works are looked upon as a co-operation with Him Who went about doing good. In the eyes of Mme Necker de Saussure, it is a grave mistake to postpone religious instruction—as Rousseau

[1] *Op. cit.* 1, 213.

would do—until the age of fifteen or even later. Religion must begin with the sentiments; it arises out of the relationship of "sympathy" between parent and child and it does this most effectively because that relationship is most akin to the relationship between God and man. Not without significance has the First Person of the Holy Trinity been given the name of "Father." To wait until the reasoning is developed and to attempt to establish the truths of religion and its moral implications by logical proof is to miss a unique opportunity. Even if religion can be imparted to any extent at this stage and in this manner, we may surely echo Mme Necker de Saussure when she says: "Remember that religion which resides only in the head is as useless for conduct as it is for happiness[1]."

The awakening of the religious sense in the child implies the establishment of a link between himself and God. Worship in all its forms is the appointed channel of communication and therefore the child at this stage must learn the use of prayer and praise. The highest form of adoration— that which realises that God is a Spirit and which seeks to worship Him in spirit and in truth—is not possible for the child. It comes at a much later stage and is the fine flower of religious education. But simple prayers are the natural expression of the child's own religious feelings. When he recognises that God is the Author of so many blessings which he enjoys, he will readily and spontaneously utter his childish thanks; and if we can encourage him to avail himself regularly of this means of communication between himself and his heavenly Father he will "grow spiritually," because he receives day by day spiritual sustenance from God. Mme Necker de Saussure pleads especially for the practice of making young children sing suitable hymns, because of the deep impression which it leaves. She attributes the undying popularity of the paraphrases of Clément Marot to the fact that for generations they had been taught in Protestant homes to children from their earliest years. She also advocates the English custom of hymn-singing in

[1] *Op. cit.* I, 212.

"les écoles modernes appelées *infant schools*[1]." But such devotional exercises are, after all, only accessory. The essential link between man and God is prayer. Mme Necker de Saussure thinks that a child, if he be "sensible et avancé," can learn to pray as early as the third year of life. His petitions will be simple and will re-assert that relationship of "sympathy" which has already been established between the child and his parents. In other words, prayer will start from the love of God for the child and the child's response to that love; and his affection for those who surround him will be sanctified by his calling down of God's blessing upon them.

With the third part of Mme Necker de Saussure's first volume ends her discussion of the "first part of infancy." She proceeds to treat of the child's development after the third year and traces it in subsequent books up to the age of puberty. But we cannot stay to follow her further. Enough perhaps has been said to establish her claim to be considered an acute observer of child life and a profound thinker upon the subject of education. She owes much to Rousseau, but between the two writers there are also many and striking contrasts. At Mme de Staël's house she may well have met Pestalozzi whose *How Gertrude teaches her Children* had appeared in 1801 and who gained a considerable influence in Switzerland and Germany long before he became known in other countries; yet her writings do not show any important trace of the educational doctrines which are particularly associated with the reformer of Stans and Yverdon. Frœbel again was a contemporary of Mme Necker de Saussure and she had probably read his *Education of Man* which was published two years before the first volume of the *Éducation Progressive*; but she cannot in any definite and distinctive fashion be classed as a Frœbelian. In short, although she took part in the inauguration of a great

---

[1] She is thinking more particularly of the work of Samuel Wilderspin, and the Infant School which he opened in Spitalfields in 1820. There exists no adequate biography of Wilderspin, but a succinct account of his work will be found in Monroe, *Cyclopædia of Education*, v, 773.

movement—the application of psychology to education—she
makes her own independent and characteristic contribution.
If her style be at times almost Teutonic in its turgidity
and the arrangement of her treatise occasionally incoherent,
there runs throughout an undercurrent of clear and logical
development which amply substantiates the claim of the
authoress to be considered a Frenchwoman. Moreover, although religion bulks so largely in Mme Necker de Saussure's
scheme of education—and for her religion is avowedly a
doctrinal system of a very definite type—yet her theological
views do not in any essential point affect her general
position. It is not true, as Compayré has rather superficially
remarked, that she "views human nature through a dark
veil[1]." Her conception of man's nature and destiny is full
of light and hope. Doubtless she takes a lofty view of what
that destiny should be, but she believes that a wise system
of education, begun from the earliest years of life, is the
most potent aid which can be given to the child in order to
enable him one day to fulfil his destiny. We rise from a
study of the *Éducation Progressive* with a conviction that
here is one of the most important products of French
educational thought. We admire in turns the philosophic
acumen, the keen and sympathetic observation of children,
the conspicuous sanity and exactitude of judgment, which
the authoress displays; and we turn back with a fresh
interest and a new insight to what is perhaps at once the
most difficult and the most important of all the educator's
problems—the treatment of the child during the first few
years of his life.

[1] *Histoire des Doctrines de l'Éducation en France*, II, 118.

APPENDIX A

ON THE COINS MENTIONED IN THE TEXT

As reference is made several times in the text to coins which were current in France during the period covered by this book, it has seemed advisable to deal with this matter once and for all in a short appendix rather than to insert a number of foot-notes.

The unit of the monetary system was the *livre*. Previous to 1667 there were two kinds of livre—the livre tournois and the livre parisis. Each was divided into 20 sols (or sous) and each sol into 12 deniers; but 20 sols parisis were equivalent to 25 sols tournois, and one sol parisis to 15 deniers tournois. In 1667 the livre tournois, which was in general use throughout France, became the only unit of currency and the livre parisis was abolished. It remained in use until after the Revolution and was then replaced by the franc. In this book when the word *livre* is used it refers to the livre tournois. It is, of course, almost impossible to assess the exact value of coins of former times. According to Avenel (*Histoire économique des prix*, etc. Paris, 1894) the following table is approximately correct:

About 1600 the livre was equivalent to 2·57 modern francs.

,,	1650	,,	,,	,,	1·82	,,	,,
,,	1700	,,	,,	,,	1·48	,,	,,
,,	1750	,,	,,	,,	0·95	,,	,,

Even this does not settle definitely the modern equivalent of the purchasing power of the livre, but it is helpful to be informed that the day labourer's wage in 1600 was 12 sols, in 1667 14 sols, in 1675 16 sols, and in 1720 18 sols.

The *écu d'or* was a coin the value of which varied considerably. In 1570 it was equivalent to 3 livres; in 1615 to 3 livres 15 sols; in 1636 to 4 livres 14 sols; in 1640 to 5 livres 4 sols. After this date no more *écus d'or* were coined.

The *pistole* of the Franche-Comté (see p. 65 n.²) was a gold coin the normal value of which was 10 livres; in 1628, however, during the wars, this rose to 14 livres.

The Genevan *florin* (p. 78) was a silver coin and the equi-

valent of 12 Genevan sols. Its value in French money varied
greatly from time to time. Apparently in the days of Calvin
it was worth more than the livre, but by the middle of the
eighteenth century it had sunk to less than half its value.
(Consult Abot de Bazinghen: *Traité des Monnoies*, I, 514, 645.)

APPENDIX B

A LIST OF COLLEGES OF THE UNIVERSITY OF PARIS WHICH WERE IN EXISTENCE AT THE END OF THE SIXTEENTH CENTURY, WITH THE DATE WHEN EACH WAS FOUNDED

[*Collegès de plein exercice* are shown in CAPITALS.]

Collège des Dix-Huits ... 1180	C. d'Hubant (*or* de l'Ave-Maria) ... 1339
C. des Bons Enfans ... 1209	C. d'Autun (*or* de Bertrand) 1341
C. DE LA SORBONNE ... 1256	C. de Mignon (*or* de Grandmont) ... 1343
C. du Trésorier ... 1270	
C. de Calvi (*or* La Petite Sorbonne) ... 1271	C. de Cambrai (*or* des Trois Évêques) ... 1348
C. D'HARCOURT ... 1280	C. de St-Michel (*or* de Chanac) ... 1348
C. des Cholets ... 1295	
C. DU CARDINAL-LEMOINE 1302	C. de Boncour ... 1353
C. DE NAVARRE ... 1304	C. de Justice ... 1354
C. de Bayeux ... 1308	C. de Tournai ... 1354
C. de Laon ... 1314	C. de Boissy ... 1358
C. de Presles ... 1314	C. DE BEAUVAIS (*or* DE DORMANS) ... 1370
C. DE MONTAIGU ... 1314	
C. de Cornouailles ... 1317	C. de Maître-Gervais ... 1370
C. de Narbonne ... 1317	C. de Daimville ... 1380
C. DU PLESSIS ... 1322	C. de Fortet ... 1393
C. de Trégnier ... 1325	C. de Reims ... 1409
C. des Écossais ... 1325	C. DE LA MARCHE... ... 1423
C. de Marmoutier ... 1329	C. de Séez ... 1428
C. d'Arras ... 1332	C. de Sainte-Barbe ... 1460
C. de Bourgogne ... 1332	C. de Coquerel ... 1463
C. de Tours ... 1334	C. du Mans ... 1528
C. des Lombards ... 1334	C. DES GRASSINS ... 1565
C. DE LISIEUX ... 1336	

[In 1661 there was also founded the COLLÈGE MAZARIN *or* DES QUATRE-NATIONS.]

In the year 1600 there existed also in Paris the following colleges belonging to religious communities:

C. des Jacobins	...	... 1221	C. de Cluny 1269	
C. des Cordeliers	...	... 1230	C. des Blancs-Manteaux ... 1297	
C. des Bernardins	...	... 1244	C. de la Merci 1515	
C. des Prémontrés		... 1252	C. DE CLERMONT (Jesuits) 1563	
C. des Carmes	...	... 1259		

In 1682 the Jesuits changed the name of the Collège de Clermont to that of Collège Louis-le-Grand. After the expulsion of the Order in 1762 the University of Paris transferred its official seat to the home of its former rivals and all the colleges which were not *de plein exercice* were amalgamated with Louis-le-Grand. Thus the secondary education given by the University was concentrated in the few full-course colleges that remained. At the Revolution the collegiate system of the University of Paris disappeared and it has never been revived.

APPENDIX C

OATH ADMINISTERED TO STUDENTS EN-
TERING THE UNIVERSITY OF PARIS IN THE
TIME OF RAMUS

I. Iurabitis quod toto tempore vestræ vitæ, ad quemcumque statum deveneritis, servabitis et procurabitis servari privilegia, iura, libertates, franchisias et statuta Universitatis Parisiensis.

II. Iurabitis quod si sciveritis secreta Universitatis Parisiensis nullibi revelabitis neque dicetis in preiudicium eiusdem Universitatis.

III. Iurabitis quod toto tempore vestræ vitæ, ad quemcumque statum deveneritis, exhibitis domino Rectori honorem, reverentiam, obediendo in omnibus licitis et honestis.

IV. Iurabitis quod si sciveritis aliquam iniuriam inferri domino Rectori aut alicui magistro signanter regenti, procurabitis amendam condignam fieri dicto Domino Rectori ac magistro sic patienti pro toto posse, neque partem iniuriantium quocumque modo fovebitis directe aut indirecte.

V. Iurabitis quod toto tempore vestræ vitæ servabitis pacem et concordiam intra suppositos Universitatis Parisiensis.

VI. Iurabitis quod nomen et cognomen vestrum fideliter dicetis.

VII. Iurabitis quod secundum Ecclesiam catholicam, apostolicam et Romanam vivetis, a qua si defeceritis, privilegia academiæ privabimini eritisque expuncti.

APPENDIX D

FORM OF LICENCE ISSUED BY THE *ÉCOLÂTRE* TO A MISTRESS IN A LITTLE SCHOOL (*LETTRE DE MAÎTRISE*, 1630)

MICHAEL LEMASLE, presbyter, sanctæ sedis apostolicæ protonotarius, prior commanditarius et dominus prioratus de Rupibus Sancti Pauli, præcentor et canonicus insignis metropolitanæ ecclesiæ parisiensis, dilectæ Mariæ N...commoranti salutem in Domino.

Quum ad nos ratione nostræ dignitatis præcentoris dictæ ecclesiæ parisiensis spectet et pertineat collatio et regimen parvarum scolarum urbis, civitatis, suburbiorum, et banlieucæ parisiensis, et antea rectoris tui litteris testimonialibus et aliorum fide dignorum relata de vita, moribus, pietate, et religione catholica commendata, et examine nostro digna ad scholas tenendas reperta fueris, tibi idcirco scholas tenendi et exercendi in vulgo dicto loco de ... inibique puellas docendi et instituendi in bonis moribus, litteris grammaticalibus, et aliis piis et honestis exercitiis, iuramento prius a te recepto, de dictis scholis sedulo et fideliter exercendis, statutisque et ordinationibus nostris observandis licentiam concedimus et facultatem impertimur; præsentibus de hunc usque ad instantem nostrum synodum proximum (si intra annum habeatur) alias ad annum duntaxat valituris.

Datum Parisiis sub sigillo nostro et signo manuali magistri Petri Lecousturier, publici auctoritate apostolica curiæque archiepiscopalis parisiensis notarii iurati, Parisiis, in via Nucum, vulgo *des Noyers* dicta, commorantis, nostri scribæ et sigilliferi, anno Domini millesimo sexcentesimo trigesimo, die...mensis...

LECOUSTURIER.

For a similar licence issued to a master in a boys' Little School and dating from 1672 see Félibien, *Recueil de pièces justificatives pour servir des preuves à l'histoire de Paris* (1725), III, 463.

APPENDIX E

OF the pupils who were educated at the Ursuline schools founded by Anne de Xainctonge, many eventually took up the profession of *maîtresse d'école*. The following document was drawn up at the mother-house at Dôle in the early part of the eighteenth century and was designed primarily as a guide for former pupils who were teaching in the Franche-Comté and elsewhere. It deals not merely with school organisation and methods, but with the special duties and responsibilities which the mistress has to bear in virtue of her office. As the document thus furnishes an important commentary on the education of girls at this period and is at the same time an echo of the De Xainctonge schools, it has seemed advisable to translate the greater part of it and to include it in this book as an appendix to Chapter II.

SCHOOL REGULATIONS FOR THE USE OF MISTRESSES WHO HAVE CHARGE OF THE EDUCATION OF GIRLS

Morning school

(1) School will begin at 7.0 all the year round and end at 11.0.

(2) The mistress will place a crucifix in the most appropriate part of the room and will put on one side of it an image of the Holy Virgin and on the other an image of St Catherine.

(3) On entering the room the pupils will say devoutly: "May Jesus Christ be praised"; to which the answer: "Amen" will be made. They will then kneel at the oratory and recite a *Pater* and an *Ave*, after which they will take the places assigned to them by the mistress for the whole year and will learn their lessons.

(4) At about 7.45 those who came first into school will begin to repeat the first lesson; before they go back to their places the mistress will kneel down with the pupils to recite the *Veni Sancte Spiritus*, or some other prayer to beseech Heaven's aid

for herself and the children. Before beginning a lesson every pupil will say: "My God, I offer to Thee the lesson which I am about to repeat; give me grace to profit by it; in the name of the Father, and of the Son, and of the Holy Ghost." At the end of a lesson she will make a courtesy and say: "I thank you, mistress."

(5) After the first lessons have been said, morning prayer will be recited; this should not be done at the beginning of school because the little girls have not all arrived at that time. Those pupils who are competent to do so will recite it in turn; after the prayer, a quarter-of-an-hour for a meal during which a religious book is read aloud.

(6) Three times a week, at the end of the prayer and before the meal, the mistress on her knees will make a short commentary in an intelligible manner on some religious truth, some virtue or vice, so as to teach children to speak to God and to commune with Him by means of prayer.

(7) After grace has been said, the second lesson will be repeated, beginning with those pupils who learn writing or arithmetic and who will then go and write out their copies.

(8) When the bell goes for Mass, the mistress will put her girls in a proper frame of mind to hear it devoutly by saying a word as to the great act which they are about to perform and the feelings which ought to accompany it; this done, she will take them, two by two, to church, making them walk modestly and tell their beads as they go; on entering she will offer them the holy water and will sit behind them to see how they behave.

(9) After the second lesson has been repeated the mistress will look at the copies which have been written, will notice the mistakes and point them out. The rest of the time she will spend in teaching the smallest children their catechism and in instructing them individually in the morning and evening prayers; she will teach all who have good voices the tunes of the canticles; she will explain to them some pious usage or speak a few words about some virtue or vice, tell them some historical anecdotes, hold up to them the example of some saint, or teach them to sew or knit.

(10) When 11.0 strikes she will make them kneel and recite a *Pater* and an *Ave* to thank God, and the *Sub tuum præsidium* to put themselves under the protection of the most Holy Virgin; and she will exhort them to go home quietly, without stopping in the streets.

Afternoon school

(1) In winter, when the days are at their shortest and the number of pupils at its greatest, it is best to begin school at 1.0 and to go on until nightfall; but from Easter to All Saints' Day it will suffice to have school from 2.0 till 6.0, unless there is only a very small attendance, in which case the hours will be shorter.

The mistress should firmly realise that it is well worthy of her zeal to keep at school as long as possible girls who are likely to do nothing but annoy and worry their parents, when they are at home, and who hardly ever go out except to waste their time in the streets and learn evil from their companions.

(2) On entering the room the pupils will behave as in the morning—the same salutation, the same prayer before the crucifix, etc.; the first lesson will begin half-an-hour after the bell has rung. When the repetition is over, the children will be allowed a quarter-of-an-hour for a light meal, the same rules being observed as at the morning meal. After this the second lesson is said; that done, the children who are learning to write will go on working at their copies.

(3) The mistress will catechise every Saturday in the year on the subject of the catechism which is held on the following Sunday at Vespers. But from All Saints' Day to Easter she will do this three times a week—on Tuesday, Thursday, and Saturday—on the topics prescribed for her. It would be wise to offer a small prize for the girl who answers best so as to stimulate emulation.

(4) Afternoon school will end with a prayer and a short reading. The mistress will explain the latter to the pupils, exhorting them to think over it at night on going to bed and to remember it next morning on rising; she will make them give an account of it next day, to make sure that they are attentive, and this should also be done in the case of sermons and other instruction given in church.

(5) When school is finished the mistress will take her pupils to church, two by two, modestly as in the morning, and will teach them to visit with profit the Holy Sacrament.

(6) If any girl does not appear at school in the morning or afternoon, the mistress will take care to send one of the pupils to her home to enquire the reason of her absence.

11

HABITS WHICH THE MISTRESS MUST INSTIL INTO HER PUPILS

(1) *At home*

The mistress must tell her pupils again and again that when they awake they must think about God and consecrate their hearts to Him; that they must offer to Him their first thought, word, and deed, and in fact their whole day; that they must take holy water and make the sign of the cross; that they must dress modestly by the side of their bed, remembering that they are in the presence of God Who sees them, and of their guardian angel who is also witness of their actions; and that they must kneel for a moment before going to school and commend themselves to Jesus Christ, the Holy Virgin, and their guardian angel. The mistress will tell them to salute their fathers and mothers respectfully, when they meet them on leaving their bedroom, with the words: "May Jesus Christ be praised"; to feel for them at all times a deep respect, to obey them promptly without grumbling or arguing, to be content with what is given them at mealtimes and not to complain like dainty children who are never satisfied; to live in peace with their brothers and sisters and other inmates of the house; to endure their faults and, so far from addressing harsh words to them—which are signs of great pride in those who use them and only cause trouble in a family—to speak to them in a gentle and friendly way. The mistress will forbid her pupils to go out of their home without the permission of their father or mother; she will tell them to salute their parents before retiring, to take holy water before getting into bed, and to fall asleep thinking of some pious theme which she has suggested to them.

(2) *In the streets*

The mistress will instruct her pupils to walk sedately and modestly and forbid them to run like little madcaps and then stop to chatter and play. She will tell them to salute everyone they meet, especially their elders, and to greet them by saying: "May Jesus Christ be praised," reminding them that our Holy Father the Pope has granted indulgences to those who give greetings in this manner. She will forbid them to talk, unless it be necessary, to little boys, and will strictly prohibit them from associating with them—and especially laughing, playing, and wantoning with them.

(3) *In Church*

She will often speak to her pupils of the deep reverence with which they ought to enter God's house and the special devotion which they ought to show in the presence of Jesus Christ Who makes there His dwelling amid the angels who adore Him with the deepest reverence. She will accustom them to take holy water devoutly and to hate their sins by a firm act of contrition, by making the sign of the cross. She will tell those who can read to keep their *Book of Hours* in their hand, and the rest to tell their beads, adding to each *Pater* an act of contrition, and to each *Ave Maria* an act of love towards God. She will keep watch upon them during the church services; and on the following day she will punish such as have shown lack of devotion and will praise such as have prayed devoutly.

OTHER HABITS WHICH MUST BE INSTILLED INTO GIRLS

A mistress must give her pupils high ideas of the majesty of God and speak often to them of His adorable perfection; she must accustom them often to make acts of faith, hope, and charity, and inspire them with a deep love for Jesus Christ.... She will make them fear and avoid any occasion of sin—bad companions, dances, staying up late at night, vanity in dress, etc. She will encourage them to love chastity, modesty, reserve, simplicity in dress, obedience to superiors, respect for those who are consecrated to God. She will forbid them to be curious or to pry into their neighbours' affairs, and will make them love silence. She will inspire them with a horror of scandal and accustom them to speak well of everybody and evil of nobody, to avoid idleness, and to love work. She will forbid them ever to show themselves to anybody—even to their family—without being completely and modestly dressed.

With regard to this subject the mistress should remember that she cannot too often or too strictly make her girls keep the rules of modesty in dress and she must punish the smallest fault in this important respect. She will advise them never to dress or undress by the fire in the presence of their family, but by their bed in their own room. She will keep strict watch to see that nothing unseemly passes between her pupils in school, whether it be in words, deeds, songs, or vulgar jests—

and this is always a danger when they are allowed to go out.

She will accustom them to go frequently to confession and teach them very carefully how to prepare themselves so as to do this profitably....

THE MISTRESS'S CONDUCT TOWARDS OTHER PEOPLE

(1) As to the parish in general, she must continually edify it, and honour and respect everyone in it.

(2) She must assist those whose business it is to adorn the church and help to make the house of God seemly and worthy of the majesty of Him Who dwells there.

(3) She must visit those of her own sex who are ill and see if they have need of her help.

(4) She must speak with great seriousness and kindness to those whom she is bound to visit.

(5) She must receive with the utmost courtesy the mothers of the girls whom she teaches if they come to see her, and tell them the progress which their children make in knowledge and virtue, and inform them of their faults, idleness, carelessness, or frivolity.

(6) She must never enquire what goes on or is said in the families, nor ever report anything to the priest about what goes on in the parish. The *curé* has no need of her help in finding out the shortcomings of his parishioners. She must not visit the parents of her pupils unless it is necessary to tell them of serious faults committed by their children; nor must she visit other houses unless there are sick persons of her own sex who wish her to call upon them. She must not enter the *curé's* house unless there is a necessity for so doing or she is sent for —which will not happen without good reason. Finally, a good schoolmistress does not confine her zeal to the girls who are sent to her school; she extends it to those who do not as yet go to school, to those who cannot do so, and to those who no longer do so. She invites all alike to come to her house and form a class, so as to instruct some and to remind the others of what they have already learnt from her, to encourage and strengthen them. She asks their mothers to let them come and to all she addresses the words of the psalmist: "Come, ye children, hearken unto me; I will teach you the fear of the Lord." (*Ps.* xxxiv. 11.)

RULES FOR THE MISTRESS'S OWN CONDUCT

(1) She must be persuaded that the best way to arrive at the perfection which God demands of her and at which she must aim, is to fulfil properly the duties of her position. To that end she should make it her sole aim in all that she does to glorify God and to sanctify her girls, and to endure with great patience and courage the worries and dislikes which she will encounter in this laborious task.

(2) She must show her pupils the tenderness of a mother and speak to them with great kindness and affability, so as to gain their confidence and win them by love rather than by fear. She would not be employing the proper means for arriving at perfection if she were to show ill-temper, impatience, anger, or passion towards her children. By censuring them for their faults and speaking roughly or angrily to them, she would make them hate her and so spoil their disposition and their affection. When she is obliged to have recourse to stern measures and to correct them, she should make them realise that she does so against her will and solely out of zeal for their salvation, and that anger has no part in what she does. For the rest, she should take great pains to discover the character and disposition of her children so as to learn how to deal with each of them. She will find some who will do whatever she wants by kindness and with whom severity spoils everything; there are others who will do nothing unless a little severity is used (this is an important point). The mistress must remember that they should rarely be punished with the cane, and that certain small punishments which would humiliate them, will as a rule have more effect than the hardest blows; for example, if they have offended their companions they may be made to ask pardon of them, kneeling in the middle of the school-room; or they may be separated from the rest and put at another bench, or be made to recite an act of contrition with folded arms. Never use slaps, blows, or kicks; never threaten to report them to the *curé* or the *vicaire*.

(3) She must give herself to the practice of sincere and genuine piety, avoiding affectation no less than frivolity. Too serious and severe a devotion would expose her to ridicule or contempt; a careless, irresponsible and worldly air would cause scandal and ruin everything; to avoid these two extremes and keep the right mean she must behave with the greatest

simplicity, modesty, and openness, seeking God with a single mind, loving prayer and solitude....

Such are the good and wise regulations necessary for school-mistresses (*maîtresses d'école*) to enable them worthily to fulfil the duties of their calling, to sanctify themselves and the children in their charge. I beseech you, in the name of God, to observe them with the utmost care. To inspire you and to uphold you in the rigorous observance that is required of you, keep continually before your eyes the importance and the usefulness of the office which is entrusted to you. Remember that you can do nothing more glorious for Jesus Christ, nothing more glorious for Mary, nothing more valuable for your neighbours, and nothing more profitable for your own sanctification than to devote yourselves whole-heartedly to the Christian education of girls. The prophet has said: "They that turn many to righteousness shall be as the stars for ever and ever" (*Daniel*, xii. 3).

APPENDIX F

THE HUGUENOT NATIONAL SYNODS

FOR ecclesiastical purposes Protestant France was divided into a number of provinces; each bore the name of a civil province but was not necessarily coterminous with it. Each province was subdivided into *colloques* or "presbyteries." Representatives from the individual churches were elected to serve on the *colloques*, and these assemblies in turn chose deputies to form the provincial synods which met once or twice a year. The national synods, to which deputies were sent from all the ecclesiastical provinces, met at less frequent intervals. These synods should be carefully distinguished from the Huguenot political assemblies, such as that which was held at Montauban in 1584 or at La Rochelle in 1588. A list of the national synods, together with the cities in which they were held and from which they are named, is given below:

1st	Paris	1559	16th	Gergeau (Jargeau)		1601
2nd	Poitiers	1560	17th	Gap		1603
3rd	Orleans	1562	18th	La Rochelle		1607
4th	Lyon	1563	19th	Saint-Maixent		1609
5th	Paris	1565	20th	Privas		1612
6th	Vertueil	1567	21st	Tonneins		1614
7th	La Rochelle	1571	22nd	Vitré		1617
8th	Nîmes	1572	23rd	Alais		1620
9th	Sainte-Foy	1578	24th	Charenton		1623
10th	Figeac	1579	25th	Castres		1626
11th	La Rochelle	1581	26th	Charenton		1631
12th	Vitré	1583	27th	Alençon		1637
13th	Montauban	1594	28th	Charenton		1645
14th	Saumur	1596	29th	Loudun		1659
15th	Montpellier	1598				

APPENDIX G

LIST OF HUGUENOT COLLEGES

[The date of foundation, where known, is given in brackets.
Académies are shown in capitals.]

Ecclesiastical Provinces	Colleges
Île de France	Clermont-sur-Beauvoisis (1609)
Normandy	Alençon
Berry	Gergeau *or* Jargeau (1609)
	Châtillon-sur-Loing
	Montargis (1571?)
Anjou	Tours
	Vendôme (1562)
	SAUMUR (1596)
	Loudun (before 1597)
Burgundy	Pont-de-Vesle
	Pays-de-Gex (at Gex)
Brittany	Vitré
Poitou	Niort
Xaintonge	La Rochelle (about 1570)
	La Rochefoucault (before 1582)
	Melle ("mixed" college, see p. 106)
Guyenne	Bergerac (about 1610)
	Nérac
Haute Languedoc	MONTAUBAN (1597)[1]
	Castres (1596)
	Puylaurens
Bas Languedoc	Béziers
	NÎMES (1539)
	MONTPELLIER
Cevennes	Anduze
Provence	[Apparently no college]
Dauphiné	Embrun
	DIE (1604)
	[ORANGE (1573)]
Vivarais	Privas (1605)
	Aubenas
	Annonay
Béarn	ORTHEZ (1566)

Huguenot Colleges outside France

Metz (1563): became French in 1643.
SEDAN (1575): became French in 1659.
Montbéliard: remained outside France and its college therefore
  survived the Revocation of the Edict of Nantes in 1685.

[1] The *académie* was afterwards moved to Puylaurens.

MAP I

MAP I SHOWING DISTRIBUTION
OF HUGUENOT COLLEGES

SEDAN ●

● Clermont-sur-
Beauvolsis

Metz ●

● Alençon

● Vitré

● Montargis

Vendôme Gergeau ● Châtillon-
                 sur-Loing

SAUMUR ● ● Tours

Montbéliard ●

● Loudun

● Niort
● Melle
● La Rochelle

Gex ●

Pont-de-Vesle

● La Rochefoucault

● Annonay

● Bergerac

Privas ● ● DIE
● Aubenas

Embrun ●

● Nérac
● MONTAUBAN Anduze ● ● ORANGE

● ORTHEZ Puylaurens ● ● Castres ● NÎMES
                     Béziers ● ● MONTPELLIER

The boundaries shown are those at the end of the reign of Louis XIV,
i.e. in 1715. Montbéliard was not included in France until the year 1793.

APPENDIX H

LIST OF ORATORIAN COLLEGES, WITH DATE OF FOUNDATION OF EACH

Dieppe ...	...	...	1614	Boulogne 1629
Langres ...	...	...	1616	Grasse 1629
Riom ...	...	...	1618	Troyes 1630
Forez (N.D. des Grâces)			1619	Bordeaux 1639
Angers ...	...	...	1619	Juilly 1639
Frontignan	...	...	1619	Salins 1641
Pézenas ...	...	...	1619	Rouen 1642
Joyeuse ...	...	...	1620	Clermont... 1644
Vendôme	...	...	1623	Rumilly 1653
Le Mans ...	...	...	1624	Bourg-Saint-Andéol ... 1654
Montbrison	...	...	1624	Hyères 1655
Beaune ...	...	...	1624	Provins 1672
Saumur ...	...	...	1624	Soissons 1676
Nantes ...	...	...	1625	Agde 1676
Marseilles	...	...	1625	Poligny 1685
Toulon ...	...	...	1625	Saint-Martin-de-Miséré... 1705
Effiat	...	...	1627	La Ciotat... 1707
Condom ...	...	...	1628	Niort 1716

The following Jesuit colleges were handed over to the Oratory after the expulsion of the Society of Jesus in 1762:

Lyon ...	...	...	1763	Tours 1778
Tournon ...	...	...	1776	Agen 1781
Arras ...	...	...	1777	Autun 1786
Béthune ...	...	...	1777	

MAP II

MAP II Showing Distribution of Oratorian Colleges

The boundaries shown are those in the year 1790. Rumilly is in Savoy and had been captured by Louis XIII in 1630, *i.e.* 23 years before the Oratorian college was opened there. In 1713, by the Peace of Utrecht, Savoy was restored by France to its Duke, Victor Amedeus II; in 1740 the Oratorian college at Rumilly was dispersed by his son, Duke Charles-Emmanuel III.

BIBLIOGRAPHY

THE following list comprises all those works to which reference is made in the text or notes of the present volume. It does not, of course, by any means include all the available authorities or all those which have been consulted for the purpose of this book.

Abot de Bazinghen (François). *Traité des Monnoies.* 2 vols. (Paris, 1764.)
Acton (Lord). *Lectures on Modern History.* (London, 1906.)
Adamson (John William). *Pioneers of Modern Education, 1600–1700.* (Cambridge, 1905.)
—— *A Short History of Education.* (Cambridge, 1919.)
Adry. *Notice sur Juilly.* (Paris, n.d.)
Aquinas (St Thomas). *Opera.* (Cologne, 1482.)
Arens (B., S.J.). *Anna von Xainctonge, Stifterin der Ursulinen von Dôle.* (Freiburg-im-Breisgau, 1903.)
Arnaud (Eugène). *Histoire de l'Académie protestante de Die en Dauphiné.* (Paris, 1872.)
Arnauld (Antoine). *Œuvres.* 50 vols. (Paris and Lausanne, 1775–1783.)
—— *Règlement des Études dans les Lettres humaines,* in vol. XLI of *Œuvres.*
—— and **Lancelot** (Claude). *Grammaire générale et raisonnée.* (Paris, 1756.)
Arnoulx (Charles-Bonaventura). *La Vie de la Vénérable Mère de Xainctonge.* (Avignon, 1755.)
Augustine, St (Bishop of Hippo). *De Civitate Dei.* Trans. by F. R. M. Hitchcock. (London, 1898.)
Avenel (Georges de). *Histoire économique de la propriété, des salaires, des denrées, et de tous les prix.* 6 vols. (Paris, 1894.)
Aymon (Jean). *Tous les synodes nationaux des églises réformées de France.* (La Haye, 1710.)
Baird (Henry Martyn). *The Rise of the Huguenots in France.* 2 vols. (London, 1880.)
—— *The Huguenots and Henry of Navarre.* 2 vols. (London, 1886.)
—— *The Huguenots and the Revocation of the Edict of Nantes.* 2 vols. (New York, 1895.)
Barbier (Edmond-Jean-François). *Journal historique et anecdotique du règne de Louis XV.* (Paris, 1847.)

Barnard (Howard Clive). *The Little Schools of Port-Royal*. (Cambridge, 1913.)
—— *The Port-Royalists on Education*. (Cambridge, 1918.)
Barthélemy Saint-Hilaire (Jules). *De la Logique d'Aristote*. 2 vols. (Paris, 1838.)
Bausset (Louis-François de). *Histoire de J.-B. Bossuet, Évêque de Meaux*. 4 vols. (Versailles, 1814.)
Berthault (Pierre). *Florus Franciscus*. (Paris, 1630.)
—— *Florus Gallicus*. (Paris, 1644.)
Bérulle (Pierre de). *Lettres*. (N.pl., 1668.)
Binet (Rev. P., S.J.). *La Vie parfaitement humble et courageuse d'Anne de Xainctonge, institutrice des Ursulines du Comté de Bourgogne*. Unpublished MS., 1635.
BOARD OF EDUCATION. *Special Report on Secondary and University Education in France*. Vol. 24 of "Special Reports." (London, 1911.)
Boissier (Gaston). "La Réforme des Études au XVIe siècle," in *Revue des Deux Mondes*. Vol. 54. (Paris, Dec. 1882.)
Bongars (Jacques). *Lettres Latines*. 2 vols. (Paris, 1681.)
Bossuet (Jacques-Bénigne). *Œuvres*. (Versailles, 1819.)
—— *Correspondance*, ed. Regnier. 9 vols. (Paris, 1909.)
—— *Epistola ad Innocentem XI*, in vol. XIV of *Œuvres*.
—— *Epistola ad Innocentem XI*, trans. by J. T. Philipps. [Part of *A Compendious Way of Teaching Ancient and Modern Languages*. London, 1723.]
—— *Discours sur l'Histoire Universelle à Monseigneur le Dauphin*. (Paris, 1681.)
—— *De la Connaissance de Dieu et de Soi-même*. (Paris, 1846.)
—— *Politique tirée des propres paroles de l'Écriture Sainte à Monseigneur le Dauphin*. 2 vols. (Paris, 1709.)
—— *De Incogitantia*, in vol. XXXIV of *Œuvres*.
Bouchel (Laurent). *Decretorum Ecclesiæ Gallicanæ ex conciliis eiusdem œcumenicis libri viii*. (N.pl., 1609.)
Bréchillet-Jourdain (Charles-Marie-Gabriel). *Histoire de l'Université de Paris au XVIIe et au XVIIIe siècle*. (Paris, 1862–1866.)
—— *Index chronologicus chartarum pertinentium ad historiam Universitatis Parisiensis*. (Paris, 1862.)
Brisac (E. Dreyfus). "Petits Problèmes de Bibliographie pédagogique," in *Revue Internationale de l'Enseignement*. (Paris, October 15th, 1892.)
Calvin (Jean). *Institutio totius Christianæ Religionis*. (Geneva, 1550.)
Caradeuc de la Chalotais (Louis-Réné). *Compte rendu des Constitutions des Jésuites*. (? Rennes, 1762.)

Caradeuc de la Chalotais (Louis-Réné). *Essai d'Éducation nationale, ou plan d'études pour la jeunesse.* (N.pl., 1763.)

Castellion (Sebastianus). [Châteillon, Sébastien.] *Dialogorum sacrorum libri quattuor.* (London, 1605.)

Castiglione (Baldassare). *Il libro del Cortegiano.* (Venice, 1528.)

Caylus (Mme de). *Souvenirs et Correspondance.* (Paris, 1889.)

Chateaubriand (François-Réné de). "Letter to the Duchesse de Berry," in *Revue rétrospective.* (Paris, Dec. 1884–July, 1885.)

Cimber (M.-L.) and **Danjou** (F.). *Archives curieuses de l'histoire de France.* 27 vols. (Paris, 1837–1840.)

Comenius (John Amos) [Komenský]. *Orbis sensualium pictus.* (London, 1659.)

Compayré (Gabriel). *Histoires des doctrines de l'Éducation en France.* (Paris, 1904.)

Condorcet (Marquis de). *Esquisse d'un tableau historique des progrès de l'esprit humain.* (N.pl., 1795.)

Condren (Charles de). *Œuvres complètes.* (Paris, 1857.)

Crétineau-Joly (J.-A.-M.). *Histoire réligieuse, politique et littéraire de la Compagnie de Jésus.* 6 vols. (Paris, 1844–1846.)

Crevier (J.-B.-L.). *Histoire de l'Université de Paris.* 7 vols. (Paris, 1761.)

Descartes (René). *Discours de la méthode pour bien conduire sa raison.* (N.pl., 1637.)

—— *Tractatus de Homine et de Formatione Fœtus.* (Amsterdam, 1677.)

Desmaze (Charles). *L'Université de Paris, 1200–1875.* (Paris, 1876.)

Despauter [Van Pauteren, J.]. *Grammaticæ Institutionis libri septem.* (Cologne, 1574.)

Diderot (Denis). *De l'Éducation Publique.* (Paris, 1762.) [This book is attributed to Diderot; see p. 233.]

Dubois (*Valet de chambre* to Louis XIV). *Nouvelle collection des Mémoires.* (Paris, 1836.)

Du Guet (Jacques-Joseph). *Lettres sur divers sujets de morale et de piété.* (N.pl., 1708.)

Dumoustier de la Fond. *Essais sur l'Histoire de la Ville de Loudun.* (Poitiers, 1778.)

Du Plessis (Armand-Jean), Cardinal, Duc de Richelieu. *Mémoires,* in *Collection des mémoires relatifs à l'histoire de France.* vol. 9, ed. Petitot. (Paris, 1810.)

Edgeworth (Maria). *Life and Letters,* ed. A. J. C. Hare. (London, 1894.)

Evelyn (John). *Diary and Correspondence.* (London, 1871.)

Félibien (Michel). *Histoire de la Ville de Paris.* 5 vols. (Paris, 1725.)

Fénelon (Salignac de la Mothe). *De l'Éducation des Filles.* (Paris, 1763.)

BIBLIOGRAPHY

Fischer de Chevriers (Ph.). *Histoire de l'instruction populaire en France depuis les premiers siècles jusqu'en* 1789. (Paris, 1884).

Fléchier (Valentin-Esprit). *Œuvres complètes.* (Nîmes, 1782.)

—— *Oraisons Funèbres* in *Recueil de Diverses Oraisons Funèbres.* (Brussels, 1682.)

Fournenc (Jacques). *Mathematica.* (Paris, 1635.)

Gaberel (Jean). *Histoire de l'Église de Genève.* 3 vols. (Geneva, 1853–1862.)

Gerdes (Daniel). *Historia Reformationis.* 4 vols. (Groningen and Bremen, 1744–1752.)

Golding (A.). *The Lyfe of Iasper Colignie Shatilion.* Translated out of Latin. 𝕭.𝕷. (London, 1576.)

Gran (Gerhard). *Jean-Jacques Rousseau.* Translated from the Norwegian. (Edinburgh and London, 1912.)

Haldane (Elizabeth). *Descartes, his life and times.* (London, 1905.)

Hamel (Charles). *Histoire de l'Abbaye et du Collège de Juilly.* (Paris, 1868.)

Haton (Claude). *Mémoires.* 2 vols. (N.pl., 1857.)

Houbigant (Charles-François). *Traité des Études.* (Paris, 1732.)

Huet (Pierre-Daniel). *Memoirs.* Translated by J. Aikin, M.D. 2 vols. (London, 1810.)

Jervis (William Henry). *The Gallican Church.* 2 vols. (London, 1872.)

Joly (Claude). *Statuts pour les petites écoles.* (Paris, 1670.)

La Chalotais See CARADEUC.

Lamy (Bernard). *Entretiens sur les sciences.* (N.pl., 1684.)

—— *La Rhétorique, ou l'Art de Parler.* (Paris, 1688.)

—— *Élémens de Mathématiques.* (Paris, 1734.)

—— *Traitez de Méchanique, de l'équilibre, des solides, et des liqueurs.* (Paris, 1679.)

—— *Traité de Perspective, où sont contenus les fondemens de la peinture.* (Paris, 1701.)

Languet (Hubert). *Epistolæ ad J. Camerarium fratrem et filium.* (Leipsic and Frankfurt, 1685.)

Lavisse (E.) and **Rambaud** (A.). *Histoire générale du IVᵉ siècle à nos jours.* 12 vols. (Paris, 1893–1901.)

Le Dieu (François). *Mémoires et journal sur la vie et les ouvrages de Bossuet.* 4 vols. (Paris, 1856–1857.)

Leti (Gregorio). *La Vie d'Elizabeth, reine d'Angleterre.* 2 vols. Translated from the Italian. (Amsterdam, 1694.)

Locke (John). *Some Thoughts Concerning Education,* ed. R. H. Quick. (Cambridge, 1902.)

Louis XIV. *Œuvres.* 6 vols. (Paris, 1806.)

—— *Mémoires écrits par lui-même,* in Cimber and Danjou, *Archives curieuses de l'histoire de France.* 2ᵉ série. Vol. 8. (Paris, 1834.)

Magnum Bullarium Romanum. 8 vols. (Rome, 1727.)

Malebranche (Nicholas). *De la Recherche de la Vérité.* (Paris, 1674.)

Marot (Clément). *Œuvres.* 3 vols. (Paris, 1824.)

Martin (André) [Ambrosius Victor]. *Philosophia Christiana.*

Massillon (Jean-Baptiste). *Œuvres,* in Migne, *Orateurs Sacrés,* vol. 43. (Paris, 1854.)

Millet (J.). *Histoire de Descartes avant* 1637. 2 vols. (Paris, 1867–1870.)

Milton (John). *Artis logicæ plenior institutio ad Petri Rami methodum concinnata.* (London, 1672.)

Monroe (Paul). *Cyclopædia of Education* (ed.). 5 vols. (New York, 1913.)

Morley (John). *Rousseau.* 2 vols. (London, 1873.)

Mourath (Rev. P. Jean, S.J.). *Vie et Vertus d'Anne de Xainctonge, fondatrice de la Société de Ste Ursule en Franche-Comté.* Translated from the German. (Zug, 1681.)

N***. *La Vie de M. le Duc de Montausier.* 2 vols. (Paris, 1729.)

Necker de Saussure (Adrienne-Albertine). *L'Éducation progressive, ou Étude du cours de la vie.* 3 vols. (Paris, 1864.)

—— *Cours de Littérature dramatique.* Translated from the German of Schlegel. (N.pl., 1814.)

—— *Notice sur le caractère et les écrits de Madame de Staël.* (London, 1820.)

Nicole (Pierre). *Essais de Morale.* 14 vols. (Paris and Liège, 1781.)

Nisard (J.-M.-N.-D.). *Histoire de la littérature française.* 4 vols. (Paris, 1844–1861.)

Orset (Rev. P., S.J.). *La Vie de la vénérable et dévote Mère de Xainctonge de la Congrégation de Saincte Ursule en le Comté de Bourgogne, d'après les mémoires inédits du Revd. P. Villars, Jésuite, et des contemporains de la servante de Dieu.* Unpublished MS., n.d.

Pasquier (Étienne). *Les Recherches sur la France.* (Orleans, 1665.)

—— *Lettres.* (Paris, 1586.)

Perraud (A.-L.-A.). *L'Oratoire de France.* (Paris, 1865.)

Plato. *Republic.* Davis and Vaughan translation. (London, 1903.)

Poirson (Auguste). *Histoire du Règne de Henri IV.* 2 vols. (Paris, 1856.)

Poisson (Nicolas-Joseph). *Traité de la mécanique de Descartes.* (N.pl., 1668.)

Pont-Aymery (Alexandre de). *Institution de la noblesse françoise.* (Paris, 1595.)

Port-Royal. *Supplément au Nécrologe de l'Abbaïe de Notre-Dame de Port-Royal.* (Paris, 1735.)

Procès-verbaux des Assemblés du Clergé de France. 8 vols. (Paris, 1767–1778.)

BIBLIOGRAPHY 307

Quesnel (Pasquier). *Le Nouveau Testament en français avec des réflexions morales*. (N.pl., 1693.)

Quick (John). *Synodicon in Gallia reformata*. 2 vols. (London, 1692.)

Quick (R. H.). *Essays on Educational Reformers*. (London, 1890.)

Ramus (Petrus) [Pierre de la Ramée]. *Scholæ in liberales artes* [i.e. Grammar, Rhetoric, Dialectic, Physics, Metaphysics, and Mathematics]. (Bâle, 1578.)

—— *Ciceronianus et Brutinæ quæstiones*. (Bâle, 1577.)

—— *Dialecticæ libri duo, sive Institutiones*. (Paris, 1560.)

—— *Scholarum Dialecticarum libri xx*. (Frankfurt, 1594.)

—— *Aristotelicæ Animadversiones*. (Frankfurt, 1594.)

—— *Rhetoricæ distinctiones in Quintilianum*. (Paris, 1549.)

—— *De Studiis Eloquentiæ ac Philosophiæ coniungendis oratio*. (Paris, 1546.)

—— *Arithmeticæ libri*. (Frankfurt, 1599.)

—— *Gramère*. (Paris, 1562); there is another revised edition dating from 1587; see p. 35 n.

—— *Grammatica* [i.e. a Latin grammar]. (Paris, 1572.)

—— *Proœmium reformandæ Parisiensis Academiæ ad Regem*. (Paris, 1562.) This is translated in Cimber and Danjou's *Archives curieuses*. 2e série. Vol. 5.

—— *La Remonstrance fait au Conseil privé*. (Paris, 1567.)

—— *Testamentum*. (Paris, 1576.)

Ratio atque Institutio Studiorum Societatis Jesu. (Rome, 1606.)

Ratio studiorum a magistris et professoribus Congregationis Oratorii Domini Jesu observanda. (Paris, 1645.) See p. 157.

Richelieu. See **Du Plessis.**

Roland de la Platrière (Mme). *Mémoires*. 2 vols. (Paris, 1864.)

Rolland d'Erceville (B.-G.). *Recueil de plusieurs de ses ouvrages sur l'éducation*. (Paris, 1873.)

Rollin (Charles). *De la Manière d'enseigner et d'étudier les belles-lettres, par rapport à l'esprit et au cœur*; usually known as *Traité des Études*. 4 vols. (Amsterdam, 1745.)

—— *Opuscules de feu M. Rollin*. 2 vols. (Paris, 1771.)

—— *Histoire ancienne des Égyptiens, des Carthaginois, des Assyriens, des Babyloniens, des Mèdes, et des Perses,. des Macédoines, des Grecs*. 13 vols. (Paris, 1730–1738.)

—— *Histoire Romaine*. 7 vols. [An 8th and 9th volume to complete the work were added by CREVIER; see p. 213.] (Paris, 1738–1741.)

Rousseau (Jean-Jacques). *Émile*. 4 vols. (Amsterdam, 1763.)

—— *Émile*, trans. by W. H. Payne. (New York, 1908.)

—— *Confessions*. (Paris, 1875.)

Rousseau (Jean-Jacques). *Rêveries d'un Promeneur Solitaire.* (Paris, 1882.)

—— *La Nouvelle Héloïse.* (Paris, 1830.)

Sainte-Beuve (Charles-Augustin). *Port-Royal.* 7 vols. (Paris, 1888.)

—— *Causeries de Lundi.* 16 vols. (Paris, 1885.)

Sainte-Pierre (J. H. Bernardin de). *Œuvres complètes.* 12 vols. (Paris, 1818.)

Saint-Simon (Duc de). *Mémoires.* 20 vols. (Paris, 1879.)

Sanctius [Francisco Sanchez]. *Minerva, seu de causis Linguæ Latinæ Commentarius.* (Amsterdam, 1704.)

Santeul (Jean-Baptist) [Santolinus Victorinus]. *Operum omnium editio tertia.* (Paris, 1729.)

Satire Ménippée, ed. Ch. Marcilly. (Paris, 1882.)

Sauval (Henri). *Histoire et recherches des antiquités de la ville de Paris.* 3 vols. (Paris, 1724.)

Schonæus (Cornelius). *Terentius Christianus.* (Cologne, 1620.)

Sévigné (Mme de). *Lettres.* 10 vols. Ed. Régnier. (Paris, 1862.)

Sully (James). *Studies of Childhood.* (London, 1903.)

Thomassin (Louis). *Méthode d'étudier et d'enseigner chrétiennement et solidement les lettres humaines, par rapport aux lettres divines et aux Écritures.* 6 vols. (Paris, 1681–1693.)

Vallet de Viriville (Auguste). *Histoire de l'Instruction publique en Europe et principalement en France, depuis le Christianisme jusqu'à nos jours.* (Paris, 1849.)

Villemain (Abel François). *Cours de littérature française; tableau du dix-huitième siècle.* (Paris, 1838.)

Voltaire (F.-M. Arouet de). *Dictionnaire philosophique et Traité sur la Tolérance.* (Geneva, 1763.)

—— *Correspondance.* (Paris, 1883.)

Vossius (Gerardus). *Grammatica Latina.* (N.pl., 1644.)

Waddington (Charles). *De P. Rami vita, scriptis, philosophia* (Paris, 1848); also a French translation of this: *Ramus; sa vie, ses écrits et ses opinions.* (Paris, 1855.)

Watson (Foster). *Religious Refugees and English Education.* (London, 1911.)

Woodward (William Harrison). *Studies in Education during the Age of the Renaissance.* (Cambridge, 1906.)

INDEX

INDEX

313

Henri IV, 2*n*., 40, 55, 56, 86, 95, 146, 149, 194; reform of the Univ. of Paris, 185, 191, 207, 211
Henrietta, wife of Charles I, 152
Hersan, Charles, 197
Histoire Ancienne (Rollin), 212
Histoire Romaine (Rollin), 212–213
History, study of (by the Grand Dauphin), 127–130; (in Oratorian schools), 161, 163–166, 179–180; (in military schools), 177; (in academies), 194; (advocated by Rollin), 211–213; (advocated by La Chalotais), 237–238, 240*n*.
Holidays, school (Univ. of Paris), 8, 190; (Little Schools), 45; (Ursuline schools), 70; (Calvin's school at Geneva), 77; (Huguenot schools), 92; (Oratorian schools), 168; (*académie militaire*), 195
Holy Orders, training for, 145–148, 150, 152
Homer, 127, 190, 209
Homunculus conception of childhood, 250–253
Houbigant, Charles-François, 181
How Gertrude teaches her children (Pestalozzi), 283
Huet, P.-D., 120*n*., 126
Huguenots, 25, 26, 27, 43, 73–108; their schools, 78–108, 298; list of their National Synods, 297
Hymn-singing, 282

Ignorantins, 235
Imagination, power of the child's, 277–279
Imitate, child's tendency to, 271–272, 273–274
Infant schools (Wilderspin), 283
Innocent XI, Pope, 125
Inspection of schools (Huguenot schools), 98–99; (Oratorian schools), 173; (Univ. of Paris), 198; (recommended by La Chalotais), 242
Institutio Christianæ Religionis (Calvin), 75

Italy, education of women in, 39; Renaissance in, 109–110, 112–113, 117

Jansenism, 196, 201, 202, 219, 226; relations of the Oratory with, 153, 175, 176, 178, 181; relations of Rollin with, 198, 199–200, 202–203; influence of, upon Univ. of Paris, 206
January, Edict of, 82, 83
Jesuits, schools of the, 26, 149, 165, 170, 181–182, 184, 191–192, 300; organisation of their schools, 227–229; their influence upon Anne de Xainctonge, 53, 55–56, 57, 58, 60–61, 64, 68, 69; their opposition to Huguenot schools, 101, 107; — to Oratorian schools, 153, 156, 160; — to Port-Royal, 199; their expulsion from France (1595), 55, 56, 88; their return to France (1603), 61, 95; their expulsion from France (1762), 155, 176, 226, 245, 247, 253; suppression of the Society, 227; attack of La Chalotais upon the Society, 219–232
Joly, Claude, 42, 145*n*.
Joyeuse, Cardinal de, 154
Juilly, Oratorian College of, 116, 149, 157–158, 159, 162, 164, 166–172, 181

Kant, 257
Kipling, Rudyard, 249

La Chaise, Père, 105
La Chalotais, Caradeuc de, 223–249
La Flèche, Jesuit college of, 149, 177, 222*n*.
La Fontaine's *Fables*, 122
La Rochelle, 85, 97; Huguenot college at, 84, 96; political assembly at, 87, 297; national synod at, 94, 297; capture of (1629), 99, 113
Laboureur, Pierre, 195
Lambert, Marquise de, 258

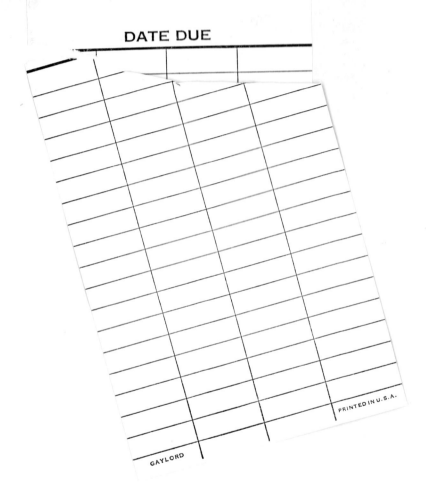

DATE DUE

GAYLORD

PRINTED IN U.S.A.